A LAND FULL OF PEOPLE
Life in Kenya Today

A LAND FULL OF PEOPLE
Life in Kenya Today

JOHN S. ROBERTS

FREDERICK A. PRAEGER, *Publishers*

New York · Washington

BOOKS THAT MATTER

Published in the United States of America in 1967
by Frederick A. Praeger, Inc., Publishers
111 Fourth Avenue, New York, N.Y. 10003

Library of Congress Catalog Card Number: 67-27673

Printed in Great Britain

Contents

Illustrations

PLATES

MAPS

ACKNOWLEDGEMENTS

The right to reproduce the following plates is gratefully
acknowledged: Africapix, Nos. 2b, 5a, 7b, 8a, 10b, 11b,
12a, 12b, 14a, 14b, 15a; Kenya High Commission, Nos.
4a, 4b, 13a; John Perry, No. 15b; John Roberts, Nos.
5b, 6, 11a; Nick Russell, Nos. 1, 2a, 3, 7a, 9, 13b.

A LAND FULL OF PEOPLE
Kenya Today

Introduction

The old cliché 'out of Africa always something new' might have been invented as a comment on publishers' lists, every one of which seems these days to contain at least one book, and probably several, about some aspect of African affairs.

New or not, Africa *is* important, as well as being interesting. Nearly everything is in a fluid state of experiment, and experiment in any part of the world is bound to have repercussions of one sort or another in the world at large. Moreover, Africa today is the result of a long and fairly thorough period of meddling by one civilisation with another; it is so to speak a trial run for the world-wide readjustment and breakdown of cultural compartments which is already in progress, and which – if mankind does not succeed in putting a nuclear stop to it – is likely for better or worse to continue at an ever-increasing pace. Lastly, and perhaps in the long run most important, Africa may yet prove to be the third force between East and West of which so much has been spoken since the last war, and which has been so slow in materialising.

Most of the books written about Africa – discounting those which are purely a product of sensationalism or bigotry – have been limited to a particular aspect of one country or of the continent as a whole, to economic or even more frequently political analysis, to personal reminiscence, or to such relatively unimportant matters as big game – for which English writers especially seem to have an almost unhealthy passion. Africa has figured in turn as Dark Continent, as case-book of economic underdevelopment, as political maelstrom, but almost never is it – or are any of the countries which make it up – treated as a

more or less arbitrary yet cohesive collection of peoples whose
concerns both individually and collectively are much the same
as those of any other part of the world.

Kenya especially suffers from this tendency to think of Africa
as somewhere different – somewhere possibly exciting, possibly
dangerous, but emphatically 'other'. In Kenya colonial rule and
the resistance to it was marked by violence on a scale so far
surpassed only in Algeria. Kenya is the first English-speaking
ex-colony with a sizable permanent immigrant population,
so her future is of particular interest to Great Britain; and what
happens in Kenya arouses particularly powerful passions and
prejudices.

Unfortunately these passions and prejudices are too often
unsullied by fact, or even by any awareness that Kenya is a
country in which *people* live. There seem to be two approaches,
that which sees everything in terms of the Cold War, and that
which sees everything in terms of elephants. I am not writing
about a land full of politics or a land full of animals. I am writing
about a land full of people. In this sense, this is not a political
book. On the other hand, politics in fact enter into every department of human life, directly or indirectly. That is why people
who say 'what is needed is less politics and more economics' are
dodging the issue. Economics *are* politics. So is farming. In this
sense, this is a political book. At least it may put the items about
Kenya which crop up in the papers from time to time into their
proper perspective.

In most writing about Kenya too much space is devoted to
the Europeans, who are after all no longer at the centre of the
stage. This being so, it was tempting to avoid any discussion of
their role and attitude today, especially as the mere mention of
Europeans in Africa arouses prejudices (for or against) which
have even less connection with reality than most prejudices.
Still, the job must be done, if only because Kenya's success or
failure in race relations may have its influence on the rest of the
continent. What is important in this context is specifically
African attitudes. If Kenya proves that three racial groups can
live in harmony – and the likelihood is that she will – credit

will be due to the minorities for a real change of heart; but
most credit will belong to the Africans, for remarkable patience
and humanity.

Given that no one person has the final answer to anything, and
that Kenya is still very much in a state of flux, I have attempted
to do no more in this book than take some of the more important
aspects of the country's affairs and examine them by discovering
the views of a number of people directly involved as well as by
describing what is being done, and what I have seen of its
workings. The stress has been laid on the present and the future.

The real problem and potentialities of Kenya frequently do
not coincide with the popular picture of them. For example,
the political scene is much less overshadowed by the Cold War
than many journalists like to make out. What is often at stake
in any particular issue is the theoretical problem of power – how,
why and by whom it should be wielded. This is why I have
included a chapter on politics. I have dealt with the arts at
length because art is fundamental to the continuing process of
self-definition in any society, quite apart from its intrinsic
validity. In the national dialogue artists have a great deal to
say, and they may well have more to say in the future. The
involvement of Kenyan artists in their society is admirable to
one used to the sheepish detachment of so many creative minds
in Europe.

Inevitably much has had to be left out, or to be treated only
briefly. To those who complain that I have ignored this or that
of vital importance, I can only say that this is one book, not six.

Many of the world's delusions about African countries have
also had to be disregarded, or dealt with only obliquely. The
theory, for instance, that in Africa leadership is provided by a
small educated oligarchy ruling an ignorant and indifferent
uneducated mass is possibly true of some countries: it is certainly
not true of Kenya. Indifference there may be; but as in most
parts of the world – and to a greater extent than in many –
comment, if sometimes uninformed comment, is more common
than 'no comment'. Kenyan public opinion is if anything too
active, though usually sensible enough. But this is not the sort

of proposition which can be satisfactorily proved: it can only emerge indirectly.

One last thing. Though I have tried to be as impartial as possible, this book is not written in a spirit of Olympian detachment. I make no apology for the fact since I believe it impossible even to start to understand any person or group unless one is emotionally involved with them in one way or another. The people of Kenya, with all their faults, seem to me admirable in their drive, their tolerance and their sense of purpose. Their problems are great and their spirit in tackling them equally great. This book is dedicated to them.

Historical Note

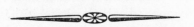

The East African coast was fairly well known in Ptolemy's days, and traders have sailed the Indian Ocean between Arabia, India and East Africa for at least two thousand years. After A.D. 740, when the first Muslim Arabs arrived, Kenya's coastal strip was part of an Arab civilisation whose centre was Zanzibar. Mombasa and Malindi are both almost a thousand years old.

Socially this Afro-Arab Islamic civilisation, first described by the Greek guide to the Indian Ocean known as the *Periplus of the Erythrean Sea*, was one of considerable sophistication; politically it was a handful of city-states in an endemic state of rivalry and warfare – a state which made possible the two hundred years of Portuguese domination after Vasco da Gama's arrival in Mombasa in 1498, during which all Arab trading was forbidden. By the end of the sixteenth century Portuguese power was beginning to crumble, and after a series of revolts the Arabs gained control again at the beginning of the eighteenth century. The Portuguese left few traces except Fort Jesus in Mombasa, a fort with a history as romantically bloody as any.

During all this time the hinterland, which represents about ninety per cent of modern Kenya, was regarded as a source of ivory and slaves, a barbarous area about which the less said the better (an attitude still prevalent in Mombasa). In fact a good deal was going on, mostly tribal migration and concomitant strife. Though it is nonsense to say (as people have only recently stopped saying) that countries like Kenya had no history until the Europeans came, research has only just begun into the collation of tribal legends, archaeology and so on. Broadly speaking, various groups here as in the rest of Africa were moving slowly towards their present areas of control. In Kenya's case much of the movement was from a westerly and north-westerly direction.

British influence in East Africa began with the arrival in 1823 of HMS *Barracouta* in Mombasa, whose rulers – threatened by Oman and Muscat – put themselves under British protection. Thus began a long period of increasing British involvement, the principal aim of which was the destruction of the slave trade. The East African slave trade was less large-scale than the Atlantic, but it was equally horrifying – during the nineteenth century about 30,000 slaves were captured each year. Kenya escaped relatively lightly, since owing to fear of the Masai there were no Arab slave routes north of Mount Kilimanjaro.

While the British were extending their influence on the coast during the nineteenth century – both diplomatically with the aim of destroying the slave trade, and through the work of missionaries – interest in the hinterland was limited. Then Joseph Thomson was financed by the Royal Geographical Society to explore a direct route from Mombasa to Lake Victoria. The reports which he brought back in 1884 gave the first inkling of Kenya's potentialities, and also of the possibility of what was to be the most important factor in the country's development – the railway from the Indian Ocean to Lake Victoria, designed to open up Uganda in accordance with the Nile-based foreign policy of the era.

The survey for the railway began in 1892, and the first rail was laid in 1896. A year earlier, the East African Protectorate – covering an area a good bit smaller than the present boundaries of Kenya – had been declared. The country remained a protectorate until 1920, when it was formally annexed to the British Crown and given the name of Kenya.

With the railway came the European and Indian immigrants. A large number of Indians were brought in to build the railway, and a few hundred opted to stay in East Africa when their term of service was up. The farmers came because the railway opened up the highlands, which were ideal for European agricultural methods.

From the beginning of large-scale immigration almost until the start of the Emergency, Kenya's history was largely a struggle between the White settlers and the Indians. The White settlers wanted Kenya to advance rapidly to Dominion status, on the Rhodesian pattern, and the Indians considered that their number and their contribution to commerce entitled them to a fair share in public affairs. The first Indian representation in the Legislative Council was provided in 1919, when two Members were nominated. The Indians regarded this as quite inadequate and the battle was on.

European attempts to have Kenya recognised as a 'White Man's Land' included a plan in 1922 to rebel (if proposals regarded as pro-Indian were accepted) worked out down to details of where to hold the Governor after his kidnapping. The British Government reacted to this treasonable venture by withdrawing the offending proposals. Nevertheless, though the Colonial Office knuckled under to the settlers in many questions, they did not gain their main objective.

The following year, thanks to Indian agitation, a political document of major importance for the future of Kenya was published – the so-called Devonshire White Paper, which stated that Kenya was primarily an African country in which the interests of the Africans were to be paramount, and (perhaps most important) that the British Government's trust could not be delegated or shared. At the same time the Indians put paid to settler demands for the legal enforcement of urban segregation, though they were unable to break the racial exclusiveness of the White Highlands (which remained in force until October 1959).

It was at about this time that the young Kikuyu later to be known as Jomo Kenyatta joined the East African Association, which soon became the Kikuyu Central Association. During the twenties a number of African political and semi-political organisations began to spring up. In spite of a good deal of agitation, however, African nationalism was of little importance in Kenyan politics (except by hindsight) until after the Second World War. At worst, from the point of view of settlers and administration, it was a nuisance.

B

In 1929 Mr Kenyatta visited Britain to present Kikuyu land grievances to the Colonial Office, and in 1931 he went again to Britain as permanent representative of the KCA. While there he studied anthropology at London University, spent four months in Moscow, during the war worked as a farm labourer in Sussex, and in 1945 founded and became first president of the Pan-African Federation with Kwame Nkrumah as his right-hand man.

It was really with Mr Kenyatta's return to Kenya in 1947 that the country began the slow and difficult journey towards independence. Many Africans had served abroad during the war, and a new social and political awareness of the potentialities of the modern world was in the air, as well as a simpler feeling among men who had fought for other people's freedom that they should be entitled to their own. Mr Kenyatta therefore returned at an auspicious moment. He took over the leadership of the Kenya African Union, a successor to the KCA, from Mr James Gichuru (now Minister for Finance).

The KAU in 1951 presented a memorandum pointing out to the then Colonial Secretary the absurdity of having four Members of the Legislative Council to represent 5,000,000 Africans. It also sought a common voting roll (though not universal suffrage). At the same time the European elected Members demanded an assurance that 'African nationalism on the lines of West Africa was not Her Majesty's Government's policy for Kenya and that any statements which suggested such a thing was possible should be considered as seditious'.

While African politicians were beginning to press their modest demands, a considerable undercurrent of unrest was developing, in which African frustration over land and lack of a voice in their own country were important factors. Oathing, which had been a traditional Kikuyu method of achieving unity in any cause, began to increase. There were major strikes, and sporadic minor riots in various parts of the country, in one of which a European officer was killed. It was at this time that the word 'Mau Mau' first appeared, in the annual report for 1948 of the District Commissioner, Nakuru.

On October 20, 1953, Jomo Kenyatta was among 183 political and trade-union activists detained at the start of the State of Emergency. He was later convicted of managing and being a member of Mau Mau in a trial which aroused considerable dispute. A retrial was ordered, but countermanded apparently for political reasons.

Though much is still unclear about the Emergency in general, it seems that Mau Mau as an overall organisation never existed. The name (which was used only by the administration until quite late in the day) described a complex of interrelated and unrelated political and semi-political activities. If there had been any sort of overall plan, let alone a plan devised by anybody as astute as Kenyatta, the resistance movement (backed at least negatively, as it was at the start, by virtually all Kikuyu and a very large number of other Africans) could have massacred most of the Europeans overnight, or at least disrupted the Central Province (the heart of Kenya) by concerted sabotage.

The groups involved in subversive activities had motives ranging from purely political aims to straight thuggery under a political cloak. That Kenyatta was regarded as the symbol and leader of African nationalism by virtually all Africans including those in the forests does not mean that he 'organised Mau Mau'. In fact it is now clear that Mau Mau was not organised – it grew.

Whether the Emergency helped or delayed the African cause is open to argument. Certainly Kenya was the last of the East African territories to become independent. On the other hand, it was the only 'settler' country, and the White farmers had in the twenties shown their willingness to rebel to gain their wishes. There is little reason to suppose that they would not in the fifties have been prepared to act as the Rhodesians have done, and although their problems would have been greater, they might conceivably have succeeded. The Emergency brought several thousand British troops into Kenya, the last of whom left only after independence – and the lack of British troops in Rhodesia was what made UDI possible.

One aspect of the Emergency which has been ignored is that

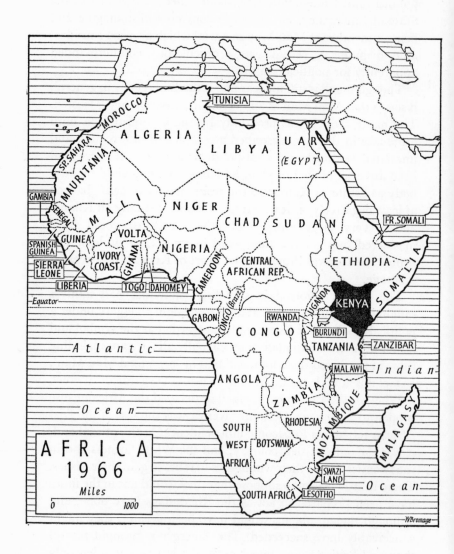

AFRICA
1966

Miles

0   1000

WBromage

its declaration and the arrest of most of those leaders who had mass support made the degeneration of the situation into guerilla war and atrocity fairly inevitable. Though civil disturbance and riots would undoubtedly have increased, the Emergency itself brought about the conditions which are thought of when the word is mentioned. Moreover the KAU demands whose rejection led to the growth of civil disturbance and thus to the Emergency were extremely reasonable. However much one may appreciate the problems (and condone the blindnesses) of the settlers and the Colonial Office, I do not see that one can get round the fact that the Emergency (and thus Mau Mau as it developed) was their fault.

At least Mau Mau and the Emergency brought a positive flurry of new constitutions and a steady advance towards African rule, helped by African refusal to accept the minute concessions which each represented while exploiting each in one way or another with considerable political astuteness. The Lyttelton Constitution of 1954 marked the end of Official Government and set up a Council of Ministers (one African). The first election was brought about by the Lennox-Boyd Constitution of 1957 which was disrupted by the African Members, who boycotted it and refused to take office.

This boycott was the prime cause of the Lancaster House Conference in 1961, which made clear to the Europeans what should have been obvious for a long time, but was not – that African rule was imminent. This conference led to the first Legislative Council with an African majority. It also led to a crisis of confidence among the Europeans, and an outflow at its worst of £1,000,000 a month.

The first mainly African Government was a minority one, since the Kenya African National Union refused office until Mr Kenyatta was released. The Kenya African Democratic Union, whose leaders were Ronald Ngala, Masinde Muliro and Daniel Moi, was the result of the smaller tribes' fear of domination by the Kikuyu and Luo, who provided most of the mass support for Kanu. Kanu's leadership by now included younger people like the extremely able union leader Tom

Mboya, whose introduction to politics was by way of the unions rather than tribal fellowships.

When Mr Kenyatta was released in 1961, there was at first hope that Kanu and Kadu would be reunited under his leadership. This proved impossible, however, and so he took over the leadership of Kanu. In January 1962 he entered Parliament as Member for Fort Hall, a few weeks later led Kanu at the Constitutional Conference in London, and in April became Minister of State for Constitutional Affairs and Economic Development.

Apart from the recognition that independence would not be long in coming, the most important feature of the constitutional conference was the 'Majimbo' or regional constitution which resulted from Kadu demands reflecting continuing fears of Luo–Kikuyu domination. There followed elections in 1963 in which Kanu gained clear majorities in both Houses, and internal self-government was achieved on June 1, 1963, with Mr Kenyatta as Prime Minister. Independence was granted on December 12, 1963.

Apart from all the social difficulties faced by any emergent nation, and the relatively minor but complex problems posed by the Europeans and Asians (especially by their monopoly of the economy), the first independent Government of Kenya inherited a secessionist movement among the Somalis of the North Eastern Province encouraged more or less openly by the Somali Government, which broke off diplomatic relations with Britain over the question. The Kenya Somalis boycotted the 1963 election, and guerilla warfare – apparently involving infiltrators from Somalia itself – continued after independence.

The principal result of this and the consequent State of Emergency in the area has been that a backward region has been virtually closed to development. It is impossible in such a confused situation to sort out the rights and wrongs of the Somali and Kenyan cases, but irredentism (however sound the ethnic arguments for it) has been recognised as potentially disastrous in Africa, where almost every frontier divides some tribe or social group.

One year after independence, Kenya became a republic – a development made possible without a referendum by the withering away of Kadu, whose last Parliamentary Members had crossed the floor a few days before.

What has happened since independence is the subject of this whole book: the only other important event to note here is the resignation (under pressure) of the Vice-President, Mr Odinga, his formation of the radical Kenya People's Union and its subsequent apparent decline.

On an East African level, there has been a seeming drift away from Federation, which was to have been one of the primary aims of the independent governments. The three territories had always been in close consultation, and in 1948 an East African High Commission and a Central Legislative Assembly to discuss matters of East African interest were set up. The High Commission controlled services like the railways, posts, customs and income tax. The currency was already joint. When Tanganyika became independent, the East African Common Services Organisation was formed to take over these functions.

This would have formed a very good basis for political federation, and indeed could still do so. Unfortunately successful federations take a long time to achieve (in the case of Australia, a century or so), and fears have been expressed that Eacso might etiolate in the meantime, to everybody's detriment. There has so far been little sign of this, though Tanzania was responsible for the splitting up of the East African currency. It is however very noticeable that Federation, which just after independence was popular enough to be a theme for songs, is rarely mentioned nowadays even in Parliament. It is certainly quite as possible as it ever was to consider Kenya as a separate entity and not merely as a region in a larger grouping.

I

Sisi Wananchi

We the People

Kenya is our land
Swahili song

We intend to show
that Africans have
much to offer the world
Kanu Manifesto

Okia, in the heart of Kamba country, might be almost anywhere in Kenya. From Machakos, the nearest town, you drive
over an alarming mountain dust-road with a near-precipice
on one side clothed in scrub and dwarf trees. Across the valley
more hills rise in banks of dark undergrowth patched with
segments of a different green where an acre or so has been
cleared for cultivation. The road is only entirely safe when it is
more or less impassable because of heavy rain. At other times
heavily laden country buses in too much of a hurry make
travel an alarming business. If it were not for the marks of
cultivation one might take the valleys for uninhabited, there is
so little sign of humanity. But around lunch time the side of the
road fills up with children on their way home from school,
with women carrying machetes and hoes, perhaps with baby
on back or with a bundle of firewood suspended from a strap
round the forehead. Then, if one is observant, one notices the
footpaths which wander away from the road, apparently going
nowhere, and below in the floor of the valley the thatched roofs
of huts or the tiles of a more substantial building half-hidden by
trees.

There is nothing to Okia itself. Two lines of open-fronted
shops are set back so far from the road that one can hardly call

them a street. A few trees cast their shade over the hens which potter in the dust and over a couple of boys leaning against a trunk chatting of nothing. There is a bar, the Okia Clean Hotel, which though it is only three walls and a corrugated iron roof, offering nothing stronger than bottled beer and fizzy orange, lives up to the first part of its name. At the rough scrubbed tables there seem to be more children watching the customers than there are customers. The menu – chicken, goat, a stiff dough made of maize meal known as posho which, with red bean stew, is the Kenyan's staple diet – is written in Kamba instead of the Swahili which is used wherever two tribes meet.

Okia is not a village, it is a market. Its like are to be found in their thousands all through Kenya, apparently dead for six days out of seven. On the seventh one sees why they are there, and why the two rows of shops are set so far apart. On market day these places are magnets which draw people from miles around with fruit, with vegetables, with goats and chickens, to bargain and gossip and meet the acquaintances who live a whole day's walk across the valley.

Kenya is still a countryman's country. The normal way of living is on the farm, surrounded by one's own land. Where there are villages they are for the most part random clusters of huts without a focus. The exceptions are usually in fact the labour lines of a big estate. Even the markets big enough to boast a few permanent shops or a post office are sleepy all week, preparing for the day when the world comes alive. This sleepiness also affects small towns like Naivasha. Naivasha has a railway station, its lake is a favourite place for fishermen's week-end outings, there is even industry – a Kenya Co-operative Creameries factory, a plant for processing vegetables and another for processing fish. Yet the whole place looks impermanent. There is one street straggling along one side of the main Nairobi–Uganda road, and a couple of turnings off it which peter out almost immediately. The buildings are single-storey and – with the exception of the Bell Inn – a little seedy. In spite of the stalls selling curios, the bright oil-company signs on the two garages and the goods trains fussing in the station, Naivasha feels as if it might vanish as quickly as it sprang up.

Only the towns which are centres of local government achieve a settled and deliberate air. Fort Hall, for instance, is spread over a series of ridges and seems almost more park than built-up area. But its hospital, its police headquarters, its administration offices and its tiny church-turned-cathedral give it substance. Yet here too the shopping streets, though the two main ones boast a traffic island of a sort where they intersect, are half-deserted except at the week-end. Fort Hall appears less a town than a collection of amenities for the surrounding country-dwellers.

For all that, any of these places – so much are they rooted in the immediate area which they serve – gives an impression of complete cohesion. Each of them (except the markets, which count officially as 'country') has its Asian shopkeepers and its little enclave of red-brick, bougainvillead bungalows which was once the preserve of the local Europeans, built rather apart from the rest of the town like a self-imposed ghetto. But in spite of these and their Asian equivalents, Fort Hall is Kikuyu, Machakos is Kamba. None of them reflects the extraordinary variety which is Kenya. For this one must visit the big towns: Mombasa the Islamic city and international port; Nakuru the 'farming capital', where Kikuyu and Luo and Kalenjin meet and which until recently boomed on the wealth of the European settler-farmers; Thika, which though it is basically Kikuyu has drawn people from many tribes to work in its factories; and above all Nairobi.

To the tourist in Kenya for a few weeks, the commercial and administrative centre of Nairobi, with its broad main streets and its impressive new buildings, is a symbol of modern Kenya. The fine Ministries, the offices – whether matchbox style like the Norwich Union building or with mezzanine balconies like the blocks down Government Road – disguise the fact that Nairobi is as small as a provincial English town. The impression which the main streets give is not a false one in so far as Nairobi is an international city, the commercial focus of East Africa.

Yet the commercial centre is not, in human terms, the centre of Nairobi. It is in the scruffier streets that the true Nairobi displays itself and that the true symbols of modern Kenya are to be found: in Racecourse Road especially, for Racecourse Road leads to 'the locations' – the districts where the mass of Nairobi's working population lives – and to the country bus station, where most people coming to Nairobi arrive.

Racecourse Road is lined with little, open-fronted stores offering a jumble of cheap cloth, tinned foods, enamel plates. Everything a poor man could want is there. Near the top is a row of shops which the symbol-addict might see as reflecting the changing face of Kenya. There is the National Christian Council of Kenya reading room, where those whose home is a single room filled with children can go and try in relative peace to make up for the education they have missed in childhood. There is the retail outlet of Kenya's main pig factory, delightfully called the Supaduka (*duka* being Swahili for a shop). There are an impoverished-looking bar, with bare and greasy tables and a row of shoeshine boys outside; two doctors' surgeries from which issues a constant stream of headscarved women with crying, freshly injected babies on their backs; and a row of workshop-garages giving off an intermittent flickering of oxy-acetylene.

The traffic too is more varied and representative than the traffic in the centre of town. There are middle-class cars, African, Asian and European. There are buses on their way to Kisumu, to Embu, or to the nearby areas of the city itself. Some of the country buses, privately owned, are so rickety that it seems impossible they will make the top of the next hill; others, equally privately owned, are of an awe-inspiring modernity. All are filled almost to bursting, all piled high with luggage ranging from suitcases and bicycles to sugar-cane and anonymous, lumpy bundles. There are lorries ancient and modern. There are swarms of handcarts, the poor man's Carter Paterson, heaped with a factory-delivery of chairs or an evicted tenant's worldly belongings.

The pavements of Racecourse Road offer as much variety as

the road itself. There are competent-looking, bespectacled women in sensible suits – social workers or teachers perhaps. There are gay groups of African or Asian youths in tight trousers wearing cheap Sinatra straw hats and carrying transistor radios. Kikuyu women from the nearby country districts tramp dourly along under a load of vegetables hung from a strap across their foreheads, or cast a critical eye over the goods in the little shops. A Masai in a blanket, visiting Nairobi to see a doctor or sell a shield, stands relaxed in the flow of people, looking around him with faintly superior tolerance. Two young men in business suits talk respectfully to a very old man apparently wearing only an old Army greatcoat. An Asian woman in a sari gracelessly topped by a cardigan tows a train of children. And as a background, Nairobi's working population in its semi-uniform of white shirt and grey or khaki trousers streams past: chatting, walking abstracted, laughing in groups. This and not the neat European and Asian suburbs or the tall offices is the Nairobi and the Kenya of today – a town and a country as full of optimism as they are full of troubles.

All too rarely in talk or writing about a country like Kenya is there any apparent recognition that it is inhabited by rather ordinary people who share the emotions and interests of all mankind. Europe knows from its cinema screens the nomadic herdsmen of tribes like the Masai or the Turkana, and at the opposite end of the scale the Ministers, the UN representatives, all those whom one sees prosperous-looking and dark-suited getting in and out of aeroplanes or urbanely submitting to television interviews. These two extremes exist, but by definition the number of Kenyans who are international figures is to be counted on the fingers of two hands. The number of Kenyans who live a life which is really like that of their great-grandparents in all respects – who never touch a shilling piece or catch a bus from one year's end to the next – is almost equally small. In between lies a land of nine million people.

Roughly speaking, Kenya is divided into four types of country. There is the coastal strip, and the barren plain which lies behind it. Then the land starts rising to the south-western plateau. This area is in itself very varied, ranging from arid plains shared between big game and the pastoral Masai to the fertile landscape of Kiambu, in the heart of Kikuyu country. Then there are the lands bordering Lake Victoria – strictly speaking, in the south-west also, but geographically separate. Going by road from Nairobi to Kisumu, there is a fairly dramatic descent from Kericho, the tea-growing centre of Kenya, which is high and chilly, to the plain floor which is the last bit of the journey. Historically speaking, the lacustrine tribes living in the area whose centre is Kisumu have more to do with what is now Uganda than with the rest of Kenya, so that the Luo or the Bakusu of Kenya and the Lwo or the Bagisu of Uganda are brothers separated by the vagaries of colonial geography. Lastly there is the vast north-eastern region – an area which the visitor (and indeed Kenyans themselves) tends to leave out of account, and yet which is on the map almost half the country. This is, to generalise, desert country. Its peoples are divided into the camel-using Muslim Somalis and those like the Boran whose links in pre-colonial days were with Ethiopian tribes. This area has always been something of a *terra incognita*. Today, when there is a quiet war going on between Kenya security forces and *shifta* – armed gangs whose motives range from a desire to secede to Somalia to outright banditry and armed from Somalia if not actually stiffened by Somali troops – this is even more the case. The region has a romantic, *Beau Geste* quality which appeals especially to Englishmen with 'desert sickness'; but in terms of modern Kenya it can as yet hardly be said to exist except as a headache.

Kenya's physical diversity is matched by the traditional patterns of its people. On the coast and the lake, people farmed rather lackadaisically and fished: in the areas which had poor soil or lacked water they drove cattle; in the more fertile areas (by and large the south-western quarter) they tilled the soil. Depending partly on whether they were Bantu like the Kikuyu and Kamba of central Kenya, Nilotic like the Luo of the Lake, or Nilo-Hamitic like the Masai, they differed in communal organisation – though even in pre-colonial days the ethnic divisions were not water-tight. The Bantu Baluhya picked up many customs from the Luo just because the two groups lived next to each other, and the same is true of the people on most tribal 'frontiers'.

Nobody can say quite how many tribes there are in Kenya. One group of peoples closely related by language and culture, the Baluhya, is divided into groups such as the Bakusu and the Maragoli, with about a dozen other major units. Is the tribe the Baluhya? Are the Bakusu a tribe or a subtribe or what? Either or both, depending on what you take the word 'tribe' to mean. Similarly, the question of whether the Chuka who live near Mount Kenya are a tribe or a subgroup of some sort is in factual terms unanswerable. This being the case, one can only say that there are something under fifty tribes in Kenya. Each of these had a strong sense of communal separateness. Groups which seen from a distance were very similar in origin, traditional social and political structure, language and so on – such as the Kikuyu and the Kamba – saw and still largely see themselves as quite distinct. None the less the differences, relatively minor from the point of view of an observer from another continent, were always dwarfed by resemblances which make possible generalisations about a 'Kenyan' (and for that matter on a wider scale an 'African') way of life. The sole really significant division was between cattle-breeding and crop-farming groups.

The only exception to this is the coastal strip, which is an entity on its own and in many ways is quite unlike the rest of the country. Racial terminology has only a limited meaning on the coast, the essence of which – especially in the towns of Mombasa and Malindi and on the island of Lamu – is Islam. Its rhythms are the rhythms of the Muslim year, of Ramadhan, of Idd. In Mombasa itself attempts to make divisions between Arab and African – or for that matter Arab, African and Indian Muslim – are largely pointless. The situation was neatly if caustically put by a Hindu friend whose family had been in

Mombasa for several generations, and who thus stood in Mombasa society but also, for religious reasons, a little separate from it.

'It amuses me,' he said. 'Ten years ago Mombasa was full of people who looked pure African, who went around insisting that they were Arabs. Now things have changed politically, the same people are as loud as can be in their protestations of Africanness.'

Outside Mombasa, tribal links are more recognisable. The Digo tribe, for instance, is Muslim by religion. Socially, however, the Digo, though Muslim-influenced, have preserved many specifically tribal customs, which presumably survive from a pre-Muslim era. Even so, anybody thinking too rigidly in ethnic terms would soon be perplexed to notice that of a group of Digo women all dressed similarly and all chatting away at the same well, one might look almost pure Arab in facial structure and another what I can only describe as West Indian.

Important as they are, there has in general been too much harping on tribal divisions as an inherently divisive factor, whether present or past. A Kenyan may still think of himself as a Kikuyu or a Luo or whatever, but there is an overriding similarity which provides the ground for a growing sense of 'Kenyanness'. Essentially the same day-to-day existence is shared by everybody. The average man is a peasant working a small plot of land which still provides largely subsistence crops, but whose life is none the less profoundly and increasingly influenced by a cash economy; a situation which can have its advantages – a reasonable degree of economic autonomy when harvests are good, for instance – but which is productive of a good deal of insecurity, as much social as economic.

Every official document in Kenya, every planning survey, reiterates the fact that Kenya, an overwhelmingly agricultural country, is in the process of changing from a principally subsistence to a principally cash economy. In the past, a family ate what it produced and bartered the surplus. Such a family was remarkably self-sufficient. Although special skills did exist, they were not at the heart of economic life. The Kamba, for example, were noted chain-makers: but the chains they produced were used entirely for ornament. In the future even the most backward areas of Kenya will abandon subsistence for cash-crop farming.

This fact has important economic repercussions; but it also has social results which make the ordinary Kenyan's life very different from the ordinary European's, whether in Norway or in Greece. The basis of existence is the *shamba*, a smallholding which feeds the family. Certain foods, such as sugar and tea, are bought; but most are grown at home. Thus there is a certain freedom – at least in good growing years – from the need for money. But there is a whole range of things for which money is essential. Tax must be paid, clothes, education, medicine, all have to be bought unless one lives entirely as if the colonial days had made no impact, which fewer and fewer Kenyans are prepared to do. Then there are all the things which may not be strictly necessary, but which make life sweeter if one can afford them, ranging from cigarettes to transistor radios.

Naturally this transitional stage raises a vast array of problems, but there is a good deal of security in the day-to-day circumstances of peasant existence the world over. The rhythm of country life is pretty regular – with a regularity which these days takes in the details of life in a modern State, such as the date the taxes fall due, as well as the patterns of sowing and harvest. This life in its broad outlines is shared by all peasant Kenyans whatever their tribe, whatever the differences in their culture patterns. A Luo peasant may view his Muluhya counterpart with a wary eye, mindful of the tales his grandfather told him, but the two have most things in common from farming techniques to food. And the similarity between different country areas extends beyond the rhythms of peasant life. Even in its incongruencies this likeness of one part of the country to another remains. Everywhere modern life is superimposed on traditional. One will suddenly come across a group of remarkably smart secondary-school pupils carrying satchels along a dirt road which has apparently been going nowhere for miles. A woman laboriously breaking turf with a mattock will pause to chat with the driver of a bright red, shining-new tractor on its way to a nearby agricultural co-operative. All over the country things are changing, and the challenges and problems – and the excitements – posed by the changes are common to all Kenyans. The very fact that, owing to the speed of this transition, the present is somewhat unsettling encourages the breakdown of barriers. Unsettledness is an incentive to opening the eyes and looking around. Given that past social factors emphasised people's differences one from another, this process is in itself a unifying influence by which even the remotest areas are affected.

Many parts of Kenya are still distant from main roads, let alone railways – so that I was once told by an education inspector that there were schools in the Embu District which he had not visited in three years because to reach them meant a day's journey on foot from the nearest road open to cars. But almost none is so isolated that new ideas have not penetrated. Young lads and girls leave the local primary school and cross the ridges into the outside world or wait in the dust for a country bus to take them to the nearest town and the nearest secondary school: when they come back they are not quite children any longer. They are listened to. Perhaps they even come back with a skill, or revisit their home as agricultural extension officer for the area. The place to which they return will already be open to the ideas which they bring back, partly because since independence a great curiosity has replaced the vague apathy of colonial days, partly because, however remote the area, some of its men will have left it to join the forces or to work for money in the towns. And what the soldier or the labourer only gathers from what he sees himself – which in the circumstances of the Army or domestic service may be very little – those who leave for education can explain and relate to life at home.

This process has, of course, been going on for a long time. The adventurous have always sallied forth, though all too

C

frequently they left never to be seen in their home areas again. In the years leading up to independence, however, a vast new expansion of opportunity was brought by political change in general and Africanisation in particular. Nowadays an area does not just have one great man, a hero vanished into the outside world to become a legend at home. The outlying district and the centres of modern life are linked by a network of officials, M.P.s, agricultural officers, school teachers, and by those of its own inhabitants who have either gone for education and returned, or have stayed in the city to work. And personal contact is not the only contact. The Okias, the little markets everywhere, have their bars, and many of these bars have radios, even if the cheap Japanese transistor sets are too expensive for the people of an impoverished area. The country buses bring the national newspapers within reach almost everywhere, to be read aloud or explained for the benefit of the illiterate. Just as the countryside of Ukambani, at first sight unpopulated, turns out to be full of people, so in all but the most isolated spot – if one waits long enough – somebody will pass with a radio or a newspaper. If certain areas still carry on very much as they have always done, this is not because they are unaware that things are different nowadays, but because they cannot relate their general knowledge to their own experience.

And of course, most of Kenya is not cut off even in this limited sense. While it is probably still true that many people never travel more than about twenty miles from their homes, the need for money sends many of the men into the towns or to the large-scale farms to look for work. If they live near a town they may get home every week. At the least they usually manage to get home once a year. There is a constant flow of people between the towns and the country, acting as messengers, perhaps taking a dozen eggs to a friend or a dress for somebody's wife, and keeping every corner in contact with every other. Kenya is not a country like the Congo, where there may be large areas whose people live without any knowledge of the outside world at all. Even the illiterate have a pretty fair working knowledge of what goes on at the centre – and often very definite views about it.

The popular song can give a fair idea of the concerns of ordinary men and women. Kenya's Swahili-language pop music is still very much of the people. The singers are almost all semi-professional. Even the professionals do not earn very much (the average payment for a recording is an outright £7 10s), and they share the life of the man in the street. On the whole these musicians do not come of subsistence peasant stock, but their backgrounds are very ordinary. The father of Fadhili William, who wrote the hit song *Malaika*, was a carpenter. Other musicians' parents worked as household cook, railway foreman, police sergeant-major, greengrocer, waiter. The singers themselves have held jobs which were only a little better on the whole: railway apprentice, telephonist, travelling salesman, barman. They come in fact of the same background as most modern Kenyans – semi-skilled or unskilled, scuffling for a living, getting along as best they can. These men sing largely for people like themselves.

What makes the Swahili songs interesting is that their public is not principally the young townees – these go for Jim Reeves, for Elvis Presley, for the Beatles, like teenagers anywhere. The average buyer of a Swahili pop record is between twenty-five and thirty-five years old and lives in the country, in the Western or Nyanza Provinces (from where, incidentally, most of the singers hail). They speak, in other words, to the Kenya – not just the Nairobi – Everyman.

The songs themselves are on a wide range of subjects. There are of course a large number of love songs, but many deal with less banal topics. Quite a number, especially around independence, were political (a reflection not of the singers' public-spiritedness, since most of them are entirely apolitical, but of their awareness that a record with the word Uhuru in it was bound to sell at the end of 1963). But much more interesting are the songs with a directly social context. These give a very clear picture of what the ordinary Kenyan has to worry about. There is unemployment: 'Where will I get work? I went to

Moshi looking for a job and couldn't get one. I reckoned if I went to Nairobi my luck would change. Now I'm in Nairobi and I haven't got work yet. Now what do I do?' Education also crops up quite frequently in these songs, since it is something of which most people are short, and yet more and more necessary if they are to get on in the world. As one singer put it, 'You used to see the work of the police and the army being done by people without education. Now the only people who are wanted are the educated. What work will there be for those who can't read?'

Many of the songs have a familiar ring. There is for example, the man whose wife has ideas above his pay packet: 'Woman, don't run me out of money – I haven't had a rise yet. When I get one I'll buy you a scooter. I know you see your friends riding out on scooters, but their husbands have fat salaries. When I get a rise I'll even buy you a car!'

These lyrics cover a wide range of social comment. Even more interesting than the main topic of the song, quite often, are the casually mentioned details which reveal how the ordinary man lives. As an example, since most people are poor a man who can afford to wear a suit is a somebody. Many lyrics dwell on the snob-value of suits. One song, underlining a man's poverty, says: 'He hasn't even got bus fare.' 'He hasn't even got a bed in his place' is a phrase so common as to be a cliché. The song about the scooter is interesting. To attain a car – however old – is still beyond most people, but a scooter is no longer quite out of the question. Even cars are now coming within the reach of a few more people. The élite of course all have them: but one sees more and more ancient models crammed with quite ordinary people. This impression is borne out in strange ways. According to a senior traffic policeman in Nakuru, the number of prosecutions for unroadworthy vehicles has risen sharply because more people can buy a beat-up old car without being able to afford to look after it!

The song which best sums up the concerns of Kenya's Everyman (and, for the matter of that, international Everyman) is called simply: *Misery*.

'What is misery for the men of this world? It's a man without land, a man without a child, a man without wealth. What is misery for the women of this world? It's a woman without a husband, without a mother, without a brother. I've no father, no mother; on the day I die who'll weep for me? I feel bad, when my fellows suffer, to think that I've land, I've a child, I've wealth.'

Kenya is often said to be a half-way house; to be hanging fire between the simple certainties of a peasant life and the complexities of industrialisation. Although this remark is something of a glimpse of the obvious – we are all hanging fire between our past and our future – the sense of evolution is naturally stronger in a land hurrying to catch up than in European countries. But one can draw over-facile conclusions. Once at the house of a very senior civil servant, as the men drank beer and talked about their jobs and the women and children watched television, a servant offered us something which might have been offered to guests a hundred years ago – a plate of roast goat. A bar and restaurant which is a favourite haunt of everybody from politicians to publishers serves, as well as the usual salads and roast meats, pork curry with posho. People have found it tempting to see symbols in these things, but philosophising about the search for a society which will have the best of Europe and the best of Africa is idle. There is such a search, without doubt: but on a personal level Kenyans are not so self-conscious. They just happen to like goat. Moreover, though traditionally African elements do filter through into modern life, the general tone of society is all too much the other way.

Except on the most obvious level – that of big game and nomadic herdsmen – Kenya is a most unexotic country for one with forty tribes and four races making up its citizens. Even the herdsmen, if one gets to know them, are usually consumed by mundane cares. If there is any single word which sums up the Kenyan African character, it is the word 'worthy'. Kenyans on the whole lack the glamour, the air of natural urbanity and sophistication possessed by the Baganda, or the Yoruba of

Nigeria. Nor do they exude an air of dignity (a lot of individuals do, of course, but this is personal dignity, possessed by old men or rather stout middle-aged women; there are some peoples whose babies manage to look dignified). They are 'weekday people': they do not charm the birds off the trees, but they are a good deal more reliable than many charmers.

As a friend who is himself half Kikuyu and half Scots remarked, when I was once rather tactlessly singing the Baganda's praises: 'Yes – very charming, very gay, very sophisticated. Never get anything done. . . .' There is something in this; ridiculous as group descriptions can be if taken too seriously, they are not entire rubbish. One meets enough hail-fellow-well-met Luo, with a tendency to talk loud and a definiteness of speech just this side of the opinionated to believe that these traits are perhaps group traits. A sufficient number of Kikuyu are a little reserved, polite but less immediately matey than many Luo, with a tendency to moods unconnected with outside events. Naturally there are many neurotic Luo and many jovial Kikuyu, as there are many Baluhya who are neither blunt nor straightforward. Generalisations about different tribes can cause a lot of trouble, but only if people start taking them as a rule of thumb in their approach to individuals. There is a charming story of a Kipsigis who came up to a settler-farmer and said: 'You know, Bwana, we Kips are awfully like you Europeans. We love to watch other people work.' As a wild exaggeration there is something in this, just as the remark that the Taita are at their best at parties, and playing stringed instruments, is a slander with a grain of truth.

The worthiness noticeable in so many Kenyans is part of a general tendency to what I can only describe as a positive ordinariness. They lack that charming fecklessness which fascinates and infuriates so many Englishmen in more romantic places. A phrase sometimes used by Europeans in Kenya is 'the land of *bado kidogo*' (in a little while). The remarkable thing about this expression is its inappositeness. The *mañana* spirit is probably less in evidence in Kenya than almost anywhere else in the world outside northern Europe and North

America. This is not to say that all Kenyans are models of efficiency. But there is a definite general inclination to get on with things. Where one meets the opposite tendency it is usually due to special circumstances. The Income Tax Department, for example, is undoubtedly in a state guaranteed to drive anybody mad who wants a return in a hurry, but this is not caused by Bado Kidogoism as such; it is lack of experience and organisation.

Of course these average characteristics are overlaid by all sorts of other influences. Off the beaten track (and to a large extent on it) you will find a great deal of relaxed friendliness. Once, making a tour of a friend's home district, we stopped at a little bar for a late lunch. It was a little more sophisticated than the Okia Clean Hotel, and even boasted a back room in which we were to eat. We sat at the bar while we waited for our roast goat (rather disconcertingly served with stale sliced bread out of a packet) to be cooked. On the boardwalk outside the open door hens clucked and stalked. Occasionally a donkey would plod past in charge of a little boy, on the way to the well to have the four-gallon cans on its back filled with water. There was a tendency for children to cluster in the doorway and gawp at us, but the wizened old man in shorts and a very tatty shirt, and the family man in mechanic's overalls, did not let curiosity overcome their civility. We were in an area where strangers of any sort – let alone stray Europeans – were pretty uncommon, but they refrained from asking (what clearly interested them most) what the hell we were doing there. Which way did we come? Was the road very bad with all the rain we'd been having? Not an exciting conversation, but relaxed and welcoming. It might be tempting to draw all sorts of conclusions as to Kenyan virtues, from this, and from the similar easy friendliness that one meets everywhere in the little eating houses and bars where Europeans still rarely penetrate. But this courtesy is not Kenyan alone, nor even African. It is a quality found in any land where a peasant culture still exists. And if Kenyan peasants are much like peasants anywhere, so are other groups very like their counterparts all over the world. A Muluhya petty clerk trying to keep himself a cut above his neighbours on too small a salary shares with a Muluhya peasant woman or a Muluhya Cabinet Minister little more than a language and a childhood background, but he much resembles his English opposite number. The fact that petty bourgeois attitudes are a new thing in Kenya has less to do with national character than with the fact that until very recently petty-bourgeois jobs were not open to Africans.

None the less, Kenyan qualities there are: and if they sometimes seem a bit dull, a bit stuffy, to feel so is a foreigner's luxury. For the inhabitants of a country which is trying to haul itself out of a semi-subsistence economy, a certain doggedness and hard-headedness are a good deal more to the point than exoticism or aristocratic indolence.

2

In the Corridor

We foster the resurgence
and adaptation of all that
is valid for the 20th century
in our indigenous customs
Kanu Manifesto

Solve Nairobi's
problems and you will
have solved all the
problems facing Kenya
Mwai Kibaki

Kenya is an exciting but also an unsettling country. It is like a house at spring-cleaning. There is bustle, there is noise, there is confusion more apparent than real. Everything is subject to doubt. Are the curtains too old? Is the husband's favourite armchair an anachronism or a tradition? It is hard to see how anything good can come out of all this chaos, yet when the brooms are back in the cupboard the overall result is usually for the better.

The elements of Kenya's revolution are more practical than ideological. Few people are obsessed with change for change's sake, and on the whole (though with exceptions, particularly concerning the social re-Africanisation of a country more influenced than most by its former colonists) the changes sought are economic. For every politician who exhorts his hearers to preserve the African personality, ten exhort them to listen to the advice of the agricultural officer.

Since it is difficult to get hysterical about the advice of agricultural officers, the spring-cleaning atmosphere is not immediately to the fore. The effects, both exhilarating and disturbing, are largely on the subconscious level. It is rather as though one were reading a book in the room being spring-cleaned. One is only half-aware of what is going on, but the requests to move one's feet and the smell of dust make their impression.

The revolution, though quiet, is none the less genuine, and its effects reach far beyond its immediate goals. For example, people need to be persuaded to plant their crops in rows, not just dotted about anyhow. If the persuasion is successful, a fundamental idea will have been upset: that what was good enough in the past is Holy Writ for the present. Once this notion – the underpinning of much traditional dead wood – is gone, new energy is released and every compartment of life comes under inspection. The trees in the middle of the shamba, once valued for the shade they gave, get in the way of the planted rows. Do we uproot them, or – still needing shade – do we resite them?

The colonial administration had only hazy ideas as to its role *vis-à-vis* the Africans except on a day-to-day basis, and such ideas as it had often contradicted each other. As a result it neither effectively upheld the traditional way of life, nor brought about any logical progression into the money economy. Such efforts as it did make in either direction lacked conviction and were liable to cease if the settler farmers protested, which they often did. Traditional life was crippled not only in the White Highlands, where the settler influence was strongest, but all over Kenya. The African population became a *lumpen*-peasantry. By the time a serious attempt was made to rationalise the agricultural situation in the early 1950s, African life was pretty well set in the worst possible social pattern, in a state of uneasy suspension between two worlds.

This suspension is still the basic fact of the country today. In administration, in law, in agriculture, in social life, Kenya's pattern is one of Western superimposed on traditional structures. Since they belonged to a subsistence economy which the country is leaving behind as fast as it can contrive to do so, the old patterns of society are disappearing at a rate which – while it creates an atmosphere of aliveness, even of derring-do – puts a strain on the community and every individual in it.

All over Kenya, people of all sorts are coping – remarkably

successfully – with the changes of attitude demanded by the country's burst of energy after independence. To a large extent this process is subconscious. Commentators sometimes talk as though the choices involved in the transition between an old life and a new were on the conscious level. Except in the very limited sense that a man has the choice between deciding to plant in rows and continuing to scatter seed all over the place, this is not the case. When it is said: 'The fact that two cultures are meeting in our present time makes it more than difficult for our youth to find the right standards' (National Christian Council of Kenya Youth Dept: Project Strategy Report, January 1965), one should not get the idea that any active process is involved. People in transition between two cultures are in a corridor. They may get a tantalising glimpse forward and back through half-open doors, but a glimpse it remains. What lies in the room ahead is the subject of guesswork and wishful thinking. What lies behind is half-forgotten and its relevance – if relevance it has – misunderstood.

The ordinary people of Kenya are fairly well aware of the practical implications of the 'Western' technological world to which they are advancing, but there are signs that they lack the psychological sure-footedness to make the best use of it. Of 'Western' culture in the deep sense – that mishmash of *idées reçues*, ethics, aesthetics, assumptions about oneself and the world which so enweb the least educated European that his mind is almost irrevocably set in a 'European' mould – they cannot be expected to possess anything. The ethical poles to which they have access – Christianity and Hollywood, to over-simplify – cancel each other out.

At the same time what remains of traditional culture has become entirely superficial. Its precepts have lost the combined religious and social power which they once possessed and operate on a level hardly above 'it's not cricket'. The ethical and social positions – the extended family, communal responsibility and so on – are still recognised, but more and more they are becoming the subject of lip-service and keeping up with the Kamaus.

Some of the most obvious results of this situation are relatively

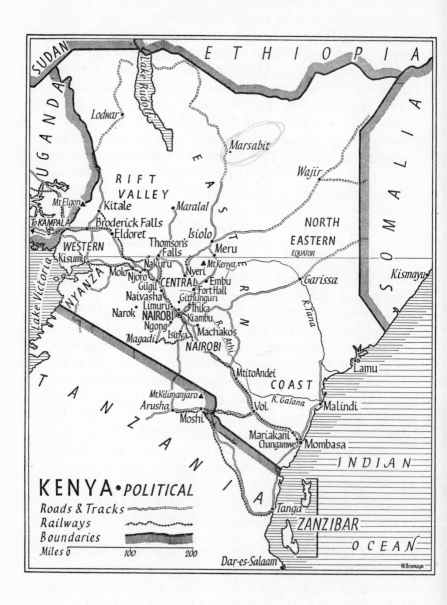

KENYA·POLITICAL
Roads & Tracks
Railways
Boundaries
Miles 0   100   200

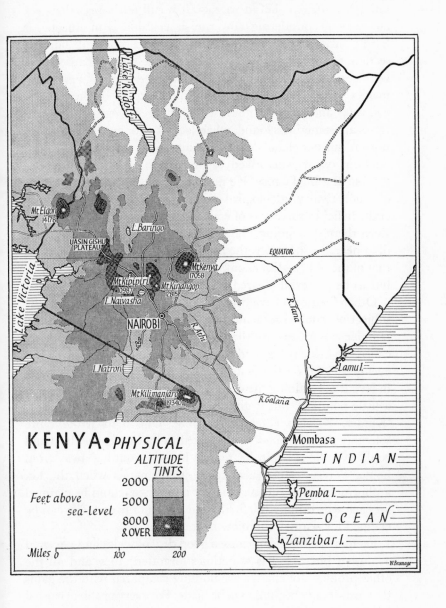

KENYA • PHYSICAL

ALTITUDE TINTS

Feet above sea-level

2000
5000
8000 & OVER

Miles 0 100 200

Lake Rudolf

Mt Elgon 14178

UASIN GISHU PLATEAU

L. Baringo

EQUATOR

Mt Kenya 17058

Mt Kipipiri 10987

Mt Kinangop 12815

L. Naivasha

Lake Victoria

NAIROBI

R. Athi

R. Tana

L. Natron

Mt Kilimanjaro 19340

R. Galana

Lamu I.

Mombasa

INDIAN

Pemba I.

OCEAN

Zanzibar I.

W. Bromage

unimportant. A belief in witchcraft is still fairly prevalent – a fact which, considering how rife superstition is in Europe, is hardly surprising. A report on social conditions, in its housing section, mentions a young man who moved house because 'there were certain Luo women who they believed were playing them magics – they found things they didn't know in their room, e.g. roots and pieces clothes'. Even apparently straightforward issues are sometimes found, when looked into, to hide a witches' brew of sinister elements. An acquaintance who is an industrial relations expert was asked to investigate some major labour trouble in a big factory. He uncovered an extraordinary tangle of union rivalry, ideological dispute, tribal rivalry and witchcraft. Belief in sorcery is of course stronger in country districts. Even there it is fading, though it will take a very long time to disappear. In the towns the most common attitude seems to be that of the old English countryman: 'Us don't believe in ghosts, but us be powerful afeared of 'em.'

Other features of traditional life are from time to time the subject of much argument in the correspondence columns. Two popular evergreens are the dowry system (rather inaccurately called the bride price) and the role of women. Opinion is pretty evenly divided on the first issue, though with a slight majority in favour of retaining the dowry. The 'women's rights' dispute is a little pointless, but it gives rise to some splendid examples of 'Kinder, Kirche, Küche' reasoning. One man wrote quite solemnly that if women were elected to Parliament no husband could ever sleep again for fear of his wife running away from home. Polygamy can also cause problems, as when the tax authorities had to rule on whether allowances could be claimed for each wife or only the first. In the event only one wife can be claimed for – a definite blow to tradition.

Factors like these can cause a good deal of social and personal confusion but (what is sometimes forgotten) they and all the other problems of change are nothing compared with the gains that are already beginning to be made. For every problem caused by transition, there are ten inherent in the situation out of which the country is trying to develop. A period of stress is a small price to pay for freeing people from disease, illiteracy and poverty, from a life in which work is a back-breaking ten hours in a dried-up maize patch and relaxation gossip by the roadside or a jug of home-brew. There was much dignity and joy in the traditional way of life, but the future offers a good deal more dignity and joy. Moreover, the life that most people live today is not really traditional. It is camping in the corridor, and the sooner everybody is out of it the better. The rush to the towns is a sign that the people themselves consciously or unconsciously recognise this, since most people equate modern life with city life.

The effects of change are most dramatic and easy to isolate in the cities, but the impact of change on those who remain in the country is hardly less profound. Traditional life there still seems stronger because the countryman, except on the very edge of a tribal area, is surrounded by his own people. Nevertheless, even in the country – except perhaps in the most 'backward' areas of the pastoral tribes – the old ways have lost much of their power. Even the pastoral tribes, in spite of their complex and special problems, are beginning to feel the impact of change.

The real division between farming groups in Kenya is between the static and the nomadic. Elsewhere in fact, whatever local rivalry may claim, there is little difference between livestock and crop farmers. But the wanderer perforce develops a way of life entirely different from that of the stay-at-home. This is all right while the tribe remains a self-contained unit. Unfortunately, what broke into traditional patterns was a more advanced stay-at-home culture. This left the pastoral tribes at a severe disadvantage. Even though progress may kill it with time, the Kikuyu do not need to abandon their whole way of life overnight. The nomadic Masai do. Their life is essentially opposed to progress. The nomad does not stick with an area and improve it, he uses it and moves on.

This fact, no other, has put the pastoral tribes behind in modern Kenya. And behind they are. Without using the term as any sort of cultural value judgement, if one accepts that the goal (right or wrong) of a developing country is prosperity within the money economy, then they are backward. Equally important, if one accepts that a first-class citizen is a citizen who contributes to his country, rather than a man who is treated well by it, then the pastoral tribes are (again without value-judgement) second-class citizens. The fact that an individual Masai chief once wrote a cheque for £1,000 to pay for something he wanted and could do it again tomorrow is neither here nor there – except in so far as it points a contrast. Few Masai know what a cheque book is. Most Kikuyu, these days, do. Although they don't have one, the co-operative does.

The cattle tribes, then, are backward. Even where the word is objected to, the fact is accepted. They are backward principally because their way of life is not compatible with the modern world. This is not really their fault. Setting aside the fact that it is not blameworthy to fail to see that something is to your advantage, the pastoral tribes were hampered by attitudes common in colonial days.

From time to time just after independence a back-bencher would make a reference to the colonial Government 'treating the Samburu and Masai like animals in a zoo'. That some Masai themselves believed this is shown by a speech made by Chief Edward Mbarnoti, then Chief of the Masai, in 1961.

'If Uhuru means anything,' he said, 'it means that we are going to be treated like human beings and not like animals!' This is an overstated accusation, but it contains some truth.

Behind the very ambivalent attitude to the pastoral tribes of the colonial régime, which was an attitude shared by very many individual Europeans, lay the myth of the Noble Savage. These fine men have something that I lack, the feeling went. It must be the primitive splendour, etc., etc. The Masai have suffered badly from a subconscious European confusion of fact and fancy. The European did not want to be the snake in the Garden of Eden, tempting the Masai with the fruit of knowledge. Unfortunately, where the Eden myth is concerned the Masai are on the same side of the Angel's burning sword as we are.

There is of course a good deal more to it than this. Human beings are usually prepared to let their consciences go hang if

1 President Kenyatta's interest in farming is not just a matter of policy. He farms himself at Gatundu, his country home, and gets a good deal of pleasure out of the visits to farms which are part of his up-country tours.

2a The road to Ocia – or almost anywhere else in Ukambani. Kamba women, like the Kikuyu, carry fantastic loads from straps across their foreheads. The tree-trunk is only one of thousands used for firewood by people who do not see the point of the Government reafforestation schemes.

2b Street scene in Pumwani, one of Nairobi's more slummy areas. The buildings would not be too bad – at least they are solid – but overcrowding makes an already bleak housing situation worse every month in the main towns.

there is profit in it. 'There's no doubt that the Masai have been terribly mucked about.' The speaker is a man who knows the pastoral tribes well. 'Before the European administration came here they roamed all over Kenya. Evidence of that is that in parts of the Meru District there are people whose language has bits of Masai – they've got isolated there. And all those queer little offshoots of the Masai . . .

'When you think that they could roam all over the country to some of the best grazing ground in the world, and then were persuaded to agree to go down to areas which were not so good, it's really very remarkable that they've been as docile as they are, in my opinion – but then they are docile people, they are not warlike. They are very soft-spoken and kindly natured.'

Having been left to the dubious blessings of self-containment, the Masai have another handicap when it comes to advancement. They do not know what they are missing. This is sometimes put forward as an argument for leaving them in peace – a line of thought rather like not telling a man suffering from malnutrition to eat meat because if he doesn't know about protein he won't miss it. Now at last the pastoral tribes are finding out what they have been missing, and the best comment on the Noble Savage myth is the speed with which they are trying to get out of their ancestral life. In his study *Nandi Work and Culture*, published in 1951, G. W. B. Huntingford could describe the Nandi of Trans-Nzoia as a people who 'on the whole have remained aloof from our way of life'. Six years later, the District Commissioner reported that 'Nandi farmers are proving successful as a result of proper farm planning, crop rotation and proper grazing'. The man in charge of Isinya Training Centre, who was brought up in a Masai manyatta, remarked to Mr John Dearden of the National Christian Council of Kenya: 'How we ever lived in those extraordinary beehives, I don't know.' When you don't know anything better you don't want anything better – because you do not know what to want.

The evidence of a desire for advance (in the ordinary, question-begging sense) is everywhere. The Samburu were reported in 1951 to have built Baragoi and Wamba hospitals

D

with their own money. The Wanderobo, perhaps the obscurest tribe in Kenya, acquired a health centre in 1959. They paid for it largely themselves, by contributing one steer each. The people of Ngong did less well by their health centre – the second in Masailand – which was opened in the same year. Even so they provided nearly a quarter of the money by a 10s. special rate.

Of course, progress is patchy. People are always ready to abandon things like starving to death or dying of the plague. They are less willing to drop the aspects of their life which they regard as fun, even though it may be necessary if they want to get on. The only way to avoid the pox at one time being to abjure fornication, the pox became the ailment you love to get. The Masai moran are a sort of warrior age-group. In some clans one had to prove one's right to enter it by cattle-theft. The Masai used to believe that God gave all the cattle in the world to them. Thus to take a Kikuyu cow was to reclaim one's own property. How many moran believe this today I do not know, but it makes a very good excuse for a bit of fun. As a result, the Masai are prepared to give up many things, but this will be among the last. The District Commissioner for Narok had to warn a baraza in April of last year that cattle-theft was 'the greatest and most dangerous enemy facing the Masai'. He can, and will have to, say that again. This problem affects most if not all the pastoral tribes. Every month there are reports in the papers of major cattle raids, many of them very bloody affairs. In May 1966, for instance, seventeen Samburu were killed by a gang which made off with 800 head of cattle.

It would of course be false to think that pastoral lack of contact with the 'outside' world is either inherent or complete. The former Vice President is half Masai. His successor in the post is Kalenjin. A number of senior civil servants are Masai, including the Director of Medical Services. There are growing numbers of ordinary people from the pastoral tribes who have settled down. The man on the petrol pump at Kajiado is a Masai. Thousands of Nandi, Kipsigis and others are more or less indistinguishable from the rest of the farmers in town for market day. A clerk at my bank is Somali. Keino, a world-record runner, is Kalenjin. The pastoral tribes not only fill the ranks of their own tribal police: hundreds of them are in the ordinary police force and the Army. All these people have relatives who still live in the old way, and when they return home they cannot help introducing the seeds of change.

For all these reasons the nomadic way of life is being abandoned. It was not adopted by choice in the first place, but of necessity. As John Dearden remarked, 'They're nomadic because of the grazing – they have got to move to new pastures. But if you can show them that they can get all the grazing they want within a restricted area, they won't want to move. I'm sure they don't really *enjoy* their old way of life in contrast to the new.' Kenya Europeans are fond of little anecdotes about Masai graduates who go back to the manyatta at week-ends as if this proved anything about the Masai way of life. If they want to go home and see their parents, where else can they go?

Although all the pastoral tribes are beginning – some more than beginning – to show that they want what the modern world has to offer, it would be absurd to pretend that they are not going to have to make a far greater adjustment than the crop tribes. The nomadic way of life must be abandoned – there is no other way out. Until it is, everything else which is wanted must wait. Until a tribe settles down in one place it is very hard to give it much in the way of social services. Those who happen to be near a clinic or a school will use it, but the need to exist is more important than clinics and schools. When they have to move on to new grazing, they abandon clinic and school. Thus whereas a thoroughly unreconstructed Kikuyu or Luo can benefit from welfare services, a pastoral tribesman who is still living nomadically cannot.

Another factor which slows down development is poverty. Pastoral tribes are poorer than most others. The Turkana are so poor that the lowest Graduated Personal Tax rate in their area is 20s. a year instead of the usual 48s. In such circumstances over-ambitious, and thus unsuccessful, development can be literally fatal. The Turkana are tougher than almost anybody in the world except perhaps the Australian Aborigines and the

Bushmen of South Africa, because they have to be. They can go for days without food or water, under a merciless sun, because these are the conditions in the semi-desert in which they live. This has an effect on development.

'When those Turkana come into the European farming area as some of them do round Kitale,' I was told, 'they daren't ever go home. They have become softened and they couldn't survive.

'Now this is what we've got to be very careful of in developing Turkana. Whatever we introduce has got to be as nearly permanent as it can be, and not at the vagaries of hard seasons. Because if you softened them up for three years and then things went wrong, they would just expire.'

This is truest of the Turkana, but it applies to most of the pastoral tribes. Caution alone therefore dictates that a major stage in their development must be to improve the way in which they manage the things which they know. Since, however, what they know is cattle, and cattle alone are not enough, they must at the same time branch out. This is not just a matter of their own convenience – one of the things which they have to learn is to be useful members of society, not just ornaments.

Though the pastoral tribes face the greatest problems of adjustment these problems are common to all Kenyans. Not all of them, of course, are problems in any disagreeable sense. Difficult as a transition stage may be, it does have advantages. Traditionalists in the industrial countries mourn the passing of a sense of community, of a place in the world, of personal dignity irrespective of material possessions. All these are lost and we are the worse for it, they cry – and rightly. But in Kenya these things are not entirely gone. It should therefore be possible to preserve for an industrial society the features of her traditional life which really have value.

Preservation must not, however, be a mere pickling process. Stravinsky, in his *Musical Poetics*, writes: 'A real tradition is not a relic of a past that is irretrievably gone; it is a living force that animates and informs the present. . . . A real tradition is carried forward in order to produce something new.' A good example of this procedure is the use of self-help in community development. One of the ill legacies of the colonial era is a tendency for people to sit around and expect things to be done for them. That this is due to colonial government, which by its nature kills initiative since it takes over the responsibilities for one's future, does not make it any the less a nuisance. The solution proposed is a return to the communal labour traditional in African life, translated into a modern idiom. 'We welcome the self-help schemes,' a NCCK-Christian Churches Educational Association working party wrote, 'for in this way our people are being subjected to grapple with their own problems and are trying to solve them.'

The self-help movement is as practical in 1967 as it was in 1867. Properly applied, it allows a great deal to be done which would otherwise be too expensive to be considered. Most self-help schemes are small in scope and individual projects sound trivial, but they mount up. In the Western Province in 1965, for example, 1,695 self-help groups involving 60,445 people were established. They completed 96 access roads, 129 bridges, 75 school extensions, 958 housing improvements, 1,118 pit latrines, 324 fish ponds, 322 protected springs and 12 nursery centres, and cleared 5,866 acres of bush for farming. This makes a lot of difference to an area short of amenities. On a larger scale, 300 members of a coffee-grower's co-operative agreed to a fifteen per cent deduction on coffee sales income in order to build a coffee factory. The Government early in 1964 announced a major plan to co-ordinate and encourage self-help. Committees were to be set up at local, provincial and national level. The Government would give financial help only 'for materials not available locally or the employment of skilled artisans'. When this scheme gets under way – and planning such things takes a long time – self-help could become a major factor contributing to advance.

The notion, implicit in self-help, that what people want is probably what they need is of immense value in a poor country. Since only a fraction of what needs doing can be done in the foreseeable future, priorities are of the first importance.

Self-help can of course go off the rails for lack of planning. The sad experience of the Harambee secondary schools, many of which were built at great effort and sacrifice although they had no hope of finding adequate teachers or the money needed for upkeep, curbed the first rather indiscriminate enthusiasm. A good deal more emphasis is now laid on working in step with central planning. Nevertheless, this is a real case of a tradition with a new role in the modern world: for the self-help schemes are merely a modernisation of the system in the past whereby, if anything major needed doing, everybody in the community turned up and lent a hand. With rare exceptions at the village-hall level, self-help of this type is unimaginable in Europe. In Africa it works because it is not new.

Though the effects of change – both decay and growth – are to be seen even in the remotest country areas, events in the cities show most clearly the breakdown of tradition and the building up of a new way of life, and the manner in which this process affects ordinary people. For this reason if for no other, it is worth examining at some length.

The Church Meets Life in the Town (the report of a joint Christian Council of Tanganyika and All Africa Conference of Churches seminar) deals in detail with the impact of the city on East African life. One of the contributors, the Rev. Andrew Hake, after pointing out that 'Nairobi is growing at 6 per cent every year, compared with Kenya at 3 per cent a year, and will reach 1,000,000 inhabitants in about 1984', examines the effects of the change from country to town life: a loss of tribal unity (replaced by a tribally mixed society), of the traditional pattern of rural daily life, and of traditional moral authority (or what is left of it); the sudden confrontation with the pleasures and interests of city life on a material level – cinemas, dance halls etc.; and the development of a degree of self-reliance, individualism, independence (and indeed selfishness) unneeded or even anti-social in the village.

To this can be added the confusion of values, norms and status symbols caused by having one foot still in the country.

These are fairly self-evident ways in which confusion between

two ways of life can affect the individual. Others, equally
important, are less obvious. To return to Andrew Hake: 'We
note the peculiar problem of time. For a person living away
from town life, clock time does not present itself as a problem.
Rather the passing of a day, a week or a lifetime is measured by
particular events, as we find in both the Old and New Testa-
ment. Yet, woe unto him who comes to work late. Town life
is measured largely by the moving hands of the clock and not
events.'

The peasant come to town is the theme of many jokes. In
Africa, where this theme is repeated a hundred million times –
so that Kenya itself is in international terms 'the peasant come
to town' – the affair is serious. Strangely enough, its effect on
standards of public efficiency is relatively slight, for reasons
which may be exemplified by the bank worker 'who was noted
for his orderly efficiency, for his abilities and promise'. As
Andrew Hake says, 'His employers looked on him with great
favour and hope for the future. And yet when four o'clock came,
something happened. It was as if he stepped from one world to
another. He was completely unable to handle his affairs at home.

'The focus of the failure came in his financial affairs. He
could not handle them. This situation seemed incongrous and
paradoxical. Why should this person, an expert from 8 a.m. to
4 p.m., be a dunce at home? We have no solutions. We offer
only the slightest shaft of light.

'His background was such that in the village he was con-
tinually in the supporting "arms" of his mother and father, the
whole family, the clan and tribe. The way of life was one, things
were familiar and offered considerable support to him as a
member of a community. In a small way, the eight-to-four bank
job substituted. There he was surrounded by the security of
having only a particular job to do, the time in which to do it,
and others to tell him what to do.'

This story could be repeated a thousand times. The results of
uncertainty can be subtle and profound. Eliot's 'hollow men'
exist everywhere, but Kenya is strikingly full of people whose
professional skill – considering their lack of experience – is

remarkable, but who have no notion of what their life is about on a deeper level; who have, in fact, no culture. The insecurity which this causes makes them draw into their shells. Without being aware that they are doing it, they fend off intimacy. One can greet a quite old acquaintance and have precisely nothing to say to him after the initial 'How's your wife?' So far, this is largely confined to the professional classes of whom a young writer once remarked: 'My great concern is the breakdown in personal relationships: I feel somehow – I don't know whether it is the education that people have received, or whatever it is – there does seem to be a kind of deadness about people one has known. They almost have become something other.

'And this I find to be a very distressing sign, because you just don't know what the younger generation is going to be brought up to. You meet people you knew very well at college, and they are doing this and that job, and most of the time you can't get past the official level – what have you been doing of late? what trips have you made? what car do you drive? This type of thing.'

A breakdown in personal relationships perhaps inevitably follows a breakdown in the accepted social relationships. Moreover, this writer's remarks contain an implicit comparison with social relationships in a traditional way of life, and this way of life is showing signs of being distorted into a Golden Age. Another cause of social deadness is that people are a good deal too busy nation-building for much leisure life. One can only hope that when there is time to relax, they will not have forgotten the art.

The degree to which Kenyans succeed or fail in adjusting to modern, urbanised life has an importance out of proportion to the present numbers of city dwellers. Kenya Europeans (especially the 'old up-country hands') are fond of the saying 'Nairobi isn't Kenya'. Superficially this is true enough, but behind it lies a fundamental misunderstanding of events. In what concerns the future, the contrast between 'foreign' Nairobi and 'Kenyan' countryside is a false one.

'While we accept wholeheartedly the need to raise the efficiency and output of the rural-agricultural sector, we cannot escape from the fact that, if we seek a high standard of living in a modern economy, we thereby accept that such a goal is inseparable from a dramatic increase in urban-industrial employment. The typical modern man is a city-dweller; the world is moving toward "metropolis" as its characteristic unit of civilisation.'

The NCCK-CCEA report *Opportunities for Employment and Training in the Urban-Industrial Sector* in which this passage appears goes on:

'In spite of the many perversions of city life, a properly organised urban community offers greater opportunities than rural life, for us as men and women to grow to the full potential of our humanity.

'We therefore accept that the migration of young people to the towns is fundamentally *with the stream* of the movement of mankind. This movement is sometimes described as a "drift" to the towns; we see it as a purposeful *drive* towards urban living.'

If the city represents not only the normal existence of the future but an enrichment of life, Nairobi is no alien city except in the most limited sense. To the saw, 'Nairobi isn't Kenya', we must add, 'but it will be'. What is happening in Nairobi is happening everywhere in Kenya, though at a slower pace outside the towns. The countryman avoids the traumata of sudden change, since his whole community changes with him and around him, but the process is the same.

Nairobi is not entirely typical of Kenyan towns – it is too big – but the same problems face its smaller sisters. The only exception is Mombasa, whose citizens tend to regard the whole of the rest of Kenya as an uninteresting and barbarous hinterland. The difficulties caused by the fact that most town dwellers are still psychologically countrymen lie behind the comment in the report quoted above that 'Social policy should in our opinion be directed towards the stabilisation of genuine, long-term town-dwellers, and the reduction of the floating element who are rooted neither in a rural nor an urban situation'.

The original tendency among Africans to regard the towns as work-camps was prolonged by the colonial government, whether because it was thought that Africans belonged in the country or purely through short-sightedness. 'African housing' was – and still largely is – totally inadequate to permanent family life, being, to quote Andrew Hake again, 'designed on the basis of the bachelor bed-space; 40 square feet – 5 ft × 8 ft. Either men brought their families, and acute overcrowding resulted, or else they were prevented from living with their families, thus leading to pressures to split the family, or for a man to work for only a short period in town.'

In effect therefore Nairobi's working-class suburbs are designed for the 'half-and-half' family. Whatever happens the results are not likely to be desirable. Either the present half-way house will continue with consequences bad for both town and country, or as city-dwellers bring their wives and children to live permanently with them overcrowding will reach unhandleable proportions. Already Nairobi City Council has had to clear away small shanty towns which sprang up in odd corners. While shanty towns are not a feature of Nairobi as they are of some African capitals, one which was pulled down two years ago was large and squalid enough to represent a plague risk. With the city growing at six per cent a year, and with almost no building going on because money is so short, it is not impossible to imagine Nairobi's becoming, as Mwai Kibaki put it, 'one big slum'. This danger is increased by the people's sense of impermanency. If you do not regard a town as home, you have little incentive to keep it as it should be kept.

Though the move to the town weakened traditional social patterns, its effects can to some extent be cushioned by them. Tribal society evolved a form of social insurance which in part worked through the extended family – that complex of inter-locking relationships taking in 'second mothers', aunts, uncles, grandparents and a host of others of which the nuclear family was only a part. Like practically everything else in the past, this was considerably battered by the impact of colonialism. None the less, it still has its uses.

When their education ends – which for more than ninety per cent of them is after seven years' primary schooling – about

90,000 children a year are without the chance of further education or training or work. Many of them travel to the towns – in practice, mostly to Nairobi or Mombasa – to hunt for jobs which they have virtually no hope of finding. Those who live in areas near these towns can travel home often, or even return home at night. The others, those who stay in the cities, represent a major social problem. But at least, in the words of the NCCK Youth Secretary, Zadok Otieno, 'With this extended family in our society there would be people who would be content to look after them for at least a year. So that you can safely say that at least for one year the boys are being looked after by their relatives.'

When one considers the possible fate of a horde of adolescents – jobless and moneyless – left to their own devices in a large city, the value of this becomes clear. Unfortunately, the extended family is capable of standing just so much strain. 'We shall be beginning to have difficulty when the family is not only going to look after one, but is going to look after four. That is where we are going to have a breakdown. . . .'

For most people nowadays the extended family means hardly more than an obligation to put up one's nephews and nieces when they come job-hunting – an obligation which most Englishmen would accept – and to contribute to the schooling of poor relations. Ideally suited to peasant existence, it is if anything a drag on people who are trying to make their way in modern life. In the old days, as one European rather caustically put it, 'you didn't serve yourself, you didn't serve your immediate family, you served the extended family. Now all that has gone by the board.

'Whether it would have been possible for a wise administration to preserve the extended family idea, I don't know. All we have preserved of it now is the least desirable factors – that is to say, if you've got a good job you are expected to educate your ne'er-do-well brother's children.

'But take most of the Luo. As soon as opportunity arises they get out of the extended family and set themselves up in Nairobi or somewhere else.'

This is not entirely regrettable. The broad bosom of the extended family can suffocate initiative. A man with an idea who wants to make use of family funds, for example, may well find his way blocked by an unholy alliance of conservative grannies, jealous uncles and brothers who want to do it their way. But regrettable or not, the decline of the extended family is inevitable.

To return to Mr Otieno, 'So long as a person has got his feet in the reserves and in the city, the extended family system will still be perpetuated. So long as a man feels insecure in his job, which many still feel – that he does not regard his job as a full-time job, and that whatever he is doing here (in Nairobi) is temporary – then he has to have some contact back at home.

'But there is rising a class of African people who are now beginning to feel secure in their job, and who are thinking in terms of making their home here in Nairobi or in Mombasa, buying a house here. That man is not going to think again in terms of reserves.'

Such people are still mainly of the professional classes – but as wages go up more workers will become permanent town-dwellers.

Meanwhile the effects of urbanisation on the family are far-reaching. In one of his lectures on urban community development given at the Kenya-Israel School in Machakos in 1965, Andrew Hake summarised them.

'(The family) is the basic unit of community life, in which we all learn how to live in community. Yet it is under great pressures in the towns of East Africa. The "normal" family is the "extended", including several generations and collateral relatives.

'In towns we have the "contracted" or "nuclear" family – father, mother and children – that is if we have a family at all. We have seen that often we have a man living as a bachelor, while his wife spends much time away in the rural home. The reasons for this are (i) lack of a family wage, (ii) lack of a family house, (iii) lack of security in the towns and (iv) other reasons such as preferences for rural education for children, psychological attachment to the soil, and cultural traditions.

'As a result we have in Narobi the "nusu-nusu" family, half here, half there; this is an adaptation to very difficult pressures and circumstances. There are patterns varying from casual prostitution, liaisons, "Nairobi marriages", to permanent town-dwelling families. This temporary, interim family life is insecure, and it is agreed that it has a bad effect on children, and on the community as a whole.'

The 'nusu-nusu' family and other unorthodox marital relations are common enough to provide themes for a good many Swahili pop songs. The impermanency of many town ménages is bewailed by one man who sings:

'In the world I wander, and it makes me think:
When I married my girl, oh mama, she ran off.
I don't know why it is, but three women have run away
   from me!

'How shall I marry a girl who will stick to me all our
   lives?
I don't know if I've bad habits or if I'm bewitched.'

Another singer issues a warning about the temptations of the city:

'If you live in Nairobi don't start walking out with pretty
   girls,
If you do you'll forget your wife and your children will
   suffer.
A pretty girl loves you while you've got money;
When your cash is gone the friendship's over!'

A natural result of the breakdown in family life is a younger generation lacking in respect for its elders. This is a very popular theme with Kenyan singers, who like to adopt a rather avuncular, moralising tone:

'Youths these days despise their parents: we say bad
   things about our parents every day.
When they're drinking youths abuse father and mother;
When they're drunk they don't love their parents,'

The undoubted decline in sexual morality in Kenya can only partly be blamed on the pressures of town life, even of 'nusu-nusu' town life. A more fundamental cause is the breakdown of tribal authority, which has not yet been satisfactorily replaced by anything else. In this as in a number of other ways, the tribe represents an 'X factor' of considerable importance at Kenya's present state of development.

3

The Naughtiest Word

The dark forces
of tribalism . . .
Any anti-Uhuru speech

It just makes one
feel uplifted . . .
Church worker

The word 'tribe', like most words with a political sense, has acquired emotional overtones which amplify and frequently obscure their original meaning. Many Europeans, brought up on 'Doctor Livingstone, I presume' and the Dark Continent, still regard the tribe as being a social unit in feathered head-dresses and up to no good. When an African hears the word 'tribe' these particular overtones are naturally missing. There are however others, especially in connection with its modern derivative, 'tribalism', which is high on the list of useful rude words for the aspiring politician. Like racial prejudice in England, tribalism is something practised by the other man – everybody is convinced that the country (with the exception of his own group) is teeming with tribalists. A recent public opinion poll showed that sixty-eight per cent of the people interviewed considered tribalism existed in the Government of the country, and only twenty-five per cent definitely believed it did not exist.

The Government itself takes tribalism very seriously. Its dangers are mentioned, if only in passing, in a high proportion of speeches made by public servants ranging from the President to District Officers. On a less responsible but equally public level, it is a shouting-point beloved of writers of letters to the Press, groups gossiping on street-corners, chronic nosers-out of diabolical-liberty-taking, and the sort of M.P. who feels that an irrelevant speech is better than no speech.

In traditional African society, the tribe was the ultimate community. There was nothing bigger. Though there might have been loose confederations of tribes, these were temporary and limited in scope. The tribe was in political terms the equivalent of a nation – a nation without fixed boundaries for the most part, but a nation none the less in that on its sanction rested the law (customary law, as English Common Law is a customary law), that war was on behalf of the tribe, that the division between 'them' and 'us' lay at tribal boundaries.

In some ways the tribe as nation was fairly sophisticated. Although of course the sanctions for it were a little woolly, resting on custom and not legislation (for legislation proper did not exist in the tribe, which depended for judgement on the system of 'elders' and for enforcement of conformity largely on the pressure of public opinion), social security was provided or at least guaranteed by the tribe. The responsibility for looking after the destitute rested on their family, or if they had no family on the clan; but the customs governing how this was done, as well as the moral pressure which ensured that it *was* done, stemmed ultimately from the tribe as a whole. The tribe could thus be said to perform some of the functions of a Welfare State, though too much is sometimes made of this analogy.

In some respects the tribe was more than a nation. In Europe, ethical and moral standards were not provided by national sanctions but rested on religious and cultural traditions common to the whole continent. But in traditional Africa – except in areas which had come under Islamic influence – it was the tribe which provided the guidelines of accepted behaviour. Naturally, since most Kenyan tribes belonged to the Bantu ethnic group, many differed little if at all in their attitudes to what was right and what was wrong. But differences could occur – whereas nothing of any importance is regarded as morally wrong in one European country which is regarded as morally right in another. The importance of the

3 Kimathis Street, Nairobi, where it intersects with Kenyatta Avenue, is typical of the city centre, with its mixture of modern blocks and older, arcaded shops. Nairobi is in many ways a dull town, but it is undeniably attractive. The streets are wide, and flowering trees plentiful.

4a Mombasa: Kenya's only town with a really metropolitan atmosphere, small as it is. In the foreground is the Old Town, an agreeably higgledy-piggledy area. The boats are dhows from southern Arabia, which at certain seasons trade along the East African coast. Many Mombasans still have close links with the Arabian coast. Zaseen Mohamed, the *taarabu* singer, was once approached by an Adeni dhow sailor. 'Do you know X?' the man asked. 'He's my father.' 'Then I'm your uncle!'

4b The peaks of Mount Kenya – less effective (if grimmer), perhaps, than when seen from any of the towns from Nanyuki to Fort Hall. Then it floats above a line of cloud in a way which makes the Kikuyu legends seem poetic truths. It dominates a surprisingly large area of the highlands – a friend in Nairobi had a house from which he could see both Mt Kenya and Kilimanjaro.

tribe to the individual was thus considerably greater than the importance of his country to the European, since it bore a moral connotation and provided an emotional security provided in Europe by a religion and ethic unconnected with a political grouping.

The tribe, then, traditionally provided social and moral sanctions as well as political and physical security. It was, in fact, all-important. In a modern State, however, these functions cannot be left to the tribe. The nation takes over the political function and indeed, for people who have not been converted to any of the ethical religions, some of the moral function. Obviously, such a take-over is immensely difficult (less practically than emotionally) and it is a cliché to observe that Kenya is in this respect as in most others in a state of rapid transition.

If one is to put the phenomenon of tribalism into perspective one must know what the concept of the tribe means to some modern Kenyans.

'Thomas Hardy writes about a very real countryside. It's a climate he has created round the characters he is writing about, and this could be tribal in a way – and this is in the best way. . . . This is what I think people should recognize when we talk of tribalism – that it is not only Kikuyuization or whatever, it is something much more meaningful than this.'

The friend who said this when I asked him about his feelings on tribalism hit on terms which I think make the whole question understandable to a European. The feeling for the tribe is no different in kind from the feeling which most English people have for the community and the place in which they were born.

'It is very difficult to define it, because I think most of the time it is indefinable,' the same friend went on.

'One little thing has occurred to me; I get irritated, however much I try to fight it, about somebody talking about Mount Kenya as being something personal to them. I grew up in a place where you could see the mountain the first thing you did when you woke up, and the last thing you saw at night.

E

And if somebody comes from, let's say, five hundred miles from Mount Kenya, you just feel they are borrowing an image which isn't valid to them.

'This kind of – well, it's quite irrational, it's quite stupid, but it's there, you know. You feel as though somebody is talking about something sacred in a kind of profane manner.

'And it is more or less on this level – little things, little responses you have to things, which you feel it is only a Kikuyu who has lived through them.'

This indefinable complex of feeling and experience makes a bond between those who have shared it, and puts those who have not in some way on the outside.

'Any two Kikuyu, I am sure, will have a different approach to their tribal background. The only thing is . . . it is the first language you learned, the first joys, the first sorrows. This type of experience did come in that particular type of language. . . .'

In no way are these attitudes inconsistent with a strong feeling for Kenya, even if at present they outdo it in strength.

After all, love for one's country is essentially love for the place in which one was born, and grows outward – from a house to a town or village to a region. It is based on very concrete things. To the Kentish man, England is, in his heart of hearts, an apple orchard and an oast house; to a Liverpudlian all that is most sacred may lie in a tangle of docks and streets which anybody else would regard as a frank slum.

In Kenyan terms, the same holds. In the last analysis the Kenya to which love and loyalty is given is not the vague shape cut out of Africa by agreement between foreign powers. It is a cluster of thatched huts set among the soft fronds and drooping leaves of a patch of maize, with Mount Kenya, a repository of beauty and of legend, rising behind. Or it is a brown plain stretching as far as the eye can see, the delicate yellowish green of the stunted thorn trees shimmering in the noonday sun as the cattle move slowly along in search of grass, the infinitely distant hills no more than an intensification of the heat haze. Or it may be the jumbled quarters of mud-and-coconut-thatched houses which burst forth in the centre of Mombasa like grass in the cracks of a pavement, and which are the city's heart: where the tiny shops and sweetmeat stalls stay open until the small hours, where the brass pots of the Arab coffee-hawkers gleam in the light of an oil-lamp, where all is chatter and warmth and the tumbledown security of a town and a way of life that are ancient and tight-knit.

Talking about the way in which – for public consumption at least – tribal ties tend to be played down even where they are a legitimate source of pride, so afraid is everyone of being thought tribalist, the friend who drew the analogy with Hardy remarked:

'I think it is quite shameful how people have ignored what the tribe means to the individual. I think I would be lost to meet a Luo friend on the level that "Oh, we are all East Africans, we are all the same", because I don't think we are. . . . You can't discount the tribe, because you can't point out one particular person in Kenya who has been brought up in a kind of cosmopolitan, tribeless society. I don't think any such person exists. . . .

'For the first twenty years of your life you grow up in one particular society; then later on you can move out, but how can you ignore the first twenty years of your life? They are the most formative, and somehow you must reconcile this with whatever other background you have absorbed, before you can get anywhere.'

In the campaign on the undesirable aspects of tribalism, the baby is too often thrown out with the bath water. As a European remarked, who has had long experience in industrial missions in the working-class quarters of Nairobi, where all men meet and where nobody is at home, 'There are its (tribalism's) positive values. I think that one of the real dangers is the de-tribalised person who has no loyalty.

'I believe there is a right loyalty to your culture, your own community, and that will remain.'

The field in which tribalism in the word's pejorative sense is a permanent issue is in that of employment, especially in the

Administration. Industry and commerce are still heavily under-Africanised, so the question of tribal distribution hardly arises. The few African-owned businesses which exist are too small to have attracted attention. The inter-territorial, publicly owned organisations such as the railways and the post offices are in much the same position as the Kenya Government.

In local government the issue is minor, since it is only to be expected that in a Taita area most if not all council servants should be Taita. Central Government's administration in country districts, on the other hand – from District Officer to Provincial Commissioner level – frequently rouses complaints of favouritism, and requests, that in, say, a Nandi area Government officials should all be Nandi. The Government's position is that this sort of demand for localisation is itself tribalism, and that anyway many tribes have too few people with the qualifications to do the job.

The issue of tribalism in the lower reaches of the Administration is raised in Parliament every so often, usually when a non-Kikuyu Member of Parliament or Senator complains that Kikuyu are being given advancement at the expense of other tribes. An alternative to this is an accusation that Kikuyu and Luo between them are getting all the jobs – a faintly ironic version of the 'big battalions' attitude, since most prophecies of tribal chaos in Kenya are based on supposedly irreconcilable Luo–Kikuyu antipathy. The fact is that at present more Kikuyu are qualified for senior posts than are people of any other tribe – not only absolutely, but proportionately. As one European put it, 'I believe if you face up to it, things being equal, you would employ a greater number of Kikuyu than anybody else, because to my mind they are the chaps with the brains – because they have lived primarily around Nairobi, and whatever little education has been going, they have got it.'

What the solution is, nobody knows. One possibility was expressed by a young European with a fairly senior position in Central Government.

'One's going to come to the point, probably, where you have the same problem as you do with Europeans and Asian citizens, that obviously they have had better educational opportunities and therefore you've got to discriminate against them in the civil service.

'You might find in time that the same is true of the Kikuyu – in fact it may already be happening. Certainly I know that in my Ministry if you can get a Somali or a Masai he's really pushed forward.'

It is at local council level that the whole issue of tribalism can become most lively. It is worth seeing what various members of the council, present and former, of one large town have to say about the problem.

This town is tribally very mixed. Does this make it a hotbed of factions? A former mayor, a European, believes it does – at times, anyway.

'I think, funnily enough, before Independence I was always very happy with this town because we were on the edge of a whole lot of tribes. I always used to think in my innocence that the town was safe because it wasn't dominated particularly by any one tribe.

'But once we got independence it became apparent that that was our danger, because in the first (municipal) elections after Independence we had, for the first time in our lives here, actual fights during the election period. And these were fights as between tribes, you see.

'Kanu in those days . . . had no real discipline on its people. They would put up an official Kanu member, to stand for Kanu, and five other chaps would also put up as Kanu members.

'You then started your election, and the Luo Kanus would support their chap and the Kikuyu Kanus would support their chap, and in between there was a great gap, and nobody thought of the Party or the dignity of the thing at all.

'They all stood for and fought for their own particular chap because he was their own particular tribe.'

Elections are far from being the whole story, of course. What matters more is the day-to-day 'set' of the council (tribal feeling may rank high in the election of a man who is himself determined to fight tribalism, for instance). In this town at least, does tribalism enter into the workings of the council?

That attempts are made to bring tribal pressures to bear, nobody denies. The present mayor, a young Kikuyu with a tough and subtle mind, laid less emphasis on this than on town gossip. He was delighted, he said, when a decision was demanded of him and he found that none of the people involved were Kikuyu.

'Suppose now in the municipal council I advertise two posts, and then I have two good Luos. If I take them, there will be nothing – nobody will say anything, they will be happy. Everybody will be happy in the town.

'But then if there are two vacancies and I take two Kikuyu – oh, they will talk! They will go round saying: "Now, look, he has taken two Kikuyu."

'But they are forgetting – it is *not* because he is a Kikuyu. We are considering – and I think the Government is doing the same thing – we are considering every case on its own merit.

'And when they try to bring this tribalism into this council, I can assure you I tell them to get out, and I do what I think is right.'

This was, without any doubt, sincerely said. But things are perhaps not quite as straightforward as the mayor made out. Other people with close experience of the workings of the council gave a picture which suggested that what he described as already in existence was in fact a situation towards which he was working.

The former town clerk – a European with nearly twenty years' experience, who was extremely sympathetic to the African council and on the whole loud in its praises – said: 'I think it's more widespread than appears on the surface. I think that a number of the councillors don't like it, but they are forced into it by opinion from the tribes.

'There are certain of the councillors – a few – who are actively against it. The others don't really like it very much, but they can't help themselves: public opinion among their tribe is so strong that they bring it in. But the position is improving. . . .

'I think they will grow out of it as soon as they are allowed to by their followers.'

Elected officials at all levels are particularly open to forces which may tempt them to tribalist actions because – to put no fine point on it – they may lose a good job if they do not comply. Alas, few politicians anywhere show much readiness to go into the wilderness on a point of principle.

If tribalism is present in municipal affairs, which nobody would seriously deny, how does it work? Is it negative, or positive? Does a man get a job because he is of a certain tribe, or does he fail to get it because his appointment would upset another tribe? How far is patronage purely tribal, and how far is it based on, say, political services rendered (which if the people involved are of the same tribe may look like tribalism though it is not)?

'It works to the effect that a chap who is the best man for the job would not necessarily get it if his appointment, being of a certain tribe, would create embarrassment or strong feeling among one of the tribal groups. I think it's quite possible – in fact I know – that he wouldn't get the job then. . . .

'The number of times when a chap gets a job because he is of a particular tribe are comparatively small. It's far more often that a chap gets a job because he's a friend of someone. I don't mean this badly, but I think that a chap would be more likely to get a job because he's done a good job for Kanu, or he's done a good job for someone – he's recommended for a job.'

This council is fairly average – if anything perhaps above average – and reflects the present state of affairs where all is going reasonably well. It is certainly efficient, and on the whole any tribalism that goes on provides the townspeople with a source of gossip rather than complaint. This is not to deny that such situations are potentially very disruptive. Tribalism, or the fear of it, bulks large in sporadic but quite serious attempts to split up the Rift Valley and Sirikwa County Councils, and the recent division of Central Nyanza into two – though an element of gerrymandering may have entered into the Nyanza split.

The complaints of patronage which are made in local government are also not uncommon at Central Government level. In a Parliamentary debate at the end of 1964, for example, Senator Lenayiara of Samburu claimed that most of the Cabinet encouraged tribalism by employing too many people of their own tribes in their Ministries, and remarked acidly that when one visited the Ministry of a Kikuyu member of the Cabinet one had the feeling of being in a Kikuyu village, so much Kikuyu was spoken. Personal impressions (from visits, the names of officials and so on) appear on the surface to bear out such complaints. Lower down, at the level of the door-keeper or driver, it is hard to deny that certain tribes appear to monopolise certain Ministries, or to escape the inference of patronage for such jobs. This may be relatively trivial, but it keeps the general public talking and hardly encourages the forgetting of tribal differences.

At central as at local government level, tribalism seems to work most strongly against efficiency in the negative sense that possible suspicions of it appear to be taken into account in many appointments and reshuffles. Thus there are certain Ministers (though not many) of whom the general opinion is that they are passengers carried for the sake of 'preserving tribal balance'. At Ministerial level this is not particularly harmful: a stuffed giraffe would make a perfectly satisfactory Cabinet Minister provided that the civil servants under it were highly qualified, and that it was content to make the speeches which other people write for it. At senior civil servant level, however, the desire to guard against accusations of tribalism can lead, if not to positive inefficiency, at least to a waste of talent which the country cannot afford. In the first independent Cabinet, there were certain Ministries whose Minister, Assistant Minister and Permanent Secretary were all of one tribe, which led to some muttering. In the first Cabinet reshuffle, certain Assistant Ministers and Permanent Secretaries were moved to other Ministries. No reasons were given, but it was pretty obvious that this was in many cases to ensure that Luo Ministers did not have Luo subordinates, Kikuyu Ministers Kikuyu subordinates, and so on. The intention was admirable, but it led to some most unfortunate results. To put an imbecile on the door because a Ministry lacks the proper ratio of Turkana is not in the same category as shifting senior Civil Servants around so as to forestall accusations that a certain Ministry is mono-tribal. Kenya, as a developing country very short of high-level skills, can afford to let no consideration deflect her from putting the most competent man available into a given job, and leaving him there until he knows it backwards.

This interpretation of the rotating Permanent Secretaries may be wide of the mark – the Government gives no reasons for such moves. But it is the least uncharitable interpretation which members of the general public put on it. Most people (most non-Kikuyu, that is) are prone if they speculate at all to shrug their shoulders as if to say 'What do you expect'. (I was once told, when I asked a certain man's qualifications for a permanent Secretaryship: 'Well, he's a Kikuyu!') If anything unexplained seems to be going on, especially if there appears to be an unwarranted posting, it will inevitably be interpreted in tribal terms – and the tendency to cry tribal 'wolf' is by no means confined to the 'outsider'. I was discussing a Cabinet reshuffle with a Luo acquaintance, a middle-aged civil servant of considerable common sense and unflappability. He did not actually see everything in terms of a deep-laid Kikuyu plot, as some people do – but time and again he would mention a Kikuyu who had been promoted and say: 'It makes you wonder, you know.'

Tribalism is no more or less terrible than any other form of nepotism, and is to be fought in the same way. At one time non-Kikuyu feared an attempt to bring them into some form of Kikuyu vassalage. This extraordinary notion was based on an atavism brought to the fore by the general air of unsettlement which preceded Uhuru, and bears no relation to the facts about either Kenya's leaders or those who might one day replace them. Their backgrounds may be different, and their tribal loyalties strong, but the people who hold key positions in the Administration are very alike one to another – some of them civilised, urbane, hardworking, dedicated to improving the lot of Kenya as a whole; some of them venal, some even treacherous; but none with much resemblance to the mythical figures of, say, Robert Ruark's *Uhuru*. It is fantastic to an outsider that these people, so alike and with exactly the same goals, should spend so much time vaguely suspecting each other. The waste of energy is the really pitiful thing about tribalism.

On the whole what obtains at the top applies, though more strongly, to the man in the street. At the most 'backward' level – particularly among the pastoral groups – tribal animosities are still strong in many areas, and kept going by such things as cattle theft. Almost every week there are stories in the local Press about tribal incidents ranging from brawls to pitched battles. These are so common that, unless particularly bloody affairs, they are tucked away down page. Such incidents, spectacular though they can be, are a lingering of the past, an echo rather than an omen.

At the level of the average man, neither Minister nor moran, prejudice is powerful but (if slowly) fading. There is still a considerable tendency to come out with group judgements in which the speakers do not really believe – at least if pressed – but which are illustrative of such prejudices. If a personal touch may be allowed, some of the attitudes of my children's nanny are characteristic. Rebecca is a Muluhya of thirty-five, intensely conservative but by no means a slave to tribal ways, with an outlook inevitably limited by the fact that she can neither read nor write, but stable and full of common sense. When she heard that we were going to live in a Kikuyu area on the outskirts of Nairobi she did not go as far as a previous nanny who had said quite firmly, 'The Kikuyu are thieves', but she was undoubtedly a little uneasy. We discovered after a week or so that she was cooking indoors instead of out (a stuffy procedure, since she used a charcoal stove) because she was apprehensive of being hit on the head after dark – at seven-thirty in the evening.

Her uneasiness soon wore off, but we were mildly surprised when she appeared to be making firm friends with our gardeneress – a woman as typical of one sort of Kikuyu peasant as Rebecca is of one sort of Muluhya. Though the two were as different as one could imagine, the friendship ripened over the two years we lived in that area and Rebecca went as far as learning to speak a little Kikuyu. After we moved to town she even went to see Wanjiku on her day off. As a result of all this, she no longer believes that every Kikuyu is a dangerous customer out to bamboozle, if not actually assault, an innocent Muluhya.

This is not to say that she has become 'tribe-blind'. She still occasionally, when asked what sort of man is at the door, answers, 'A Kikuyu'. Certainly in any description of a person's individual characteristics, his tribe would come high. And of course her tribalism has a 'positive' side as well as a 'negative', exemplified by the day my wife lent her an umbrella and she left it in a taxi. 'I'll go and get it tomorrow,' she said. 'It'll be quite safe – the taxi driver is a Muluhya.' He may have been, but it wasn't.

What has been happening to Rebecca's attitudes is what has been happening to the attitudes of everybody in the country. Even in the sensitive realm of tribally mixed marriage, things are not what they used to be. At a highly educated level, one knows tribally mixed couples (though perhaps not many more than are racially mixed). At the level of the man-in-the-shamba, 'a number of them will seriously raise questions because a girl wants to be married outside the tribe, (but) that one might marry someone from outside is not looked at with the same sort of fear, and spelling doom, as it used to be. . . . (In the past) when it came to the actual customary law and habits, things like initiation, the dances, somebody from outside the tribe would completely be a misfit. . . . But these days we have a number of women who have been married outside – they live mainly in the urban areas, so they can fit in with anybody else.'

The speaker was a middle-aged Church leader who talked from wide personal experience. The reason he gave for the breakdown of taboos on inter-tribal marriage is as significant as the actual breakdown.

In everyday life inter-tribal relations are becoming a good deal more relaxed than they once were. Some time ago I overheard a revealing sequence of jovial insults between a Kamba and a Kikuyu. They had been discussing the latest rumour, something to do with the loyalty of the Army and an alleged build-up of the police to counter it (the Army has a high proportion of Kamba, and there was a theory going around that the Government was trying to pack the police with Kikuyu).

'You wait,' said the Kamba. 'We will cut you to pieces.'

'Kamba?' said the Kikuyu. 'The Kamba are only fit for drumming and turning somersaults. If you try anything we will beat you in a day!'

I found this exchange, and much more on the same lines, remarkable. At the time there was a good deal of loose talk about various tribes and their supposed scheming, and one might well have thought that cracks like that of the Kikuyu risked at the least a clout on the ear. But no. Though the tribal factor still crops up everywhere – real or imagined – the whole issue really belongs to the past, and is slowly receding into the past. Those who do most to keep it in the present (apart from the odd individual using it to further personal ends) are the elderly, the backward, or those who have positions of prestige within the tribal hierarchy and thus a vested interest.

To be surprised at the continuance of tribalism is naïve. The tribe was until very recently the source of Everyman's social persona. Its gradual withering may have had a liberating effect in many ways (traditional society was inhibiting to individual initiative, for example) but it has led for many people – perhaps most – to a loss of safe criteria. Moreover there are many aspects of traditional life (communal concern for the destitute, a non-material scale of values) which are by common consent worth preserving. Kenya like most other African countries is still experimenting in ways of keeping the good while dropping the bad. In any experiment mistakes are made and in this particular experiment mistakes often bear the name of tribalism.

On a more fundamental level, since the tribe still provides the framework for the first twenty years of life – the years which form a man's psychology – it is not surprising that the difficult process of putting off childish things should include occasional retreats into the safe ways of childhood when the going gets rough, either on the part of the individual Kenyans or of groups. We all make such retreats from time to time.

'You don't change a society in a hurry. I mean, you can go to England and you can find just the same social – shall we call it tribal – divisions. You can't suddenly say everyone's got to choose his friends from all the different tribes. It's bound to be a slow process. But the main point is this, surely, that you do have certain points at which influences are beginning to bear, which minimise it.'

The words are those of a European clergyman whose work is in the field of African education, a man whom neither temperament nor experience incline towards the starry-eyed.

Kikuyu or Luo or Muluhya or Swahili, Kenyans of all tribes have far more to bring them together than to separate them. Their childhood worlds may differ, but their adult world is the same. Of course, any of us may destroy our adult world in a fit of regression, but most of us contrive to have our childish moments – even our continuing childish traits – without endangering our adulthood. Tribalism is disappearing. What is important is not the sum total of individual signs of its disappearance – one could produce plenty of counter-balancing evidence of its continued liveliness – but that it is the product of a structure of society which is rapidly dying. When the cause is gone the effect will go. Times of national stress may temporarily revive it, but the long-term direction of Kenya's development is more powerful than individual crises.

'This is an era of change, change of attitude. We are growing out of subsistence farming, the extended family, everything – the whole religio-social set-up of the African is changing.' The man who said this was merely expressing a cliché better than most.

The only thing that could halt the process would be a total

collapse of the country such as even the Congo suffered only temporarily, and (however shakily) survived. This is not a prospect seriously considered by even the most gloomy. If anybody is led by present wrongs to be pessimistic about progress at grass-roots level, he can take heart from a young Kikuyu friend of mine who until fairly recently earned his living as a shoeshine boy, and whose favourite football team is Luo Union!

4

Breakdown and Build-up

We Africans . . . don't have upper
class and second class
Union leader

Even I as an African cannot
mix with every class . . .
Mayor of large town

Politically important as tribalism is, it is far from being the most
significant social result of Kenya's transition from the tribe to
the nation. The loss of the tribe's moral and social sanctions has
a less obvious but more important effect – a more fundamental effect at that, since one of the first things to be altered
is mankind's first and basic social unit: the family.

A National Christian Council of Kenya paper, dated June
1965, discusses the effect of this loss in relation to traditional
marriage practice:

'Among many African tribes,' it commented, 'marriage was a
social bond as well as a contract between two families and two
clans. . . .

'The exposure of African institutions to other cultures, particularly the Western culture, has undermined the old basis
of those institutions without providing a new basis which would
be suitable to our changing society. . . .

'At the moment, marriages are either based on Western civil
contract, Christian traditions or on customary laws, but there
are no accepted traditions to control and guide them. . . .
Customary marriage while accepted lacks the traditions or
social sanctions to support it as family and clan ties have become
so fluid as to have little influence on such marriage. . . .

'To sum up all factors, we may rightly say that the structure
of the old society is unable to bear the impact of change. We are

in a stage somewhere between organisation and reorganisation.'

The General Secretary of the NCCK, John Kamau, made it clear that tribal moral authority, which in the past was so strong that only a very brave or a very reckless couple would flout it, is to all intents and purposes extinct.

'According to my tribal custom and quite a few others the actual knowing of a girl carnally, not only did it have a stigma attached to it, but the perpetrators would have been ostracised by their age-group. . . .

'Today this particular sort of excommunication is non-existent, whether in the urban areas or the others. It may perhaps have remained in very primitive groups.'

The resulting amorality is found at all social levels. As another NCCK paper puts it, 'Some élite women are reported to give their favours to several friends. Their motive is acquiring for themselves the sexual freedom of men or earning some cash for their own private needs. "You see, no woman could possibly earn as much as a man even if she is employed," an educated married woman told us, "and if men want to share their money with us why stop them?" '

Moral uncertainty is not confined to sex. The considerable crime rate is partly caused by extreme poverty – but there are many extremely poor parts of the world with a low crime rate. A combination of the lack of accepted moral authority and the less attractive features of the acquisitive society have a good deal to do with it.

'It's always struck me as quite remarkable,' an elderly European with experience of both East and West Africa observed, 'that there was no jealousy in the African society, and I've asked quite a lot of our chums here and they say, "No, but this jealousy isn't in the African make-up. If my brother is successful I say: The gods have been kind to him. He's got away with it, I can't." No question of jealousy at all.

'But our present development is *creating* jealousy. Look at the thieving in African communities, which never took place before – it couldn't, it was anathema. If you look at the police reports you'll see that there's more thieving going on in the African locations than there is in the townships. Now this is a terrible thing, but I'm afraid it's an unavoidable consequence of the sort of development we are going in for.'

Though a weakening of moral sanctions may be unavoidable, it has not reached the point at which it is a major plague. A far greater problem is posed by attitudes which in themselves are harmless and even capable of being seen as virtues. Some of these – a disinclination to take individual initiatives is one – stem from ingredients of the traditional way of life, and remain powerful even when the traditions out of which they grow are weakened. One of these attitudes is the belief in and desire for large families, without which the extended family would not have been able to function effectively.

'Whereas in traditional society it was an asset to have a big family because every pair of hands could help in production and defence, in modern society it is seen that beyond a certain point any extra children are a liability as they all require clothing, schooling and other benefits which cost money.' This sentence from an NCCK report on family planning introduces quite the most alarming problem which Kenya faces – the population explosion. According to the official *Economic Survey for 1965*, almost the whole of the country's economic growth in 1965 was swallowed by the extra mouths of a population increasing at the rate of about three per cent a year.

The powers that be are well aware of this situation, in which the economy is running to a standstill. In *African Socialism and its Application to Planning*, a sort of blueprint for Kenya's economic future, it is said that 'a programme of family planning education will be given high priority'. But custom and the needs of the past are strong. It has been estimated that such a programme would take at least twenty years to have the necessary effect, in the face of traditional attitudes – attitudes, moreover, which peasant and élite seem to share.

Fortunately there are signs, in spite of the recklessly large families started by too many people earning even a half-way decent salary, that ordinary people are beginning to respond to the need for birth control. A mobile family-planning unit some

F

time ago went to the Kiambu District, with unexpected and encouraging results. Kikuyu peasant women walked for miles to be fitted with intra-uterine devices, ten-shilling notes in hand – and ten shillings is a lot of money when a day's labour may only earn three. The demand was so great that scores had to be turned away, many of them in tears.

Events of this sort must be set off against findings like that of a family-planning research team in Central Nyanza, which discovered that local opinion held the ideal number of children to be one hundred, and the ideal number of wives twelve. The people who can least afford large families, moreover, are those who are least aware of how to avoid them. But uneducated people are not necessarily slow to adopt something new provided they see clearly its advantages, and there is growing evidence of an awareness that exhaustion and constant financial worry are too high a price to pay for domestic prestige.

One of the most valuable effects of Kenya's present state of flux is that the deep conservatism of country people is considerably shaken. The weakening of tradition naturally reduces its power to hold people back from what they consider their rights, and – perhaps more important – its power to blind people to where their interests really lie. It is perhaps over-pessimistic to talk as if, in the words of one report on family planning, 'the long-term outlook threatens to be catastrophic'. People everywhere find it difficult to correlate individual cause and national effect, as tax-collectors know to their chagrin. But birth control is one sphere in which personal and national interest work together. Intensive education is needed so that people realise that there is a way out of their difficulties, and a good deal of money must be spent on mobile clinics so that the new knowledge can be put into practice. If this is done there is a reasonable hope that the women at least, who bear the brunt of an over-large family, will be prepared to say 'to hell with what the neighbours think'. Then the gloom of the official reports may prove too deep, and masculine dreams of twelve wives be made harmless.

Socially speaking, most of the currents of Kenyan life work from division to cohesion. There is, however, one problem which was not present in the past. This is the developed nations' version of tribalism, the consciousness of class. Whether because of the system of clan and age-group structures on which most tribal organisations was based, or because subsistence farming does not allow the build-up of economic privilege, African societies were largely free of hierarchies, and certainly free of a class structure as fundamental as the one Britain is still in the process of abandoning. This does not however mean, as some optimists assume, that there is no danger of social divisions growing up. In her drive to develop and industrialise, Kenya inevitably risks the undesirable consequences of industrialisation.

'Even I as an African cannot mix with every class: there is a class I can mix with, but not everyone. Not because I hate them – I don't look down on them because they are a low class; but there is a class I can mix with, and there is a class I can't mix with even if I want to.'

This classic statement of hierarchic values was made by the mayor of a large city, during a denial that class was an issue in Kenya. His attitude rested not on birth but on position, of course – he himself had been a waiter at an earlier age in his career. It was clear that he saw the undesirable aspects of class entirely in terms of the attitude of one individual to another and not at all in terms of the equality of opportunity, since he added: 'But then I wouldn't be in a position to look down on a person just because he is not able to buy a suit as I am. I think it's a very bad practice,' and considered the subject closed.

The tendency to discuss the problem of the élite and class divisions in over-simplified terms is pretty well universal. I was given a description of the élite by one of its members, a lawyer and graduate of a British university.

'The point is, during the pre-independence days, because of a strong common goal (political independence) there was not any idea that there were élite and non-élite, if I may put it that way.

'But as soon as the British civil servants left Kenya there arose a class, of necessity, of African civil servants who – either because they were very busy or because it was not prudent for them to go and start doing the things they might have done in pre-independence days – started keeping themselves aloof.

'Now that does not, to my way of thinking, mean that there is an élite class emerging. There is a career group emerging which does not find time to go around (and which of course might be precluded by the rules and regulations of the particular employment) agitating and shouting the way they used to. . . .

'People are definitely grouping themselves into these classes, but it does not mean that there is a sort of snob outlook by the educated Africans against the mass.'

This analysis is true as far as it goes. The present generation élite, since it is 'self-made', does form a career group rather than a class. But its children may well become the first generation of a hereditary upper crust. The career group explanation is neat and reassuring, but it ignores the very real possibility of privilege by birth, because it ignores the economic and educational aspects of the question.

Kenya's new élite stands in the same economic relation to the country as a whole as any other élite. In other ways, however, it differs from the middle class in industrial countries. The basic difference is that it is a very new élite, and that it sprang to life more or less fully grown. Ten years ago there was to all intents and purposes no African middle class though there were prosperous individuals. The then middle and upper classes were defined by colour, and it was self-evident that an African could not become a member of them. Change came as part of the lead-up to independence, when for the first time an effort was made to train Africans in any numbers for élite jobs. This had an overwhelming effect on social patterns. Once Africans broke the barrier between wage and salary and acquired power at one and the same time, the way was open for a totally new bourgeoisie, a totally new upper crust, above the same old peasantry and proletariat.

Virtually everybody in the Government, virtually everybody in administration or business or the professions, is self-made. Especially among the older generation, they know from personal experience the life of the average man. Even the younger men, those who went straight from school to higher education to a profession, did so at the cost of a struggle unknown in industrial Europe for seventy years. The peasant life was theirs until higher education took them out of it. They ate maize meal like anybody else, tended goats, lived in huts, or houses little better than huts, went cold and wet in the rainy season and ragged in the sun. Such people do not hold the customary class attitudes. Their condition is the result of individual success, and they are not really cut off from the proletariat. Those who do not have illiterate brothers and sisters have illiterate parents, or at least illiterate aunts and uncles. They may well be visited, as is a friend of mine, by a grandfather wearing nothing but an Army great-coat: and they may well have grounds for respecting that grandfather's wisdom.

This situation is, however, likely to be a strictly temporary one. The key to success in Kenya is education, and this to a far greater degree than in Europe, where there is hardly such a thing as a really uneducated man. The gap between the most and the least educated is so wide as to make England seem like an egalitarian paradise. The economic gap between a subsistence farmer with his £20 a year cash and even a clerk earning £400, let alone the really skilled whose salaries are on European levels, can hardly be overstated.

The colossal disparities of wealth and education combined can even drive a wedge between parent and child – a wedge illustrated by John Kamau of the NCCK in a description which also shows how the racial superstructure of the past can have lingering effects.

'Now the young educated people are feared generally – I am using the word fear because the parents in some cases dare not criticise a person who has been through university. . . .

'The parent will say: "Well, no, this man has gone here, there and there; he is just as educated, just as powerful as that white man now." And of course they never answered anything that the white man said, when he was either the missionary or the colonial District Commissioner, or the farmer.

'So this black educated person who is more or less taking the position of these people is feared in the same way.'

Already then there is enough of a difference between 'haves' and 'have-nots', for educational as well as economic reasons, to provide a good base for problems of class. But the essence of a classbound society is that class should be transmitable. Otherwise it remains embryonic – no more than the sum of the benefits of a good job.

The question is, can it remain at this level? In Kenya, where most people still have no sort of a start in life at all, where secondary school education for ten per cent of primary school leavers is only a long-term aim, will the sons and daughters of the present élite not start so far ahead that equality remains largely theoretical?

S. N. Waruhiu, the Vice-Principal of the University College, Nairobi, argues that education should be able to prevent, if not the existence of privilege, at least its more serious rider: the growth of a belief among the privileged that they are privileged through some merit of their own.

'These things exist in every country, and we do hope that we are going to bridge the gulf, rather than allow the gulf to widen, by providing much more quickly, for example, free education than it was provided in a country like Britain – where even up to this day you find your Eton and Harrow people creating that special class of their own.

'We hope that education towards African socialism is going to close the gulf rather than allow it to widen.'

That education could in theory prevent the growth of a 'privileged mentality' cannot be doubted. Whether there is much hope in practice that the appalling difficulties facing Kenya's education system can be surmounted before it is (from this point of view) too late, is quite another matter.

Tremendous as are the social variations involved in Kenya there is a growing group which provides a wide bridge between the two extremes. In the country there are, increasingly, yeoman farmers and small businessmen who are not necessarily very highly educated, though obviously most are literate. The towns are full of their opposite numbers; clerks, telephone operators, shop assistants.

These people far outnumber the élite, and their interests and standards of life fall between the most and the least fortunate. Many of them still live in the 'locations', and will be more likely to give the 'locations' a more bourgeois tone than to move into the grand suburbs. They eat posho as do the peasants, and often have small-holdings, but none the less are on the way to becoming the main urban class though at present they form the bulk of the 'nusu-nusu' world. They are potentially the most important section of the community since their life represents what will probably become Kenya's norm.

These people are very difficult to discuss, precisely because there are so many of them and in any analysis they are apt to vanish into a number of different pigeon-holes. Some are 'workers' – skilled artisans, perhaps, of a thrifty turn of mind, bus-drivers, even head-messengers. At the other end of the scale some are journalists or minor civil servants without a social-climbing instinct. Their wives may be nurses or untrained teachers. Just because of the low standard of living of the peasant and unskilled worker, anybody who has a job above the hoe or pick-and-shovel moves into an income bracket which is high by the standards of the great majority of people, but which is still not even half that of the true élite. Such people are on the same side of the great educational divide as the élite, but they are not so very far from the proletariat. Indeed, many of the proletariat have more in common with this group than with the more backward peasants. A cook in a private house is not likely to earn much more than £10 a month, but a skilled cook with a good primary education is already in Kenyan terms almost bourgeois – as bourgeois as life in the cramped confines of the servants' quarters will allow.

The fact that this large group has a great deal in common does not of course mean that it is free from its own snobberies. The Swahili musicians poke such fun at the social climbing which goes on in a group which they know intimately because it is their own. The *karani* – the clerk – is a popular butt, thought to put on ridiculous airs because of his job and generally to make a nincompoop of himself. As one man sings:

Here in Nairobi the clerks have a lot of trouble –
They buy scooters to carry tarts around on (cha cha cha),
By the eighth of the month they are shut out of their digs,
Their food is finished and their popsy run off.

The basis of most snobbery in this group is education. The man who has more of it considers himself a cut above the ignorant, even if he is poorer. This educational snobbery centres especially on the ability to talk English:

I wanted to go with an educated girl, but as I have no
　　learning she wouldn't listen.
When I greeted her she said 'Good morning' (in English).
I couldn't answer since I didn't go to school. Then she
　　asked her friend:
'What is this boy saying' (English). Her friend answered:
'This boy loves you' (English).

Social questions arising from development are not just a matter of economic or educational differences and the status differences that arise from them. Complications are added by Kenya's having been – unlike any other African countries which have achieved independence except Algeria and Zambia – a settler colony.

The first Africans to rise into the professional class were in a slightly odd social position. In normal conditions the young man at the outset of any career imitates the social patterns of his elders – the man just called to the Bar adopting the prejudices and perhaps even the taste in sherry of the Silk, and so on. In Kenya the first African professional men had nothing African to copy, since there was no traditional bourgeoisie. Yet they needed (even more than their English counterparts, since they were under the eyes of people convinced that they could not make any social grade) a sure pattern to copy. They did the only thing they could – they followed European examples. The Black Englishman was born.

'Classes used to be in three strata. The top stratum was that of the English civil servants, the English settlers in this country, and people in the lower strata aimed at achieving that goal. A person will look at what is the topmost and highest achievement.

'I know African friends of mine who when they speak Swahili they even speak it like the English civil servants or settlers used to speak it, with a sort of Oxford accent.'

The speaker, himself something of a Black Englishman, went on:

'This will go. I see it going very quickly. We are now beginning to have graduates from American universities, from the continent of Europe, from Asia even, and they will definitely ... dilute this English outlook which might be a lingering legacy of the old days.

'I am not admitting that there is so much of it that we ought to stagger everybody; but I am saying that it is there, but it will disappear.'

It has already begun to disappear. The sudden flood of new bourgeois during the year before independence diluted the Black English. Though the phenomenon of the tyro copying his elders still applied, these new people were too many to become entirely Black English in their turn.

Black Englishness at its best produces people of considerable outward charm and urbanity. A reasonable reserve, a lack of the tendency to be too hail-fellow-well-met on first acquaintance, combine very well with an un-English relaxedness and informality. There are, of course, purely superficial qualities. Their possessors are quite as capable of being over-casual, inhospitable, downright rude, as anybody else, just as they are capable of gross incompetence. There are, moreover, negative attributes picked up from the British: the stuffy and the boorish have learned a thing or two from their English counterparts, and there is a combination of second-rateness and self-satisfaction of a very English sort.

The Black Englishman's character is not in entire contrast with that of the ordinary Kenyan. A certain bluffness and stolidity, an air of being willing to listen to reason, are all common enough to be accepted – though naturally with reservations – as part of a 'Kenyan' character. Complaints that the Black English are 'not African' are thus not very valid. None of the qualities which together give the impression of Englishness are individually un-African; they are merely blended in a rather English way.

Discussed at any length, moreover, the whole subject becomes a little artificial. The existence of a strain of Englishness is obvious to any foreigner who has been in the country for any length of time, and yet the more one tries to define or isolate it the more elusive it becomes. In truth perhaps most Kenyans have acquired something of the English in seventy years of settler presence. The traits which separate any group of humans from any other are after all far fewer and less important than those which unite them.

Much apparent Black Englishness in the Kenyan environment stems from the surface appearance of a country which at peak had 60,000 European inhabitants, mostly British, and still has 40,000. In the formerly European residential suburbs of any town most of the houses are red-brick, tiled bungalows which could have been torn from a building society advertisement. The older, wood-and-iron houses which still stand scattered among them are far more 'White African' but though many remain they have the air of relics. Brick or wood, these houses are surrounded by very English gardens – English not because of what grows there of course, but in their balance of bush and lawn and flowerbed. Since the European residential areas take up a good deal of the space in any town (a 1947 map of Nairobi showed twenty-three grid squares devoted to European living space, six-and-a-half to Asian and less than one to what is called 'native') it is hardly a matter for wonder that the casual visitor receives a powerful impression of slightly idealised English suburbia.

Kenya's new élite has moved into these suburbs, side by side with the Europeans and a few Asians. Naturally, the Africans drive the same cars as anybody else. Their dark suits are English in cut because that is what Kenyan tailors are used to. Their wives favour fairly conservative and English-looking clothes (another piece of Black Englishness this, though suited to the unflamboyant nature of most Kenya Africans). Their children in their romper suits or Tricel frillies look just like any other charming and well-fed infants out of the advertisement pages. However un-English they may be in the privacy of their rather English, television-focused homes, these people *look* Black English. Yet in fact, what is growing up is rather suburbanity than Englishness.

There is tennis, there is beer or whisky combined with office chat and talk about motor-cars, there is Monopoly. This last is something of an in-group craze. The only time I have seen a group of Black Englishmen behaving with lack of restraint was during a tense Monopoly final between a senior civil servant and a senior member of the University College, Nairobi.

Much of this, of course, is caused by the uncertainties of rapid social change as they affect the highest social group. It was described by a young African civil servant and writer in much the same terms as those used by the National Christian Council of Kenya reports.

'I feel it is all too new, the effort of getting into a job – and quite often, you know, making a little corner for yourself in a decidedly alien society. . . .

'And it isn't English either, you know, it's a kind of imitation English – terribly sad to see. . . . One would want to see it destroyed – I don't know how, but it seems to be the worst importation that we could get from the old rule.

'I think it is just a sign of insecurity. Somehow you don't know exactly what you want to make out of the new situation which you have been plunged into; and rather than grapple with the problem and come to a solution, you take the short cut.

'You know: Let's invite whoever you know round, let's have a game of Monopoly or whatever, and let's say: "We went to the Club last night", and let's go to the airport to meet so-and-so, and let's dress up for it, and this sort of oh – and let's call it life. It really seems to be a kind of death.'

The emptiness at the centre of individuals' social lives is

paralleled by an emptiness in city life remarkably reflected by the physical emptiness of the streets in any town except Mombasa after working hours. Come 4.30, everybody is off like a jack-rabbit to his suburb. Even in Nairobi (which for beauty and dullness is the Zürich of the tropics) the only areas with any after-hours life are Eastleigh (where this life is largely such as no city boasts about) and the working-class suburbs – and even there it is faintly artificial, revolving round the community centre rather than anything more spontaneous. Nairobi looks like a swinging city – but its peak social hours are those of any little provincial town: Saturday morning.

Kenya may escape permanent suburbanisation, but since the whole world seems more and more prey to it, this is on the face of things unlikely. It is, for a country with a rare chance to develop a real culture based on the best of Africa, Europe and Asia, a sad prospect. Of all the gloomy things that prophets have said would happen to Kenya the most likely is that it may become a cosy, worthy, even (by Afro-Asian standards) pros-perous desert of the spirit. Already, in spite of its beauty, variety, dignity and warmth, Kenya is in a strange way characterless. This, however, is one of the few problems about which it is hard to feel optimistic. True, the others are so complex and so colossal that at times they seem insurmountable; but the very fact of change which lies behind so many of them leads to a spirit of enthusiasm increased by the fact that more and greater prob-lems are already on the way to solution.

5

The 'They' Syndrome

They must not think
they are in a little
England in Kenya
Young African

You need good people
in an underdeveloped
country, and there are not
a great deal of good people
European woman

The popular picture of Kenya as a land of settler-farmers may once have been true in spirit, but it has not been entirely reflected in the statistics since the pioneering days. At its peak the European population of Kenya was about 60,000, of whom around 24,000 lived in Nairobi. Some of them were administrators, civil servants from the higher echelons perched on The Hill to the D.O.s in the country. Some were farmers, some were professional hunters and some were remittance men. But the vast majority were in business or the professions. There were lawyers and doctors, directors of import–export firms and bank managers. There were also proprietors of European grocers in small towns, clerks and hairdressers, Linotype operators. As was not the case in most colonies, the senior officials and the large-scale farmers – the *Bwana Mkubwa* class which elsewhere was all the Africans knew of the British – were heavily outnumbered by all sorts of humbler people from skilled artisans up.

If this was the case in the past, it is even truer nowadays. Immigration Department figures issued about a year ago reported the presence of 41,000 Europeans. While there is nothing to show what sort of people left in largest numbers, a great many were British Army. Of the rest, who were in some sense Kenyan, a large proportion were farmers or those inhabitants of the small towns who lived off the farmers.

The European dream in Kenya came to an end at the first Lancaster House conference. The awakening was not pleasant, and a general sense of unease settled over the European community – not pronounced, and certainly not strong enough to upset daily life. But, as one young man remarked, 'What usually happens is: you sit down, you have a drink, and you talk. Well, invariably the talk comes round to . . . Somebody says "Are you staying?" and the answer is "We'd like to stay, but . . ."; and there's always that "but" there.'

This was a year ago, and an encouraging difference is in the air now. It really seems as if, after setting up so many bogies to frighten itself, the European community is beginning to settle down to being an ordinary part of society. Every time the country reached a new stage, despondency used to set in – a despondency which never had much real connection with the state of the country or anything else. Now at least the tendency to jumpiness seems to be gone. Two things helped to dispel it. One was the passing of the date for citizenship by registration, with no measures taken against non-citizens. The other was the Rhodesian illegal Declaration of Independence, when in all the outrage expressed in Parliament, in print, and on street corners, the only mention made of Kenya's Europeans was on the lines of 'Why can't the Rhodesians learn from them?'

Not everybody has either gone or settled down, of course. There are those who, true colonial relics, have been unable or unwilling even to try to adapt to a new situation, and cling on unhappily in, but not of, a country they no longer understand. Now that they can do no harm, one cannot but feel sorry for these people. They come down from their farms, as an English businesswoman in Nairobi once remarked, 'and they haven't got the slightest clue what's happening anywhere else'. The woolly mammoths, she called them, and the description fits.

What does one do when the society one has known vanishes, and a new one takes its place? The answer depends in part on how old one is – since, as an African acquaintance sympathetically said, 'You see, it is very difficult to change one's attitude, particularly when you are old; it is very, very difficult, and the man you are asking me about now is that man who was here when the European set was right at the top. It is very difficult for him to forget this.'

Perhaps, like a young coffee-farming friend at Thika, you take out citizenship and enlarge your acquaintance. If you are older, perhaps you just vegetate.

'My outlook over the past couple of years has been to restrict my activities. I very rarely go off the farm, and I don't get around, and I'm not very interested in other things. It's a bit of an ostrich act, but . . .'

The speaker was an elderly farmer living near Nakuru. Although a pleasant person, he was difficult to talk to because of this 'ostrich act'. He knew so little about what was going on in the country that everything, almost, was said in a vacuum. But it was quite clear that he and his wife felt isolated and lonely. On farming he was interesting, though his cynical view of Government policies like land settlement was somewhat vitiated by his ignorance of what was in fact happening.

Even though Nakuru is in an economic depression there is still plenty going on, with an agricultural college and a co-operative training institute nearby. A man like this could well have found new interests, helping tyro African farmers, making new friends. Many men in his position have done it. If he were happy alone on his farm there would be no more to be said. As it is, he is afraid to come out of his shell because then he could no longer go on half pretending nothing had happened, that Kenya was still the country he came to – and because of his shell, he is left a prey to vague and unreal fear. 'One has to keep a guard on one's tongue these days,' he said at one point; and 'You can't be too careful'. A couple of days later a Nakuru branch Kanu official brought up this same man's name in conversation.

'Now, talking to a person like that in this job – I have had quite a lot of reports in my office here, concerning what he's said; and we wave that away as a very, very great joke. And his labour take it as a greater joke than we take it back here, because the labourers know that if they put their tools down today he won't be able to function at all. But they reckon: "Right, fair enough, let him shout." As they say, "An empty tin makes most noise". If such people don't see the trend of things, the changed times, they actually only do themselves harm. . . . If you went to the market-place now and shouted your voice out, people would just look at you and go away and say "That fellow is off his head".'

Such a man is an extreme case; but few Europeans seem to be aware of what Kenya really thinks of them. In the words of a young African friend more sympathetic than many, 'What really worries me about most Europeans is that they have not the least *inkling* that the African knows them quite well. I think they still have a kind of misguided impression that the European is still a mysterious exalted creature "up there", and at the best of times the African can only have a glimpse of the great goings on.' This ignorance may be bliss, but it is bad for any minority not to be able to assess its position in society as a whole.

In his introduction to the pre-Uhuru manifesto Mr Kenyatta wrote: 'There will be no place in the Kenya we shall create for discrimination by race, tribe, belief or any other manner.' The basis of this and the current official attitude is that *citizens* of Kenya will have all the rights of the citizen, whether they be African, Asian or European. Non-citizens will have the rights of non-citizens in any country, and no more. But, of course, the official view is not the end of the matter. For one thing, official attitudes change with the climate of acceptance or hostility on the part of the general public. In any real sense, therefore, public opinion is more important to the minority than official dogma.

African attitudes to non-Africans of course vary as greatly as individual African experience of them. This experience is a living thing, which changes from day to day and is in its turn conditioned by non-African attitudes to Africans. But certain basic trends recur.

5*a* The foreign and the 'African' are everywhere intermingled in Kenya. A young girl in a smart dress walks between two of the buildings which make up her mother's home, while her cousin with baby on back stands under the eaves of her hut. The building on the left is run together with bamboo and corrugated iron, but its overall appearance is un-African. The thatched hut is rather the equivalent of a room than a house – traditional Kikuyu dwellings consist of a number of such huts, some for sleeping in, some for cooking in, some used as stores.

5*b* A familiar sight from the back windows of any block of flats in Nairobi – the servants' quarters. Bleak as these are, they represent a step up in the world for many of those who live in them after the discomfort of a hut in the country.

6 Mamoba. The view from the author's sitting-room in Nairobi stretched for 120 undifferentiated miles. In the foreground is Wilson Airport, as untidy as the outskirts of any town. In the background is Mount Kilimanjaro, almost invisible above a collar of clouds. In between is the bush – in this case, Masai territory.

'I think if the other races behave they are going to live here peaceably. . . . I would only say about those two races that they must adjust themselves – they must not think that they are in a small England in Kenya. It is impossible.'

This remark by a young professional man sums up a view held by virtually all educated Africans. The minorities should realise that they are no longer in a privileged position, and should throw in their lot with the majority. Then they are welcome.

The nature of the change expected varies. On the whole, people are not very interested in polite social gatherings. Kenya is a country with a vast amount of work to get through, and the Europeans can play a major role in this work. Often enough, this – and a civil tongue – is all that is asked. As a Rift Valley county councillor remarked:

'The African is very observant. . . . In an office, if I come to you for advice, the way you give me that advice can tell a lot. . . . I may feel that you are really very candid in your way, and you are very genuine. Well, that's what counts a lot. You see, the African is mostly interested to get on together, to work together. When you go back home that's your private life, and when the other fellow goes back home that's his *shauri*.'*

The feelings of the man-in-the-street towards Europeans are less clear-cut than this, principally because he has far too many important things on his mind to think about them very much. In the first year or so after independence there was a certain amount of talk about the machinations of the colonialists, or their *alter egos*, the imperialists. In so far as this referred to real or suspected meddling by the British – or for that matter American or Russian or Chinese – Government, it was and is fair enough. But the accusation of imperialism was occasionally – for example in trade union disputes – levelled at individual Europeans of whom it was manifest nonsense. Such accusations were, however, not just made out of devilment. Behind them lay the illogical but understandable train of thought: 'The Europeans in the old days were imperialist in that they sup-

* Affair.

ported the colonial rulers. If they behave now as they did then socially, this must show that their attitude has not changed, and that they are still in favour of colonial rule.' None the less, the general lack of anti-European feeling which there was at independence, let alone now, is remarkable. Of course, it could easily be revived if anybody decided to stir it up as the KPU showed rather half-hearted signs of doing during the 'little General Election': though if racialism had been a 'hot' issue it would certainly have been more harped on. Nobody poor likes having a pack of foreigners making a lot of money in his country. European behaviour towards ordinary Africans – including messengers and servants as well as clerks and men in more senior positions – is not without its possible consequences, even though at present the most common African reaction to rudeness is: 'Poor chap, he can't help being a cantankerous grouch.'

It is very noticeable that the minority of Europeans who have either started with what Africans regard as the right attitude or acquired it are accepted without suspicion and without reservation. No doubt this is partly because other Europeans tend to mistrust them. There is one man in Nairobi, a former District Officer, whose dedication to the new Kenya is outstanding. He is a mild and charming person who has been led to criticise certain aspects of European behaviour, for which he earned the comment from a compatriot: 'I've no time for people who run down their own kind' – a remark of singular obtuseness. Africans notice this sort of thing, and they admire people who are prepared to make a stand on principle. A Kanu official described another such person to me, a white farmer of considerable wealth.

'He has given me an impression that I haven't ever had from anybody else. He told me: "Look, John, I am going to live here and I am going to be a part of Kenya. I am an African. . . ." Now here is a person who participates in everything. You know, English people are very good at cracking jokes, so he points at his skin and says, "Eh, look, I'm the only bloke here . . ." He's got the guts.'

To the man-in-the-street, Europeans are most of the time just part of the landscape. None the less it is surprising how often such people go out of their way to be friendly to any European who seems out of the usual run. Though a polite tendency to agree with whatever is said sometimes makes getting down to brass tacks difficult, I have rarely met any of the expected reserve when talking to uneducated or semi-educated Kenyans. The matter-of-fact friendliness and warm-heartedness of the ordinary people of this country are striking, not only considering the past but in the abstract.

A writer once said to me: 'I think people fear that the African hates the European; I don't think the African does. After all, the Africans are known to be welcoming to strangers, and it is not just a saying, it is true.'

In my own experience it is indeed true – and it is not by chance that the Swahili word *mgeni* means both 'stranger' and 'guest'.

Constant contact between the various races has in some ways helped to break down prejudice, moreover. As the same speaker said: 'I have never felt that Europeans as Europeans were bad people, because I met some good Europeans when I was at school. . . . My teachers, some of them, were very good. Of course I quarrelled with them and shouted at them and so on, but I was never bitter against them as a race.'

Since, however, the exceptions are very much in the minority, reaction to the 'difficult' European is of more importance. The antics of the more high and mighty type are greeted by laughter more often than by indignation. A friend told this anecdote of a bus journey: 'There was one European woman who didn't want to sit in the seats with the Africans: she always stood by the driver, and the Africans there were laughing and talking in Kikuyu and Swahili, saying, "Oh dear, she won't even come and sit here. . . . Let her go on like that, it's she who gets tired, who cares." That kind of feeling – they were not bitter, they were not angry, they thought she was ridiculous.'

This said, however, it must be recognised that such an attitude could change rapidly in times of stress. As another friend said: 'This is all right, you know, as long as she doesn't go and tell somebody to do this and that on the bus; then the amused tolerance becomes something quite other. . . .

'He (the European) still is a bit of a threat in that he is the employer. . . . So I don't know that the average African can quite afford to laugh.'

It is common ground that European attitudes towards Africans in the past were highly undesirable, even obnoxious – had they not been, the whole history of Kenya would have been different. There are no doubt embittered Africans, who cannot forget the slights of bygone days, but few people have time to spare on grudges from the deadest of pasts, and few are even unreasonable enough to expect the Europeans to change overnight.

'It is coming,' as an African lawyer said to me. 'You must remember that in the pre-independence days there was a concerted effort to keep people separate from one another. Now the concerted effort is the other way round. . . . You see kids coming from school – they have already started forgetting that they used to be at different schools, or live in different zones of the same city.'

Is much of a change really occurring? Such a question is almost unanswerable, since its terms of reference are the secret places of the heart, but on the whole African opinion holds that it is. Mr Sammy Maina, Kanu's Nairobi branch secretary, once said in a Press interview that 'the Europeans have identified themselves completely with the new nation'. This view is echoed by most Africans if the subject comes up – albeit with overtones not entirely agreeable to European ears. One man, a journalist, said: 'Whenever a European is defeated he admits defeat; as now he is defeated in Kenya, he admits that he is defeated and he does what he is told to do.'

The 'good loser' motif came up again in a conversation I had with Mark Mwithaga, an M.P., Nakuru councillor and the local Kanu chairman, whose political activities before independence had landed him in jail several times. Of all the people I have talked to, he was most sanguine about the change in European views.

'I'll tell you what. . . . We were good rivals in this town. I fought very hard for my camp, and they fought very hard for their camp. And here it wasn't a question of stories or paper-work or Press work. It was a question of fighting *vis-à-vis*. We met, we couldn't talk, or we quarrelled, we fought, we organised strikes, this sort of thing.

'Now their attitude today is incredible. Everybody had thought, because of their past behaviour, that they wouldn't have accepted to remain and mix with Mark and others. . . . Right now we meet in parties, we talk, they join the Party. . . . This is the flexibility of human nature. Being human, some have been completely unable to change. But they have still got time.'

It is especially difficult to assess the magnitude of changes in attitude, since they usually take place gradually. A young European described the process rather well. 'My mother has been here a long time, she's seen all these changes, and she finds it hard to accept them. But working where she does (in a dress shop) . . . a lot of African women go in there to buy clothes . . . and they are very polite, they want to learn; and my mother is surprised by this, she's flattered in a way that they will come to her and say "I'm going to a banquet, what shall I wear, how shall I do my hair?" And her eyes are being opened, so she's not so suspicious, and she realises: "Well, they are just like I was when I was a young girl" – coming . . . from a rural kind of life, and then you go to London and you want to be told things so that you won't make a fool of yourself.'

Of course a lack of overt prejudice sometimes only means that Europeans know when to keep their mouths shut. Those who have not changed will often reveal themselves to other Europeans. Thika, about thirty miles from Nairobi, is a small town with a growing industrial complex, surrounded by large farms and estates – coffee, pineapples. Although the experts who work in the factories come and go, it is probably fair to say that a higher proportion of the white faces in and around Thika have been there for a longer time than is the case with Nairobi.

'I think to a certain extent you have to distinguish between

Europeans. . . . They (farmers) are consciously hypocritical because they realise that they are only here on a short-term basis, and from a pure economic point of view I suppose that is a reasonable sort of attitude to take. But on the other hand if you . . . have established a factory, or a business which is an expanding business, then you have got to look at the situation very much more sincerely, and there I think it is a question of degree.'

The speaker, who was for a while a senior executive in a Thika factory, talked for an hour about his impressions – on the whole very unfavourable – of the local Europeans. One of his remarks summed up most of what he said: 'The majority of Europeans in the Thika district are interested in two things, and in two things only: they are interested in the money they make out of their crops, and they are interested in sport. And sport fulfils a very large role in their life because it is a form of escapism: I sincerely believe the reason why sport is so important to them is because it saves them from the real things that are going on round them.'

Another European – in Nairobi, this time – who runs a business which brings her into contact with a vast number of people, has a more tolerant outlook. Considering that, as she said, 'ten years ago there was a real colour bar here', she believes that change is taking place too rapidly for relics of the old ways to be important; though she added: 'I think there is a lot of hypocrisy, there's a lot of dishonesty. . . . I think there's a big backlog of opinion here against the African on the whole. It's just ignorant prejudice. Mark you, they have the most terrible ignorant prejudice about everything else too, it's not just about Africans.'

Though it is going, there is also still a certain amount of snideness around. The old language of prejudice is no longer to be heard. In its place there has grown up a euphemistic jargon, based on ellipses such as 'our little chums'. The tone of these remarks is not virulent. It is one of resignation or at times mild exasperation at the antics of people regarded not necessarily as *inherently* inferior, but as none the less inferior –

incompetent, over-excitable, or whatever – as things are.

The most depressing and by far the most widespread of basic attitudes is the They syndrome, or They All complex.

'If you give them a chance, you know, they all take advantage.'

'They all have wives in the Reserves.'

'They're all the same – you can't leave tea or sugar about.'

The mentality is probably epitomised by a question asked by a visitor to our house. She wanted to know how many servants we employed. What she said was: 'How many boys do you keep?' The connotations of the word 'boy' for an adult servant of from twenty to sixty years depend on the user. Our former nanny uses it in Swahili, with the plural 'waboy'. But on the lips of a European it can tell a lot about the speaker – as can the habit of entering a friend's house and walking obliviously past the servant in the front hall without a word of greeting.

The principal and depressing point about the They syndrome is that 'they' are almost all servants, office messengers, or similarly low-paid workers; and the speaker applies his limited knowledge of this limited group by extension to refer to all Africans – about whom he often knows less than one would believe possible. It is usually clear from the context that he has no social knowledge of Africans at all. Africans are 'they' – 'they' the Government, 'they' the servants, 'they' who drive old and dangerous-looking lorries or laugh loudly in the street, always 'they'. This leads to things like advertisements in the paper: 'For sale, European-owned car.' (I once even saw 'For Sale, European-owned pram'!) Even if, as may be true in the case of cars, there is a better chance of a thing's being in good condition, since Europeans are more likely to be able to afford regular servicing, the wording and the cast of mind both seem unlikely to win African hearts. This, not in a country where there are no indigenes of a high enough standard of living to be on a par with the speaker, nor where local habits of urban life are strange – there are few places socially so like Camberley as Nairobi, and this is as true of the African as of the European upper class.

The They syndrome is of course a product of ignorance – and complacent ignorance. One sometimes hears a Kenya 'old hand' come out with some remark of quite obvious folly and smugly conclude: 'But they're just spoilt children; you can't tell me, I've been here too long!' On the whole its stupidity is greater than its harmfulness, except for the unpleasantness it may cause to people such as servants who are not in a position to answer back. Even on a master–servant level, those who suffer most are the employers. People who start off with the assumption that *all* servants will 'take advantage' do not get the optimum service from their domestics, who as individuals are sensitive to this type of generalisation. As Herman Melville said: 'The suspicious man kicks himself with his own foot.' But it consorts ill with the image of themselves that most Europeans have. The 'old hands' are not the only people to blame in this respect. Contract workers – people in Kenya for a limited period – often suffer from the They syndrome.

Two sub-aspects of this sort of mentality are perhaps more distasteful. For instance, a remark made to me by a Scots secretary at a party. 'What I hate,' she said, 'is when somebody in the office finds a mistake in something, and they start swearing and saying "what can you expect, you can't trust an African to do anything right". It happened the other day, and as it happened it was my fault. So I said so. And the woman stopped shouting and said: "Oh, that's all right, Miss Macdonald, we all make mistakes." '

A former colleague of mine was involved in another incident. A public company made a muddle over a bill. When he saw the European woman who dealt with complaints, she told him confidingly that this sort of thing was always happening now that there were so many Africans starting work with them. 'You know,' said my colleague, 'she actually said: "It's those African clerks." And I found out later there wasn't anybody in the department who was African. It was all Europeans who'd made the mistake.'

The reasons for this uncivilised attitude to Africans in an

African country are complex. But it is not unfair to say that many of the Europeans in Kenya have little sense of social responsibility. The number of immigrants from Britain jumped after the Second World War, and while a large number of these were ex-servicemen who could not settle down to the relatively dull life at home, others were fleeing from the new conditions entailed in the growth of the Welfare State – not only high taxation, but the concomitant lowering in their own standards of living. It is hardly surprising that people who opted out of greater equalisation in their own country are unenthusiastic now that an independent Kenya has set out on the welfare path.

As for the contract workers, many are, as I was, in Kenya in jobs of a seniority which they would have been unlikely to attain in competitive England – this after all being one of the major motives for the upheaval entailed in emigration. They have a far higher standard of living than they could have expected in Britain, and many are not socially equipped for it. The result is that they have taken over the behaviour of the old hands for want of the knowledge of anything better. Many of these people have a sort of 'jumped-upness' which is particularly disagreeable. A middle-class African friend once observed: 'You find the kind of European who is not educated, you can tell from the way they speak . . . from the way they behave . . . especially in this area, I think you have the lower type. . . . There were bad motives. They wanted a comfortable life with servants around them and so on. . . . And they can be very rude, this kind of people . . . straight away you can tell the background they come from.'

Still, inter-racial relations in Kenya are improving all the time. This is partly because the composition of the European population is constantly changing. In Nairobi at least, there is a more international, largely more cultured, group which is not in the least concerned with a person's skin-colour, and in which Europeans (often in fact Americans), Asians and Africans mix without the least artificiality. These circles – most of whose members are in their twenties and thirties – are the prototype of what should, and probably will, happen in Kenya as a whole. Others who are ceasing to think in community terms are those who work with Africans as equals (notably Church or social workers) and who thus share in the task of building up the country. As an African social worker said:

'My contacts are with Europeans working in the Church. I know very few that work in the Government or in commercial firms, therefore my judgment may be false. By and large I think that there is a change to the good; I mean, there is a recognition that this is an African country. . . . Most of the expatriates are people who are coming on a short-term basis now, and come with that in mind. . . .

'I don't know about those who have taken citizenship. I think that some of them feel . . . well, although we have taken citizenship we are not fully accepted when it comes to senior posts.'

This last remark points to a source of worry for many of the Europeans who want to stay. As one young man put it, 'If they want me to become a citizen, okay. . . . But if I become a citizen and then within three years they turn round and say "even though you are a citizen you are a white citizen so we don't want you" . . . that's the fear I have.'

A number of people who might otherwise have taken citizenship have hesitated for reasons like this. There is a theoretical dilemma at the heart of Government policy. On the one hand it is morally right as well as politically essential that there should be a period of Africanisation in which non-Africans are bound to suffer job-discrimination. On the other hand, it is wrong that any citizen should be discriminated against on grounds of colour. If the majority of non-Africans had taken Kenya citizenship there would have seemed no answer to this dilemma, except for those Europeans who want to stay to set off the possible disadvantage of being non-African against the tremendous advantage of education and position which they will for a long time continue to have. A number are doing this. But most Europeans remain without taking out citizenship, content to live in Kenya as foreigners, like one middle-aged businessman who said eighteen months ago: 'I don't think I am going to opt for Kenya citizenship. Shall I say that I perhaps have been too long an Englishman. I do it for no reason, no disparagement of Kenya whatsoever. . . . It is just that I have been too long an Englishman to change my nationality.'

A fact about the European community which is not fully realised is that as a community it is slowly in process of becoming extinct. This makes talking about the present in terms of the future a little unreal. The only thing that is certain is that – through the Europeans' own choice – there will be no community as such in twenty or even in ten years' time, though there will still be a fair number of individuals. Those who are in Kenya as non-citizens (and only 844 Europeans have taken out citizenship of the land most claim to love so dearly) because they have better jobs than they would have in England, will go when there are citizens to take their place. Like the British Government, the Kenya Government will certainly refuse work permits to non-citizens except where they are needed. Moreover, since most of them are only in Kenya because they have materially never had it so good in England, when – as is inevitable – taxes go up to pay for giving the masses some sort of slice of the national cake, they will have no incentive to stay. The short-term expatriates will of course only be in the country as long as there is a shortage of skilled manpower. The steady trickling-away of 'old hands' continues. One of the most commonly-given grounds for departure these days is the uncertain position of the former European schools, which will be dealt with in another chapter. Others, as is their right, do not want to stay because Kenya is no longer what they knew. As one man said, 'I did think I'd retire out here; but I thought it would be part of Britain. And it isn't, and therefore I shall go home to my own country. This is a matter of taste, and certainly as far as I'm concerned, there's no bitterness about it.'

Up-country, especially, the exodus still slowly continues. One of the few European Kenya citizens in Nakuru described it.

'A great number of Europeans have gone. . . . You don't realise it . . . it doesn't sort of mount up. But they are going. The European Stores at Molo, which has been there for years and years and years, and more or less entirely depended on the farming community at Molo, lost 180 accounts last year. It's in liquidation now. . . .

'The doctors are going, the lawyers are going, the dentists are going – I have to go to Nairobi to the dentist now – and this has a sort of snowball effect. Then the elderly married couples say, "This is absurd, I can't get my teeth done here, I'll go to England", and the cycle starts again.'

These problems, real or imaginary, affect up-country people rather than those who live in Nairobi; and the result is that the European community is gradually withdrawing, so to speak, into the capital. One cannot carp at people who, thinking their comforts are going to disappear, decide to leave. Kenya is a land where at one time three per cent of the population enjoyed standards as high as any in the world, while the remaining ninety-seven per cent enjoyed practically nothing. Now that work has started on improving the lot of the majority, the three per cent is going to suffer a drop in standards, and like most human beings they are not prepared to be sacrificial.

But the fact that for these reasons the community will go on shrinking does not affect the position of those who *do* want to remain. What about people like my coffee-farming friend at Thika, who want to stay in Kenya because it is their country, who still feel themselves part of it – albeit at times a dissentient part? They may not continue in exactly the same jobs, or even at the same job-level, as before. This, in a country where nobody can be sure of a job as of right, is part of the sharing process. But men like this will be able to stay in Kenya as long as they want, to sink or swim with everybody else. For one thing, Africans too are dropping the tendency to think in group terms. As one put it, 'A person of European origin who wants to live as an individual, just to see that his rights are respected, that he has the freedom to work, that person I think will be more and more wanted. Right now there are many

Africans who have come ... to see that after all that particular DC or that particular teacher there, who was white, was giving them better service than this fellow-African. . . . What I mean is that they will now stop branding the white people all together and will start looking at individuals.'

This is, of course, not to say that everything will without question always be lovely in the Kenya European's garden. Minorities are never entirely secure anywhere; circumstances can change. In so far as they are seen as privileged, the Europeans will always risk a growth of hostility. In the rather sweeping words of an Asian friend, 'When there are Europeans and Asians living in grass huts, then they will be safe and not until then'.

While they are waiting and working to lose their dubious position as the moneyed class, the Europeans have one very important factor in their favour – the very fact of their own irrelevance, as a group, to modern Kenya. As a friend remarked, 'I think the thing of the Europeans, apart from the settlers, is not an issue. You know, the Europeans here are like a foreign community anywhere. They are not an issue – I mean, the Poles are not an issue in Britain.'

6

The Undervalued

I have never got a straightforward thing from an Asian
Middle-aged African

Even if I am not an
African I shall be a Kenyan
Young Goan

If the Europeans enjoy the relative security of irrelevance, the
Asians do not. They are an integral part of the country, and
being ethnically distinct they are open to all sorts of prejudice.
The word cannot be burked. Africans honestly believe that racial
prejudice is a European disease; but it is prejudice to extra-
polate a class of dishonest dukawallas from the existence of
individual dukawallas, and then tar the entire Asian community
with the same hairless brush.

The Asians are as integral to Kenya's history as are the Europeans. In the sense that they are to be found in every corner of
the land and at every level of society, they are more inextricably
a part of it. Even politically they have played a role more important than is usually admitted. No doubt most of their activity
was on their own behalf, and many of them viewed the rise of
African nationalism with mixed feelings (genuinely mixed, for
the emotions of a privileged group warred with the enthusiasms
aroused by India's struggle against the Empire). But their
constant agitation did far more than the vacillating sense of
duty of the Colonial Office to prevent Kenya from going the
way of South Africa and Rhodesia. In the words of a local Asian
leader, 'they kept the door open'. This is a fact which cannot be
repeated too often. Even in the mid-1950s there was a European
political movement – the Federal Independence Party – whose

policy was rooted in the Bantustan theory, with all the elements of polite apartheid ('The party believes that separation will bring co-operation. We believe that integration will bring destruction and misery to all'). The failure of this party (many of whose members, incidentally, are still living happily enough in Kenya) is in part due to Asian political activities going back to the twenties and beyond, which prevented the idea of Kenya as a 'White Man's Land' ever going unchallenged. The FIP manifesto recognised this, and abandoned its Olympian tone of fatherly love for all to remark waspishly: 'The Party believes that the Asian has no inherent right to a share in Government. ... Past experience has proved that the only result of increasing the Asian share in Government is a continual demand for more.'

If the political part played by the Asians was significant, the Asian contribution to the economy has been tremendous. It lay not so much in the wealth they created – though Asian business assets were a few years ago assessed at £100,000,000 – as in the type of activity they promoted.

An Asian leader observed in an article in the *East African Standard* a year or so ago: 'Over the last 60 years or so, as masons, carpenters, blacksmiths, builders and contractors, engineers, civil servants, traders and industrialists, as lawyers, doctors, nurses and teachers they have helped to build the nation.'

In particular, the Asians developed areas which otherwise would have remained untouched.

'When you think of the contribution the Asian has made in the remote areas in setting up industries such as cotton ginneries – small industries, shops. Europeans have tried and flopped: they couldn't stand the pace, or the hardship, or the low return. The Asian has – he's an inveterate gambler. He will through his family connections raise enough capital to put up quite a big factory in a sort of gimcrack way, and he thereby does give the community a most wonderful service, and I think it's grossly unfair that he should be accused of pinching all the trade. The European couldn't establish all those places, and the African certainly couldn't in those days.' These remarks, by an elderly European who has travelled all over the country as few people have, sum up the peculiar Asian contribution perfectly.

There are many Asian commercial undertakings which could compete anywhere in the world – the Supermarket in Nairobi, owned by an Ismaili family, is better than any that I have found in London since I returned recently. The big Asian shops in the centre of the town are only differentiable from their European rivals in that they usually give better service. Most European shopkeepers in Kenya are extremely pleasant compared with their English counterparts, but they preserve a vaguely amateur status, closing at 4.30 (just in time to be of no use to the office workers) and too often assume that because they are European their service must unquestionably be the best – an unwarranted assumption which can lead to amusing results, as in an incident related to me by Rebecca Njau, the writer.

'These European shops that look smart and clean and what not, the price is often twice as much (as in Asian shops). They are easier to get on with, you know, the Asians. We went to a European chemist and asked for a cough mixture by name, and he started saying "No, no, there is no such thing", trying to make us look fools. We went to a little Asian shop opposite and got that same stuff, and went back to the man – "Here it is!" He was ashamed of himself!' The ideal is a combination of the best Asian and the best European commerical characteristics, as one finds in the bigger Asian stores.

These Asian enterprises, and their industrial equivalents, are excellent, but they do nothing which the Europeans would not have done. It is outside the main towns that the Asians have made their biggest contribution. Debarred by law from farming – and in the country districts from trading – they made a living from service industries and from business in the small townships. They got Kenya off the ground industrially, as the Europeans got it off the ground agriculturally. Every African politician is careful to give the European contribution its due, and it is time that the Asians were treated in the same way.

One of the reasons for this general grudgingness lies in the very nature of Asian enterprise. The African man-in-the-street

7*a* Nowhere is the overwhelming Asian predominance in Kenya's trade more strikingly brought home than in roads like Bazaar Street, Nairobi, where every building is a shop and every shop bears an Indian name.

7*b* Much of Kenya's retail trade is still carried on at ground level. This sweet-potato seller might be in any of the small rural markets. In fact she is in the outskirts of Nairobi.

8a Just one of the thousands of boys who present Kenya's cities with one of their biggest problems. Unemployed and probably unemployable, they scratch a living as best they may. That Kenya's juvenile delinquency has not got out of hand is thanks largely to the extended family; but with the employment situation what it is, the position may become desperate.

8b Nairobi's unemployed complain surprisingly little – in public at any rate – perhaps because many can get at least some food from a family shamba, so their position, while unpleasant, is not desperate. Occasionally there are small demonstrations, but they often have political overtones. This one, outside Parliament, was held just before the 'little General Election' last year.

comes most directly into contact with the Asian small shopkeeper, whom he believes – inaccurately – to be both rich and
typical of Kenya Asians. The theory of the dukawalla's wealth
is wide of the mark. In the words of *Portrait of a Minority*,
'Dukawallas in remote parts of the country live on pitiful
margins of profit; work immensely long hours, get the whole
family to serve in the shop, live a life of austerity, cut off from
many amenities of modern life, and retire after a long life's
work with meagre savings. The image of the exploiting, unscrupulous, wealthy, Asian class has been so popularised that
the very real sacrifice and contribution of these small, up-
country shopkeepers has been completely ignored, to be
replaced by a long catalogue of sinful practices.'

This shopkeeper image projected on to the entire community
is pretty absurd in all the East African territories. It is especially
so in Kenya, which has about 180,000 Asian inhabitants,
sixty to sixty five per cent of whom were born in the country.
Of 'economically active' Kenya Asians, according to recent
study, just under seventy per cent worked for somebody else.
The public sector occupied thirty-three per cent of these
employees, and the commercial sector thirty-four per cent.
Thus public services, transport and communications, manufacturing and miscellaneous services account for almost as
much of Asian employment as does trade – and most of those
in trade are employees, not owners. Add the lawyers, doctors
and so on – without whom Kenya's desperate shortage of
professional manpower would be wellnigh catastrophic – and
it will be seen that not only is the image of the exploiting
dukawalla unfair, but the dukawalla image *in toto* has little
relation to reality.

If the picture of the Asians as a nation of shopkeepers is
inaccurate, the notion of the Asians as wealthy also needs
readjustment. Certainly there are one or two Asian millionaires,
but the tax figures show that most Asians can hardly be called
rich by objective standards, though they may appear so to a
peasantry living well below the poverty line. In 1962 eleven
per cent of Asian personal-tax payers earned less than £120.

H

In the private sector (where the postulated exploiters would presumably operate) only eight per cent of Asian males earned more than £900 a year. In other words, a sizable minority of Asians in Kenya earn barely enough for essentials. Apart from this near-pauper class, most Asians fall into the middle-income group, between £300 and £900 a year. Most of these people live in two- or three-room flats. For entertainment they make do with the endless tinsel nothings of the Indian film music broadcast by VOK Vernacular Service and occasional trips to see the films whose melodies they have been humming. Their lives are given colour by the sun in which they stroll by hundreds of a Sunday afternoon, and by the endless ramifications of family life. If these people are exploiters, they must be the most incompetent exploiters in the history of skulduggery.

The tax figures hint at the real economic ground for African resentment of Asians. The Asians are in the way. Any African who has primary education and the slightest head for business sees the little neighbourhood duka with its jumble of brooms and cheap crockery, its tinned food and slightly stale chocolate, its sacks of dried chilis and lentils and beans, its charcoal stoves and kerosene lamps hanging like shrunken heads from the eaves, and he knows or believes that he too could be in the relative comfort and warmth of that shop instead of pushing his bicycle loaded with the vegetables that are his stock-in-trade through mud and dust, rain and shine. He does not reflect that if the dukawalla and his relations scraped and skimped to provide the pathetic little portion of capital which underlies their sweat and labour, and that his own were too poor to help him, this is his misfortune but hardly the Asian's fault. He mutters, as he will not mutter when passing a large general store, European or Asian, because the large store is beyond his grasp and not worth wasting bile on.

The same principle applies in the public sector. The average man leaves school after primary level, if not before, but a growing number (apart from the lucky few destined for the élite) have at least some secondary education. These people are not fools, and few have ideas 'above their station'. They see the European managing director behind his nice shiny desk, and they know that they have no prospect of replacing him. They may subscribe to the political theory that he should not be there, but this is a view held without bitterness. The young Asian clerk who has reached Secondary Four, on the other hand, is in little better educational trim than many African youths. Small wonder that the lads who roam endlessly round hoping for an opening however humble, for any sort of job, see him as a rival – almost, at times, as an enemy. 'That very desk, that very cup of tea might be mine,' they think as they leave yet another office rebuffed, 'if it were not for that Mhindi there.' Such peculiarly personal feelings, born of personal woes, no amount of logic will undermine. They are more dangerous than any ideological conviction.

The Asian is in the way, and the solution to this lies largely in Asian hands. The country dukawalla is doomed. The Government naturally does everything possible to give Africans a larger active share in the economy – to wipe out the present gross and potentially explosive imbalance, in which non-Africans control virtually all the country's commerce and industry. The same process has already started in the public sector. As we have seen, the need for Africanisation produces a moral dilemma where non-African citizens are concerned. For the moment the interests of the underprivileged group have priority. Non-citizens (and most Asians for one reason and another failed to take out Kenya citizenship while it was easy) have even less chance of consideration. The clerk and minor civil servant class is having a thin time, and fears a thinner.

This does not mean – as many in their gloomier moments assume – that the Asians are finished in Kenya. If they were, it would be a double tragedy: for the Asians the outlook would be bleak indeed, with a choice of emigration to England where they are not wanted, or India which is even poorer than Kenya. For Kenya the result might not be collapse, but the loss of finance and of skills would reduce her to a pauperdom from which she might never recover. Given that Kenya's industry, peripheral as it is, is the most diversified in Black Africa, and that in general she has more hope of a prosperous future than most of her sisters, this would be a pity.

It is, however, neither necessary nor likely. Kenya's need of skilled people is such that in some categories it will not be fulfilled (assuming any sort of expansion) for decades. The Government report on high-level manpower needs in the period 1964–70 shows that in 1970 there will be too few graduate secondary school teachers, doctors, mechanical and electrical engineers, architects, surveyors, pharmacists, physical planners, vets and lawyers. There will be shortages of more than 3,000 primary school teachers, 400 nurses, 300 non-certified accountants, and an unspecified number of draughtsmen and engineering technicians, as well as a range of aeronautical *fundis*.*

All these jobs need higher education; for those who cannot afford it or are not up to it, there are other openings – though in these categories there will be far more African pressure. As the report puts it, 'we have paid too little attention in the past to our pressing need for skilled office workers such as stenographers, secretaries, bookkeepers, cashiers and speed typists. . . . Of the more than 7,000 skilled technicians that will be needed, over 1,000 are motor vehicle mechanics and about 500 telephone and telegraph operators.' These last categories provide the answer to the employment fears of the skilled but not very well educated or flexible workers and technicians. Provided that Asian parents appreciate the need in time, their children could be gently steered towards training for employment where shortages lie. If this is done Kenya, which already cannot get along without her Asians, will have no temptation to try.

People in positions of service to the community already blur the dukawalla image. A young teacher commented: 'I notice for instance a vast deal of difference between the attitude of an

* Strictly 'craftsmen', but a word which is used to describe anybody who is good at anything.

average African to a dukawalla and to me, when he knows
that I am a teacher. To me every African, from the petrol
station attendant to the caretaker of these flats here, his attitude
is one of respect – and they really respect teachers.'

As the number of Asians in 'service' professions increases and
the number of dukawallas declines, the old image should
(helped by the growth of an African dukawalla class) disappear.
A way in which the Asians, working at a communal level, can
help it to do so is indicated by the Ismailis, who combine
considerable public-spiritedness with a long tradition of working
together, and who founded the Aga Khan Hospital in Nairobi.
This is not only – in spite of staffing problems – the best and
most modern hospital in Kenya; it was the first to be open to
all races, and was indeed multi-racial from its opening in 1959.
Although it is fee-paying, the Aga Khan is still largely supported
by contributions from the Ismaili community. This hospital
is the most striking Asian communal contribution to Kenya,
but there are others. There could be yet more, and they could
well serve the dual purpose of increasing opportunities for
young Asians and for young Africans (as does the Aga Khan
in its nursing training).

Asian unpopularity is not merely a matter of economics.
Socially they are said to be clannish, snobbish and exclusivist.
As the mayor of Nairobi, Ald. Charles Rubia, once remarked:
'The Patels tend to mix only with the Patels, and the Shahs
with the Shahs.' This is undeniable. Kenya's Asians are
divided into a fairly large number of religious and cultural
groups. Roughly seventy per cent are Gujarati-speaking
Hindus, but even this apparently unified group is split into
Shahs, Patels, Lohanas, and a number of others, all regarding
themselves to a greater or lesser degree as different from each
other. There are also a number of Punjabi Hindu groups.
Then there are Muslims, Jains, Sikhs and Goans (mainly
Roman Catholic). This crazy paving of groups, most of which
are indistinguishable to the non-Asian observer, makes integration into a multi-racial society very difficult. The younger
generation is on the whole – at least theoretically – intolerant

of communal and racial divisions. In this respect it is unfortunate, however much it may be a good thing in other ways, that parental and family authority and the weight of public opinion are still so powerful in Kenya's Asian communities. It makes defiance of the older generation's feelings on integration difficult. The power of tradition – far stronger than among Africans and in many ways than in India itself – operates almost always to the detriment of initiative and individual freedom. The results are seen in boy–girl relationships except among the most sophisticated individuals and perhaps in the Ismaili community, which is the most sophisticated group. Even now a girl who takes a job other than the 'premarital fill-in' type like stenography or who shows other signs of intelligence or initiative has great difficulty in getting married – a two-way difficulty, be it said. First most Asian young men are intimidated by such a girl, and if they are not their mothers are likely to object to her. Second, most Asian young men are so limited in outlook that such a girl has the devil's own job finding one in whom she can summon up any interest. This is no theoretical equation. At least two of our own friends find themselves in this position, and one of them has left the country rather than resign herself to spinsterdom.

As in attitudes to marriage, so in most social questions. While the impact of the West on the Asian communities in Kenya is very large, it is mainly technological or superficial. As has been observed, it 'provides the form rather than the content of modern living among the Asian minority'. None of this is very obvious to the casual observer. On Saturday mornings the Ismaili teenagers, interspersed with a few Goans, chatter like starlings in every coffee-bar in Kenya. The girls are frequently extremely beautiful, and almost always well groomed and well dressed; the boys good-looking for the most part with sharp suits and good manners. They wave to friends and gossip, raise innocent hubbub and even flirt in a decorous fashion, without a care in the world.

The Ismailis and Goans are far less 'foreign-looking' to European eyes than any other Asian group. The Sikhs seem

the most exotic, though a turban looks remarkably un-
romantic worn over blue overalls and streaked with engine oil.
In casual dealings the Sikhs are remarkably open and at ease –
the men especially, but also such women as one meets. More
'Singhs' (the word Sikh is rarely used in Kenya) are to be seen
chatting on equal terms with their African employees than
members of any other group. This may be in part because there
are a large number of Sikh artisans and artisans are often more
relaxed than the bourgeoisie, but many Africans confirm the
impression that this trait is common to all classes of Sikhs.

Asian inturnedness is not of course obvious at first sight. But
when the visitor penetrates into their homes (not all that rare
an occurrence, be it said) he is entertained with the polite
but awkward hospitality which would be given to a Martian.
The most urbane would quail at the sight of the entire family
sitting stiffly waiting for the visitor or the head of the house to
pronounce, the formality broken only by the giggling of a
collection of little girls, conversation about as easy as a game
of ping-pong played with cannon balls. Even in the gatherings
of the rich a certain over-politeness is rarely absent. Once one
is regarded as a friend this vanishes, and there are individual
households where it is never present; but not many.

In all this welter of sectionalism it is hardly surprising that
the degree of Asian integration with other communities is not
marked. This in itself should not account for the bitterness with
which most Africans talk of Asian failings – as a young Goan
remarked, 'I think a person can be a Shah, not talking to a
Patel – or to an African or a European – and yet be a good
citizen of the country'. As we have seen nobody is very
bothered about how much Europeans mix socially with Africans.
But combine this social sluggishness with the economic competition which the average Asian represents to those Africans
who have managed to get a bit of education, and one can
understand – without condoning – a degree of racial prejudice
which they do not display towards the Europeans.

Prejudice is, of course, not universal. A few people have a
lot, and most people a little. The man in the street is pretty

bigoted, but is also prone to wag his head and add: 'It takes all sorts . . .' African opinion is at its silliest at minor political level, when it can come up with absurdities like: 'Most of the big Asian businessmen are engaged in corrupting the leadership of this country and undermining and sabotaging the efforts of our Government to build this country economically.' It is little wonder that Asians sometimes despair when all their efforts, when the Shah Karimjee Trusts and the Aga Khan Hospitals receive this sort of thanks.

Fortunately, most Africans are not that stupid. None the less, the commonly held opinion can be summed up in the words of a young journalist: 'An Asian is never reliable. . . . They are used to cheating. They are liars, commercially and in every way.' The poor dukawalla has a lot to answer for! Occasionally one will meet Africans who really appreciate Asian difficulties with impartiality. One such once commented: 'I feel a little sad about the isolation of the Asian community as such. . . . This kind of backwater existence worries one very much, and I think it becomes terribly apparent when an Asian wants to break away from it – the isolation he suffers as an individual. . . . A kind of closed-in smug atmosphere that "this is good for us, if only we could be left alone". Which is quite untrue: it isn't good for them.' Such understanding is, however, still too rare.

More unexpected is the reaction of many of those Europeans who as far as the Africans are concerned do most to bring about Kenya's aim of non-racialism. One of these told me: 'I have found in practice that the Asians out here are people for whom I can have no time at all . . . they live in physical terror of the African, and I think the reason is because they have exploited the African so much in the past that they are completely at the mercy of their own guilt.' These words were spoken some time ago, when passions were apt to run higher than they do these days. But they indicate something which applies equally to the present, and will continue to do so: the danger to the liberal in reaction from Kenya European norms of swallowing African attitudes hook, line and sinker.

From both sides, therefore, the unfortunate Asians attract

sub-racialist cross-fire. They themselves are not blameless, needless to say, nor are they guilty only of sectionalism. The complaint which the Mayor of an important town made to me, though sweeping enough to fall into the category of racial bigotry, contains too much truth.

'It's all right for a man like myself, holding such an office – they will welcome me. But not with an ordinary man. I hate it, I really hate it. . . . It's not a question of high class ignoring the low class. It is entire, the whole community, regardless whether they are middle class or the highest class, they still feel themselves superior.'

This sense of superiority shows itself in a number of ways. Some Asians can be guilty of a degree of rudeness towards ordinary Africans which has to be heard to be believed. The sight of a dukawalla raving (and raving is at times the only possible word) at some unfortunate peasant woman is not made less embarrassing by the fact that his colleagues are starting to extend the courtesy title Memsahib to include their poorer as well as their wealthier clients. The dukawalla is usually a man of little education, and often with a strong sense of insecurity as well: it is more distressing to hear the way in which some of one's own friends can talk to ordinary people – not shouting in this instance, but with a brusqueness made somehow worse by their appalling Swahili. At times like this even European snideness can seem preferable.

Rudeness, always fairly rare, is dying. A more frequent trait is the assumption of a sort of Euro-Asian *entente* in enduring the idiosyncrasies of the African. One meets it quite a lot in shops. At the dry-cleaner's one of my suits was once hung on the wrong rail, causing a delay of perhaps two minutes. The Asian manageress made a production of looking for it, rather in the tones of an elderly woman discussing the Youth of Today: 'Where is it now . . . Tsst tsst! . . . I'm very sorry to delay you . . . You know what it is . . . (confidingly) they lose their heads – put things on the first rail without thinking where they're supposed to go.' This sort of thing, though it is said without malice, is mildly distasteful.

In African comminations against the Asians, discourtesy is usually mentioned only as an afterthought. The allegation that the Asians are making no effort to change provides the main burden. As we have seen, this is not true. Certainly such efforts as have been made are hesitant and sometimes marred by tactlessness or over-cordiality. An absurd photograph appeared last year, in the Press, of an Asian group which called on the President. The man next to Mr Kenyatta, a rather over-jovial looking character, has his arm across the President's shoulder. The effect is unfortunate. But as the more sensitive non-Asians realise, the Asians have the weight of thousands of years of exclusivist tradition to overcome. The timid efforts which are being made – not only, though mainly, by the younger generation – should be encouraged in every way. An English friend once remarked: 'I personally am convinced that this country is making a very strong and very serious attempt to set a high international standard on race relations. . . .

'Compared with what they are genuinely trying to achieve in Kenya, they regard the clumsy and fumbling attempts in America to achieve something of racial working relationships as those of uncivilised savages.'

If this is true – and the evidence suggests that it is – then the Africans should be prepared to meet the Asians half way. Yet very many Asians believe they have been rebuffed when they have made overtures. Not only is this extremely upsetting to people who are doing what is demanded at the risk of the powerful disapprobation of the more reactionary members of their groups. Once rebuffed a man is not likely to make the effort again – and worse, others will not even make a first attempt. As a Goan friend put it: 'Being a bird of passage – I think we can accept you as that – it doesn't worry *you* so much if somebody doesn't accept you or misunderstands your overtures of friendship. But in the case of people like me, who would like to be considered part and parcel of this country, if I were to get off on the wrong foot with somebody it would upset me quite a lot. And rather than risk being upset by being misunderstood, people like me very often don't make the attempt.' This may be an over-sensitive and defeatist attitude, but the Asians of East Africa have had enough to make them over-sensitive one way and the other. Things are not helped by incidents like the broadcasting last August of what was objectively a racialist attack on the Asian communities as a whole for their lack of speed in integrating. The motive of this broadcast (and of the speeches along similar lines made from time to time) was obviously to prod the Asians into action. In fact, as one might have expected, it tended to make them retire into their shells pessimistically.

All these difficulties notwithstanding, relations between all three races, always pretty relaxed on a superficial level, are improving. The ultimate goal – a society in which race means nothing – is a long way off, but in view of the past there is a remarkable lack of overt strain. The present atmosphere was well described by a young Nakuru Asian. 'I think tension as such doesn't really exist. I think it's more an awareness of the different races, and this is the result of Kenya's history. . . . Formerly these were the talking points of everyone. The Asians were talking about integration in great fear, the Africans were talking about integration in great anger . . . the Europeans were in the same sort of situation. Nowadays people hardly talk about it – people hardly think about it in fact – except when the topic comes under discussion . . . there are so many things happening in this country, the country is developing so fast and so on, that we don't have time to think about these things.'

Provided that the tentative efforts of the Asian communities to make the adaptations needed for their continued happy existence are increased and encouraged, the gloom of the day when Pio Pinto was murdered – when, to quote a friend, 'the bar was full of blue-grey Indians huddled over beers looking round anxiously' – will be gone for ever to everybody's advantage. It will not be before time. The Asian community has had more than its fair share of worry over the last few years. For some time there was considerable fear of violence. Although this was exaggerated, events within East Africa itself added to it (while only the Congo, a country in no way comparable with Kenya, could provide gloomy examples for the

Europeans). What happened in Zanzibar during the re-volution is still not clear, but any Asian who believed even a tenth of the stories which were circulating at the time must have trembled. During the mutiny in Dar es Salaam it was Asian bazaar shops which were looted. On the day when some strikers got out of hand in Kisumu, in Kenya itself, Asian shops had their windows broken. In any future disorders the Asians would be the first to suffer, not only because there are more of them than of Europeans and they are more unpopular, but because the ordinary 'little brown man' both lives and works much nearer the African working-class suburbs than do the Europeans. True, nothing violent is very likely to happen in Kenya, but violence is not impossible in any new country.

Nowadays discrimination or the fear of it is the greatest of Asian grievances. They suffered discrimination for sixty years under the British. Now, they complain, they suffer it under the Africans. Part of the trouble is that the Asians, more of whom are at a medium level of employment, have felt sooner than most Europeans the effects of Africanisation. That this is necessary, that this is the price which non-Africans must pay if they are to live secure in Kenya, is not easy to face when the family pay packet is at stake. Europeans can return home or be welcome in any part of the White Commonwealth, and virtually all of them can afford to go. But for many Asians, Africanisation means major hardship if not ruin. Most people accept African-isation, however apprehensively. What hurts is that although little hard evidence of actual discrimination against Asians exists, undoubtedly (in the words of the leader quoted above) 'at present they are not being given full credit for their work and others appear to take advantage of their labour'. A very large number of Asians have served Kenya for years with loyalty and skill in the civil service and many other public services, and their contribution has apparently been ignored or underrated because they are Asians. Worse, so far as the future is concerned, employers have too commonly been known to engage expatriate staff for senior positions at vast expense rather than take on qualified East African Asians. This may be the privilege of private firms. When the Government acts in this way – as it has done – Asians begin to take African avowals of egalitarianism with a pinch of salt. They are wrong, since the isolated cases of this sort of thing weigh very light against all that is done to make the immigrant groups feel at home in Kenya: they are wrong, but they are hardly to be blamed. For them, the decision to stay or go costs more potentially than it does for the Europeans.

Discriminatory action on the part of the Government has a trebly unfortunate effect. First, to employ foreigners when you can employ locals is a waste of scarce money. Second, local Asians are less likely to make sacrifices to obtain needed skills if they are afraid of being passed over, and the high-level manpower situation will suffer. Third, such practices are among the reasons why many of Kenya's most highly trained Asians are emigrating to England or Canada or elsewhere. These people, most of them young, do not leave the place where they were born solely for more money. They leave because they think their motherland does not want them. In this respect at least Kenya's anti-Asianism is a material as well as a moral handicap. Still, such practices do not reflect Government policy, which is quite clearly that 'Africans' means 'citizens', of whatever colour. As always, the difficulty is that policies are carried out by human beings.

7

Give us Land

What is misery?
It's a man without land
Swahili song

Our greatest need is
for efficient farmers
Kanu Manifesto

The variety of Kenya's landscape is, for a country straddling
the Equator, remarkable. In Githunguri the banana palms
seem down-at-heel yet prospering, slightly defiant. The overall
impression is of a lushness more influenced by rain than sun.
The soil is a deep, a brilliant, a fantastic red; the grass, the
banana palms and the tall deciduous trees are a deep and
glowing green. The earth seems all-conquering. The walls of
the huts and the houses are stained with it knee-high, the little
boys herding cattle or waving at the roadside wear shorts and
shirts whose colour has long since been obliterated by it.

Driving over the Uasin Gishu Plateau or down from Kitale
to Broderick Falls, the green is less uncontrolled. Friesians or
Ayrshires graze peacefully in a scenery of meadows and
clumped trees whose Englishness is disturbing. Here, as 150
miles away in Limuru, an atmosphere almost of the British
Home Counties is broken only by the colour of the men and
women walking through it, by the drama of the sunsets and
by the bleak and uncompromising beauty of the distant hills.

The Coastal strip is the tropics of every Northerner's imagina-
tion. Driving south from Mombasa – itself a town exotic as is
no other large town in Kenya – the road leads through coco-
nut plantations whose palms are as tall as beech trees. Wayside
stalls sell green coconuts for drinking, huge pawpaws, mangoes
incredibly cheap. This is the Africa of half-forgotten geography

books and of romantic films. Even the dull little trees which
take over from the coconuts after a score or so miles turn out
to bear cashew nuts. And half visible beyond palm and cashew
lies the vivid blue of the Indian Ocean.

All this richness of landscape is dwarfed by the immensity
of bush and desert which lie between and around it, and which
produce the paradox of a country in which there are more than
fifteen acres to every man, woman and child, and yet good
land threatens to become seriously scarce. Of Kenya's
140,000,000 acres, only 26,000,000 have good enough soil and
sufficient rainfall for intensive agriculture. Other land is rich
enough for agriculture but lacks rain. Yet more – about
twenty per cent of the country's total land area – is prohibited
by tsetse fly.

The land is the only source of income for two out of three
Kenyan families. Thus the present and future depend more or
less entirely on those 26,000,000 acres of high-potential land.
This alone would explain Kenya's obsession with the soil. Land
and the Kenyan's attitude to it was a major factor in the
country's independence. Land hunger among Kikuyu dis-
placed from tribal lands – or what were regarded as tribal
lands – in the so-called White Highlands was the greatest of
the complex frustrations behind the Mau Mau rising, which
drew attention to the fact that there was something desperately
wrong in Kenya.

Though the white settlers' political domination is a thing
of the past, they still have a great economic significance. More
than seventy-five per cent of agricultural exports come from
European farms; and if their importance now is considerable,
their importance in shaping Kenya's agriculture was even
greater. European farmers gave Kenya an agricultural economy
advanced enough to serve as a basis for rapid development in
all spheres. Unfortunately, since they also acquired so much
land, a good deal of their work had to be undone in the
interests of social justice. In the former White Highlands, a
potentially desperate situation existed at independence – a
situation which led to a remarkable experiment in going in

two directions at once: the high-density settlement schemes.

'The basic purpose (of the settlement plan) was . . . the transfer of land in the "scheduled areas" from European to African owernship. . . . One must take into account the stability brought to the country in a period of political transition, marked by inter-racial and inter-tribal jealousies and prejudices, by the orderly transfer of over a million acres of land owned by 780 Europeans to 26,000 mostly landless and impoverished Africans. . . . Without such a plan undoubtedly there would have been a breakdown in race relations, and violence and theft on a very large scale and a collapse in the general economy.'

These remarks in the closing report of the Kenya Central Land Board, which was brought into existence to handle the transfer of this land, show the need for what from the purely economic point of view was a retrograde step: the return to peasant farming in an area where large-scale farming had been the rule. If this had not been done, and done very fast, Kenya might not have been the reasonably contented place it is today. It is a measure of the political success of this scheme that few people in Kenya are fully aware how necessary it was.

Settlement still goes on, for it was not just a stop-gap policy, though the first million-acre scheme – involving especially areas like the Kinangop with a large number of squatters – could be described as an emergency measure. By December 1965, 1,000,000 acres in the former scheduled areas had been bought for African settlement at a total cost of nearly £15,000,000. By June 1966, it was expected that 35,000 African families would have been settled in these areas. Not all of these are peasants with subsistence or near-subsistence smallholdings. By the end of June 1965, President Kenyatta told a Kanu conference held in March of last year, 'Africans either as individuals, co-operatives, or partnerships owned 750 former European farms'. The high-density schemes were dramatic, but they are only a small part of the total effort.

The fact that political considerations were overriding in the high-density schemes, and that among these considerations speed of transfer ranked high, led to great difficulties at first. Settlement on the Kinangop, which was part of the Nyandarua scheme in the Central Province, started in chaos. At first, owing to a gap in the plans, 3,000 families were without any basic medical facilities. This could not be remedied before 1964, because the whole area was to be transferred from the Rift Valley to the Central Region, and the appropriate authorities did not yet exist. Pneumonia and bronchitis were widespread, and children without warm enough clothes for the 8,000 feet altitude, and weakened by malnutrition, were dying. Some settlers got good plots without delay; but others had to wait – and others were given no cause to hope for a means of subsistence. There were what a witness described as 'sort of DP camps', in each of which up to a thousand families waited a year or two for their permanent plots and were expected to support themselves meanwhile on two acres of indifferent land. Things were so bad for a while that part of the Nyandarua area, Kipipiri, was seriously considered for famine relief. The National Christian Council of Kenya set up a rural aid mission and farmers' training centre without which it is possible that disaster might have been even greater.

These initial problems – caused partly by inadequate planning, but also by the limitations of the settlers – were increased by more permanent disabilities. As a report on the schemes says, part of the Kinangop 'is "difficult" land, ill-drained, subject to frost, and the techniques required for success are strange to settlers who come from other areas'. This report also showed a cautious optimism. 'Already some of the settlers are showing considerable enterprise and the signs of success. But the Training Centre is faced with a stupendous task to help all the settlers to become efficient farmers in their new and strange environment.'

It will be some time before Nyandarua returns fully to the prosperity of the days when £250,000-worth of produce a year bumped to market along its rutted lanes. The year after the settlement scheme was completed, its 'exports' dropped to £50,000. The Jeremiahs had a field day. But things are improv-

I

ing all the time. Mr John Dearden, the Agricultural Adviser to the National Christian Council of Kenya, says: 'Some of them – a few really progressive ones – I would say are really in top gear now. Generally speaking you can drive through there and you see half-built houses and people not developing the land. But I do notice that after intervals of six months I see things happening and developing. . . . I'm quite sure, given time, that place will be quite a success.'

The breaking up of big farms into small plots might have been economically disastrous. The whole concept is certainly unorthodox. When a European farmer remarked sourly to me, 'I've never really met an African farmer – I mean, what is a farmer? The majority of those sort of Africans that I've seen are smallholders . . . but anybody who's got a bit of land today in Kenya is looked upon as a farmer rather than a small-holder', he was thinking mainly of these schemes. It did not occur to him – as it did not occur to most of the critics – that in a country in Kenya's position orthodoxy gets nowhere.

There are already strong overall indications that the ortho-dox are wrong. The Government *Economic Survey 1965* reported that 'It is . . . notable that nearly all of the increased agricultural product (in 1964) was derived from the small farm sector'. This does not mean that small units are yet the backbone of the economy – far from it. They remain largely subsistence farms, and in 1964 only 16·8 per cent of their total production was marketed. Still, if one looks at the efforts of the new farmers on a wider scale than the high-density plots, the position is reasonable enough. As early as the end of 1964 the Minister for Agriculture, Mr McKenzie, was telling the FAO that 16,000 new farmers on holdings ranging from 20 to 200 acres had increased yield on their land by twenty per cent.

Most of this increase has been contributed by the larger units. The settlement schemes were divided into high-density, like Nyandarua, and low-density. The target for low-density or 'yeoman' units was to develop holdings which would yield £100 a year to the farmer after he had met all debt charges and fed his family. Once the crash settlement programmes were complete, and immediate political and social needs were met, the emphasis returned to economic farming.

The low-density schemes can be hoped in the long run to make up any economic shortfall in the high-density. Many of them appear to be improving on the production achieved by the former European owners, as Mr McKenzie's figures indicate. An example of this is the Sigona scheme, a 624-acre project financed by the World Bank. Two European farmers were brought out in 1961, and thirty-eight settlers – all with agricultural experience – moved in in 1962. They put down £30 of a total £300 settlement charges, and are repaying the rest over ten years. The estimated gross production in the last year during which the land was farmed by its former owners was £8,045. The new settlers' estimated gross production in 1963 was £12,477.

The African takeover of the former White Highlands is not a matter of settlement schemes alone. Some of the new farmers have gone in as private owners, helped by Land Bank and Finance Corporation loans. Where this has happened, things have often continued much as before. Even if the purchaser is a comparative novice, he may inherit farm workers with a great deal of experience. Africans rich or credit-worthy enough to take over big farms as individual owners are, however, rare (so much so that some farms have been virtually returned to smallholding status by the appearance of 'hidden partners' who helped to put up capital and then demanded a physical share of the land). The settlement schemes, with all their faults and virtues, were the backbone of the change.

An essential rider to the settlement schemes is the co-operative movement. A man farming a plot of twenty acres – especially if he starts without a penny, as most did – can do very little in the way of improvement by himself. If enough plotholders club together, many of the disadvantages of the small unit can be overcome. Marketing co-operatives reduce costs and also make it possible to enter into contracts for the regular supply of produce which give a guaranteed income, where an individual could only chance his luck at the local market. A vegetable-dehydrating firm, Panafprod, for example – which pioneered written contracts in this field – buys much of its intake from Kinangop settlers. Co-operatives can buy equipment which would be quite out of reach of a single farmer. They can, for that matter, buy expertise.

An example of what can be achieved by co-operatives is the Ainabkoi settlement scheme, which has about 275 plotholders on 1,600 acres. The scheme began in 1962. By the beginning of 1964 the Ainabkoi Farmers' Co-operative Association had 146 members and an average monthly pay-out of £2,500.

The co-operative movement is taken very seriously in Kenya. Actual farm co-ops, it is estimated, will take over 1,200,000 or more acres. This will enable more people to have a share in the land, without large farms having to be broken up. Co-ops have enabled smallholders to grow major cash crops where this would otherwise have been impossible. Tea, for example, was considered the plantation crop *par excellence* until Kenya showed that smallholders could grow it, and grow it well. Although in 1962 ninety-eight per cent of Kenya's tea was still produced by large plantations, the smallholder sector is growing steadily. In 1960 it was only 1,500 acres; by the end of June 1963, 8,430 acres. By 1970 it is planned that smallholder acreage should have reached 25,000, with seventeen factories (of which three were in production by September 1964).

Development targets include a contribution from the co-operatives of between sixteen and twenty per cent of the gross national product by 1970. In order to achieve this and to get rid of the troubles which still bedevil the movement, the Government, in May 1966, announced steps to cope with what it described as 'major abuses'! These included continuing inefficiency on the book-keeping side. Almost half the six hundred farm marketing co-ops were a year behind with their accounts. Loan repayments were badly behind. Apart from financial difficulties there were too many cases of corruption, particularly by committee members putting on pressure to have their own produce given a better grading than it deserved.

On the growing side, after a good start the quality of the coffee crop has gone down badly in the last few years. The fault is not all on the side of the farmers and minor co-operative officials – in Kisii, where the co-ops are particularly inefficient, by-laws are in English, which effectively prevents most of the farmers from knowing what they are. All this does not mean that the co-operative movement is a failure, but a good deal of tightening up is needed to put it straight. A new Co-operative Societies Act will give the central authorities a much freer hand in dealing with inefficiency and malpractice, as a short-term measure. The Nordic countries are to spend about £3,500,000 on aid to the co-ops in the next ten years, and between twenty and thirty Danish instructors will advise on the setting-up of regional co-operative offices, which should help to improve standards.

Education at every level is the prime need in all farming, as in all things Kenyan. At the highest stage are the agricultural colleges, like Egerton at Njoro and the farmers' colleges at Embu and Thomson's Falls. The Six-Year Development Plan included enlarging Egerton to accommodate another 120 students at a cost of £25,000, and increased local training for vets is also planned. By June 1965 Egerton had 310 students, ten times as many as in 1961. Of eighty-three who sat for their diploma, only one failed. But there is little use in training agricultural officers, vets and so on, if the farmers themselves are untrained – for an untrained farmer, even if he listens to advice, will be unable to put it into practice really effectively. The greatest need is for grass-roots training. In order to provide this at a reasonable cost, five farmers' training centres have been set up to teach up-to-date methods with a strong emphasis on local needs and possibilities, and more are planned. These centres serve the dual purpose of teaching farmers better techniques, and keeping Ministry field-workers up to date with improvements from research. Each centre has or is to have an extension officer to encourage self-help projects. These and other educative and informative activities were expected in the Six-Year Plan to cost well over £400,000 in capital costs alone.

If the Government's task in training the country's peasant farmers is rather like having to remove a mountain with a shovel, there is much help not only from such bodies as the FAO, but – more important from the point of view of Kenya's self-respect – from local voluntary bodies. The National Christian Council of Kenya in its Agriculture and Malnutrition Project runs seven agricultural training centres, including one at Limuru which comprises a boys' school teaching better farming and a centre for short practical courses for farmers and their wives (who are responsible for much of the farm work). Another NCCK centre covers health, education and agricultural training on the Kinangop Settlement Scheme, and there are others for the pastoral tribes.

Although a good deal of effort goes into training the settlement scheme farmers – especially the high-density plotholders, many of whom had no experience at all when they went on to their land – this is not the most important aspect of agricultural education in Kenya. Of Kenya's high-potential land, eighty per cent lies in the former African Land Units; and these farms, in the words of the Development Plan, 'promise the greatest return on investment and will receive first priority in allocating funds and staff for development'. These areas are in many ways more gravely in need of education than the settlement schemes, for the people farming in them have a continuous subsistence tradition which includes some very harmful habits. Modern techniques, though they are being introduced by the more progressive, are very little practised. Even soil nutrition is so little understood that the Development Plan had to make provision that 'to convince all farmers of the great advantages which can be derived from the correct use of fertiliser, a demonstration unit will be established at a six-year cost of £51,600'.

Backwardness in the African Land Unit is made worse by the attraction of the towns, which draw off the young and able-bodied especially. This situation led to the so-called 'back to the land' policy, first mentioned by President Kenyatta in a speech at Kiambu in 1964, and the subject of much exhortation since. Regrettably, this was conceived more as a short-term answer to urban unemployment than as a rational approach to agricultural problems. As was remarked at the time, 'The type of man that you are asking to go back to the land is the last man to ask . . . because he cannot develop the land to the stage in which we can have an economic springboard.'

The back to the land policy did not have very much effect, and little has been heard of it recently except in political speeches. This is probably fortunate. There are enough farmers in these areas already, without increasing their numbers. What is needed is to get at the youngsters before they desert the land, and make them feel agriculture is a career worth following. To do this it is essential that rural amenities be improved. Kenya is not like England. In many areas a visit to the cinema would mean a journey of forty miles or more. If teenagers are going to stay on the land, they must be offered at least *something* to do with themselves; otherwise they will see the countryside as something to be escaped at all costs. Again, something must be done about persuading their parents to pay them for their work. As Mr. Zadok Otieno of the NCCK put it, 'We all talk about going back to the land, but if the father is not going to employ his son and give him an adequate salary, then the son is definitely not going to stay at home'.

Just as important as brightening up the countryside is farming training, without which the new generation will merely carry on the bad old traditions. In this field the 4K Clubs, started on the lines of the American 4H Clubs by the Ministry of Agriculture and the US Agency for International Development, are doing most valuable work. Already they have about 20,000 teenage members. They work by teaching members what to do with the *shambas* they have to work on, keep interest high with competitions, and a certain amount of social activity.

That people are learning is revealed in all sorts of ways – not least in import figures. As the Minister for Finance, Mr Gichuru, once commented, 'The fact that agricultural machinery and fertiliser imports are much higher than at any time for the past three years is significant in that it shows that small-scale African farmers are adopting the modern techniques of production essential for the growth of our economy.'

But there is still a terribly long way to go.

Lack of education is not the only problem in traditionally African areas. Most farmers own ill-defined tracts scattered over a wide area. Land consolidation and land registration, which the President once described as the foundation of modern farming, are designed to correct this situation. The task is immense. In extreme cases, forty or more tiny holdings may have to be measured and recorded for one right-holder before they can be put together and registered. Although by the end of 1965 1,629,000 acres had been consolidated and registered, another 25,000,000 acres remain. When this will be completed is anybody's guess. It is hoped that by 1976 most of the high and medium potential land and a good deal of pastoral land will have been registered: and that is as far ahead as anybody is prepared to look.

Land consolidation is not just a matter of neatness. A good deal of time and energy was wasted in some areas over disputes as to who owned the land – a situation which does not encourage maximum effort from the farmer. Even more significant, given the need to advance from scratching about with a hoe to the scientific production of cash crops, is the fact that only once his land is registered can a farmer use it as security to borrow money for development. The importance of this can be gathered from the Ministry of Lands and Settlement's estimate that – 'The impact on the economy of Kenya of registration of half of the farm holdings in the former land units will be enormous: production of cash crops could well show an increase of £100,000,000 a year or more within the next seven or eight years.'

Even if this figure is over-optimistic, the scale of its optimism shows what is at stake.

Agricultural progress is rarely the subject of big headlines, and it is very easy for the inexpert eye to miss what is going on. Except in the case of very big schemes, the pattern is usually that of small advances on all fronts. Thus in April 1966 the District Commissioner for Meru made his annual report. Total agricultural exports were up thirty-eight per cent on the previous year. Coffee brought the district £2,100,000; English potatoes were second with a value of £121,250. Maize, in spite of the overall shortage in Kenya, totalled £56,297. The three farmers' training centres in the district gave courses attended by more than 2,600 farmers. A total of 270 acres were planted with trees, and two tree nurseries flourished. Settlement went on, with 270 farmers moving on to the Nkonde Settlement Scheme. It is a pity that none of this is publicity-worthy, and that the agricultural features which appear in the Kenya Press make such dull reading, for such quiet progress is the measure of Kenya's real achievement.

Ignorance in the high-potential areas is the subject of a quiet war of attrition. It is in the low-potential areas that most of the drama is to be found. Especially is this true of irrigation. The most impressive irrigation scheme yet functioning in Kenya is the Mwea-Tebere rice scheme. Thanks partly to good planning, and partly to the expatriate expert in charge, who eats, drinks and sleeps irrigation, Mwea-Tebere has progressed with hardly a setback, since it was started as a detainee project in 1954. It was opened for settlement in 1958, with the aim of turning dry land into rice-paddy by irrigation. The ultimate target at that time was 30,000 acres under water. By 1960 the scheme was producing more than the world average crop per acre, and the settlers – who knew nothing whatever about rice when they arrived, since they were chosen on grounds of landlessness – were making a net average income of £140, as much as any Kenya African farmers. By the beginning of 1964, there were 10,000 people on the scheme, in nineteen villages.

At present, Mwea-Tebere supplies ninety per cent of Kenya's rice needs. By 1970 it will provide all of them, and there is a good chance that Kenya will be exporting rice.

Mwea-Tebere, though the first, is not Kenya's only irrigation scheme. The Kano Plains scheme, which has only reached the experimental stage as yet, will be equally important. Other smaller schemes are no less valuable in transforming their areas. A case in point is Perkerra, in the Baringo District. This semi-desert area is irrigated by a very simple method. The plot-holder plunges a metal tube into the water of the irrigation channel, with his hand over one end, and works the tube backward and forward until pressure is built up. Then he takes his hand away and the water flows. It is a sort of siphoning technique, and shows what can be done without sophisticated machinery. Perkerra started off on the wrong foot, since some-body on the planning side only allowed for average water pressure when designing the headworks, and as a result the first heavy rains carried them away. The scheme has however survived that setback and a certain amount of squabbling be-tween the two tribes involved – the Njemps and the Tugen – and now supplies Nairobi with most of its onions, as well as growing bananas and maize.

The nomadic tribes present special problems. The obvious way to help them develop is to encourage them to settle down with their cattle – to ranch. This of course means training. The Masai are certainly not ignorant about cattle, but their know-ledge is limited to what works for a nomad.

'They have had their own cures for a number of diseases – not very effective, but they recognise it as a specific disease with its own cure. So it's not too difficult to implant in their minds the modern methods of dealing with that disease. . . .

'There are certain practices which are not bad for the nomadic way they lived, but they've got to change their minds about. The animal husbandry aspect of calf-rearing, for instance. If they want milk they should keep house cows and not have them part of the general herd – a lot of little things like that which they do see the point of but which were almost impossible to apply when they were nomadic.' The speaker, John Dearden, is much concerned with such matters in his work. The NCCK does as much as the Government – perhaps more – to train the pastoral tribes. It runs a rural training centre at Isinya, in the Kajiado District, together with a 2,000-acre ranch and a small area for demonstrating crop-husbandry. This was the first of its kind teaching the techniques of small-scale ranching and animal husbandry and it is doing very well.

At the other end of the country, in the North-eastern Province, the Ministry of Agriculture and the NCCK are operating a somewhat similar scheme for the Turkana, though Turkana land is mostly too arid for ranching. Here what is needed is training to make the nomadic way of life more effective. In the NEP, one of the problems is getting cattle to market. Though work is hampered by the minor war which is going on between the Kenya Army and Somali shifta, the Government is trying to set up cattle dips, and has plans for a permanent cattle route to take stock to Mombasa for sale.

Training is, of course, useless unless people are willing to undergo it. Although the number of pastoralists prepared to try ranching is still small, it is growing. A Ministerial complaint in 1964 that only sixty-eight plots had been enclosed and registered in Masailand was denied by a Masai Senator, who claimed that there were 1,000 on the waiting list in Kajiado District alone. Much of what progress the Masai are making is due to leaders like Chief Maora who set an example themselves by turning to modern techniques, and encourage others to do the same. According to Mr Dearden, these leaders 'from my experience are devoting very much of their time, to their own financial detriment, in trying to persuade their fellow-Masai that they've got to develop. This is something that is going to snowball. It's getting through, believe me.'

Efforts to coax people into doing what they should can give rise to impatience with their backwardness. One young European civil servant said: 'One's got to be fairly authoritarian. . . . You've got to divide the country up and say "Right! You go on to Ranch A, you're on Ranch B, you're on Ranch C. You're refusing? Right, off to prison, two months! *Now* are you going? Okay, you go on to your ranch. If you don't, another two months in prison." You know, to hell with the traditional way of life.'

In a country like Kenya, where bloody-mindedness on the

part of individuals can hold up schemes so important that it seems like a sort of treason, such attitudes can easily take hold. They are nevertheless disastrous. Apart from the fact that if the rights of the individual do not include the right to be mulish and unco-operative they are meaningless, slapping people in jail for not doing something of which they do not see the value is a very good way of persuading them to move heaven and earth not to do it. The pastoral tribes have been out of the main stream for a long time. If 'modern' society starts throwing them in jail for being too slow to join in, they will be convinced once and for all that they are right to stay out.

In any case, in many of the pastoral tribes the urge to kick them into action is lacking, because the desired change would benefit only themselves. The temptation is considerable in the case of the Masai, however, because they own a very large area of high-potential land. In Dearden's words, 'They reckon there's a million acres of wheat land in Masailand, and Kenya wants this wheat'. A couple of years back, when the Narok Masai were refusing to let this land be developed or to develop it themselves, there was pressure within the Government to bully them 'for their own good'. Wisely the authorities decided to wait and see. Last year four groups of Masai from Narok went to the NCCK and asked for help to grow wheat. One thousand acres at Narok have already been planted with wheat. If pressure greater than patient persuasion had been used, the whole of Masailand would by now have been refusing to co-operate – at the very least.

If crop husbandry and ranching combined are the answer for most of the pastoral tribes, the unfortunate Turkana, as we have seen, are without the necessary decent land to develop. The 125,000 Turkana eke out the barest existence in a desert area of 22,800 square miles which is reckoned capable of supporting only 30,000 people in its present state of development – and though a little can be done with the drilling of Artesian wells, irrigating enough land to make much difference is a very slow process. In the meanwhile the Turkana live in a state of endemic starvation. They do however have one asset –

they live near Lake Rudolf, once described to me as 'God's gift to fish'. This has become the basis of a most imaginative attempt at development, the NCCK Fisheries scheme at Ferguson's Gulf. It has been estimated that an annual catch of 1,500 tons of fish from the lake could be maintained, and the scheme is engaged in teaching the Turkana to fish and in finding markets for their catch. The main difficulty at Ferguson's Gulf – apart from training – is the road. There is already a big demand for the fish, which goes mainly to the fish-eating tribes like the Luo round Lake Victoria, and also to Uganda. It is hoped that processing at Rudolf will soon be possible. Meanwhile, the catch is filleted and sun-dried.

If the pastoral tribes badly need to develop an agriculture which will bring them into the money economy, cash crops are an important ingredient in Kenya's farming revolution as a whole. Prosperity will not come quickly if people merely grow enough of what they have always grown to take some to market.

It was and is therefore essential to increase African participation in produce like coffee, tea, sisal, sugar, cotton, pyrethrum, and dairying and livestock farming.

There is already a reasonable amount of African participation in some of these crops. Coffee was the first into which African growers went in a big way. Dr Kiano, when he was Minister for Commerce and Industry, once remarked that the coffee co-operatives were the backbone of the co-operative movement. Recently coffee has been threatened by a glut in the world market. Worse, by April 1966 coffee berry disease in every area of Kenya had become a very major worry indeed. Restrictions in planting because of international marketing conditions may become unnecessary – some pessimists even suggest that coffee may be wiped out.

Cotton is bedevilled by people who will not take advice. It has been claimed that Kenya's crop could be doubled within a season at no extra cost, if growers would listen to their extension officers. Though the potential is there, another factor which makes cotton prospects gloomier than some is the appalling rate of repayment (as low as one per cent or less) of Government loans for development, especially in the Central Nyanza area. As a result of this there may not be money available for further development loans. Given that the Six-Year Development Plan envisaged a tenfold increase in cotton growing, this is not encouraging.

Livestock generally, and especially dairy farming, is also due for major extension. The Minister for Agriculture, Mr McKenzie, in 1964 announced schemes costing a total of £100,000,000, including the setting-up of quarantine farms to international standards so that Kenya beef – which is excellent and staggeringly cheap by English standards – could be exported to Europe. Kenya, apart from South Africa and perhaps Rhodesia, is the most advanced country in dairy farming in Africa – a legacy, this, of the European farmers. Until 1960, just about all the produce handled by the Kenya Co-operative Creameries was produced by European settlers. Since then African participation has risen to almost half the current turnover. This is less due to the settlement schemes, where cattle-farming has declined since the Europeans left, than to the increase in dairying in the traditionally African areas brought about by development programmes financed by the FAO and Unicef. A major example of this is the Mariakani Milk Scheme on the coast, which is on the whole a depressed area agriculturally.

On quality alone, not only beef but other dairy produce should have a considerable export future in Africa and the East. Zambia has already asked for more butter than Kenya can yet produce. Kenyan cheeses are excellent and varied. The revised development plan envisages a milk output of 82 million gallons by 1970, as against 61 million in 1964, and this should increase export possibilities considerably.

Sugar, like cotton, is from time to time plagued by bloody-mindedness as well as by more normal hazards. In the words of the *Economic Survey 1965*, 'The setback in sugar-cane production is related to the difficulties of the Coast Sugar factory and a considerable loss of crop from arson in Nyanza'. People in the smallholder section have often (usually through bad yields caused in part by not taking advice) failed to keep up minimum deliveries needed if the factories are to keep running economically. With all these troubles, however, it is reckoned that Kenya should be self-sufficient in sugar by 1970. At present she imports about 180,000 tons a year. Self-sufficiency would save the country about £2,000,000 annually.

Pyrethrum, an important cash crop used in the manufacture of insecticides, has been building up in the smallholder section for a long time – peasant farmers seem to have taken to it like ducks to water. On the Kinangop at one time it was doing better than any other single crop. In 1965 pyrethrum production doubled in Nyanza. The main risk appears to be that of a bad fall in international prices – a danger to which Kenya like all developing countries is all too exposed.

In the midst of this activity in Arican agriculture it is easy to forget the European farmers, who quietly go on growing most of the country's marketed produce. With all this change, what future have they in Kenya?

On the surface everything looks quite bright. The farming communities seem to be integrating slowly. Two years ago the Agricultural Society of Kenya was widely regarded by African farmers as a colonialist body. In April 1966 the President announced that 200 new members had joined since New Year: 100 African and 100 European. For the first time, the society hoped to reach 3,000 members. Entries for the Nakuru Show were up in 1966, another sign that farmers are reasonably content.

Underneath, however, not everybody is happy. The worries are largely economic, and they are best expressed in the words of a European farmer I talked to.

'Is European farming going to carry on in Kenya? . . . Can Kenya keep going when it turns sound economic farms into subsistence units? Is a farmer going to put a lot into his farm when he's unable to sell it? I have a plot up at Kipipiri, it cost £600 ten years ago. It was wanted for a settlement scheme. I was offered £48. . . . I think farming and political expediency are at loggerheads.' Views of this kind are not normally given publicity in Kenya, whose Press rather goes in for the cult of the optimistic grin, but they are present. The Government can take over mismanaged farms, though it does not exercise this right very often – only 121, mostly abandoned, had so far been requisitioned by mid-1966. If it loses patience with farmers who just coast along, take-over orders may increase in frequency.

In balancing economic needs with political considerations the Kenya Government has so far tended, quite rightly, to-wards the economic. But both the African majority and the European farmers themselves still wonder whether white farming has a permanent place in Kenya.

The answer would seem to be: it depends what you mean. A European friend whose sympathies are with African aspirations once remarked, 'Sooner or later I am quite sure – quite, quite sure – that all this land is going to be bought up from the Europeans and is going to be turned into co-operatives as soon as they have available trained managers to operate it efficiently.'

With some reservations, this seems to be an accurate assess-ment. Certainly it is not within the realms of common sense to expect the Government to be willing to contemplate the permanent presence of a large European *community* controlling a major slice of the country's economy. But this is not to say that in twenty or thirty years' time there will be no place for *individual* European farmers. Government policy and opinions expressed publicly do not always coincide with the private thoughts of ordinary people. The views of Councillor Mark Mwithaga, M.P. for Nakuru, who is also the local Kanu branch chairman, are interesting in this connection – the more so since he was at one time regarded as a very dangerous man indeed by the Europeans of the area.

'It will depend on the individual's merits. . . . Some Euro-peans who have taken out Kenya citizenship . . . are not farm-ing because they want to make a fortune, but because they want to be settled. So I am sure some will accept to live on a piece of land, of, say, one hundred acres with a good house.'

As for popular hostility to white farmers, he commented,

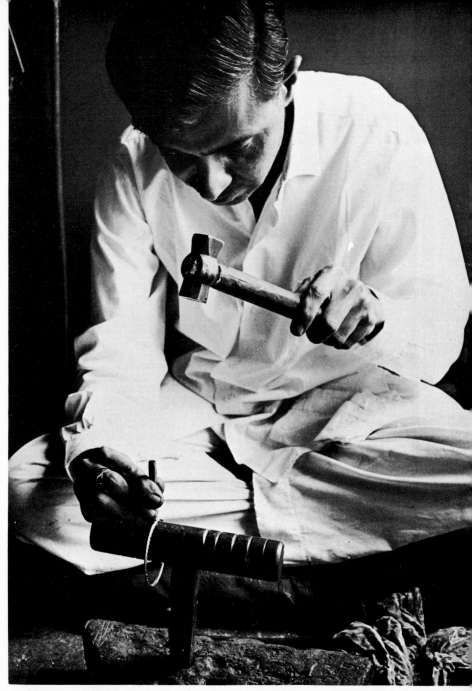

9 The Asians of Kenya are to be found doing every kind of work. Among them are to be found craftsmen like this silversmith, whose work – and way of life – would probably be little different if he had stayed in India.

10*a* Infants' dancing class. Kenya's African élite has adopted European ways with enthusiasm, but there are not many of them. What one thinks of as 'upper-class' activities are still largely a preserve of the Europeans, though this is changing slowly

10*b* A tailoring class at the Tailoring Institute of Cutting and Dressmaking in Nairobi. African commercial pressure on the Asians starts at this level – in Bazaar Street and its equivalents.

'People would still be thinking that way if land hunger keeps on growing. But if there is satisfaction to an extent, there is nobody will be looking at a person, thinking, "That's a white man, a farmer, but I am landless".'

Though most people accept the European contribution for what it is, there is a fairly sizable body of opinion which does not agree that gratitude is appropriate, or even necessary. People who feel like this believe that all European farmers should be expropriated with or without compensation.

The argument behind this attitude is roughly: 'Granted that the Europeans have brought benefit to the country, they brought it purely selfishly. The railway opened up the country, true enough; but for one thing it was built for Uganda and not Kenya, and for another it and all the other amenities were designed to help the European farmers to prosper.'

Behind this attitude to the white farmers is another argument, which expresses itself in terms of the 'land for which we fought'. Since so many Kenyans suffered to get rid of colonialism, this argument runs, they should have land, and have it without any nonsense about settlement charges. 'The land for which we fought' is an emotional concept, and not to be removed by argument. Its importance will depend on the success of Kenya's future. If the country prospers reasonably those who have the plots will soon forget the £10 or so they paid for them; and the others will be too busy coping with new jobs and responsibilities to worry overmuch about whether what they were fighting for was land or more generally the right to a decent life.

That 'free' land is still capable of being used as a political issue was shown when the Kenya People's Union was formed in April last year, and it became one of the Union's main policy planks. As a political slogan the word 'free' is vital. In practice what would be likely to happen if the policy were ever implemented is something along lines described by one Kanu branch official: 'These people could farm effectively if they were given the land without any charges right now and given all agricultural necessaries – seed, tools – for a period of about four or five years, during which they have made an income from the

K

farm, then they start reimbursing the Government. That is very different from free land, because it's only free land in the interim period.'

Even without the doubtful experiment of 'free' land, Kenya's farming revolution is bold. If it succeeds, the result will be a social as well as an economic transformation. If it fails, the results are perhaps best hinted at in the cool phrases of the *Economic Survey 1965*: 'The intensive working of Kenya's greatest natural asset – its land – would seem to be the only possible solution to the twin problems of rapid economic growth and the containment of unemployment.'

8

We Must Industrialise

You are dependent on a
Board who are encapsulated
by their office walls. . . .
Factory manager

It is economic madness for
us to continue to import
finished goods which have
been processed abroad from
our own primary products
Kanu Manifesto

Pal Singh's furniture workshop holds no secrets from the world.
Its fourth wall is the street, and the rush-hour motorist crawling
past has ample opportunity to admire the light-wood sofa and
armchair set – just like the one in the advertisements, but half
the price – which dominates it.

Singh's shop is like many small industrial concerns in Kenya.
It employs about half a dozen African carpenters, including
one who acts as foreman and deals with customers when the
owner is out. There is no real division between shop and workshop. Most of what is made is made to order, whether of
private customers or of big stores.

The Metal Box factory at Thika, a town which is rapidly
becoming an industrial centre, has a labour force of about five
hundred. Using the most modern machinery it satisfies most of
Kenya's need for tins of all sorts, as well as many types of card-
board boxes. By British standards it is not a very big factory,
but it is likely to grow rapidly since food-processing forms
an important part of Kenya's industry present and future,
and the processing plants that do not need tins will need
boxes.

At Changamwe on the mainland next to Mombasa is a shiny

new oil refinery, which came on stream at the end of 1963. With all the latest automated gadgets, it employs four hundred men. During 1964 – working at three-quarters capacity – the Changamwe refinery gave import savings of about £1,000,000. Of the crude petroleum products imported into Kenya in 1964, about twenty per cent were re-exported to Uganda and Tanzania in refined form, and another twenty-five per cent – mainly as residual fuel oils – re-exported outside East Africa. The refinery alone was responsible for half to two-thirds of a twelve per cent total manufacturing growth in 1964.

Compared with other Black African countries Kenya has a fairly diversified industrial sector, even if one ignores the multitudinous small workshops which make practically anything under the sun, but in negligible quantities. The foodstuffs industry – the most important, as one would expect – includes everything from milling to the drying, freezing and canning of vegetables, meat and fish. There is a considerable tobacco industry, and Kenya's breweries produce beer which wins international prizes. Other sizable industries include textiles, clothing, cement, wood, paper and printing, and a large number of consumer goods of all sorts.

However, the diversity of Kenya's production does not make her an industrial country. In the words of Dr Kiano, writing at the time of independence, 'Though Kenya's industry and trade is one of the most developed in tropical Africa, it still displays the basic pattern of a comparatively under-developed country, that is, production and export of primary commodities, import and consumption of manufactured articles from abroad. The process of import substitution has begun, but it is still in its early stages.'

Kenya must still import most of the manufactured goods she needs, and just about all the raw materials with the exception of cement and food. All the machinery needed by developing industry must come from overseas, as well as consumer goods ranging from lorries and bicycles to refrigerators, sewing machines, radios, razor blades – the list is endless. It is true that there are a few assembly – not manufacturing – plants, including an African-owned radio and record-player assembly plant and a factory which assembles buses. But these do not yet make much of a dent in the import bill.

An obvious choice for new industries, and for the expansion of existing ones, lies in food-processing.

Kenya is a long way from many of the best potential markets for her food products, so relatively little expansion is possible in exports of fresh food. There are already many industries based on agriculture in Kenya, mostly as yet of the obvious canning, drying or freezing variety. Dairy and pork products have already been mentioned. Two big firms make jams (as well as a number of farms which run 'cottage industry' jam production from their own orchards) and fruit juices. In both these fields quality, though variable, can be high. The orange marmalade made by one of the big jam firms is quite up to average English standards (that made by the other was at one time mainly notable for the extra protein supplied by the presence of ants and other insects). The Kenyan fruit juices are all excellent. Other products – especially frozen vegetables – are still not as good as the imported varieties. This is partly a matter of inexperience: from personal observation, the standard of pea-freezing, for instance, has greatly improved in the last two years, and the tomato juice, which used to be abysmal, is now very pleasant.

New food-processing industries are being set up in connection with major agricultural schemes. The expansion of sugar production for example, demands the building of sugar-processing plants. The one at Muhoroni, whose foundation stone was laid in January 1964, is an example of this. When it is in full production, it will cause a considerable rise in employment in an area which sorely needs it. Though the numbers employed in the factory itself will be small, it will provide indirect employment for about 4,500 people. Muhoroni will also be an example of the increasing importance – and diversification – of co-operative enterprise. Local cane-growers, organised into co-ops, will own more than forty per cent of the factory's equity. When cotton really gets under way, it will also provide the basis for a considerable expansion of Kenya's textile industry.

Though not strictly agricultural, industries based on fishing fall into the same general category. A great advantage of fishery industries from the point of view of the country as a whole is that they affect a number of areas which are on the whole lagging behind in development. The Turkana scheme is one example. The processing plant at Naivasha also handles lake fish. But the area which will benefit most is the Coast. According to the Development Plan, 'External markets for deep sea fish are extremely promising. The world demand for canned tuna in particular is considerably in excess of the present supply, so the canned tuna industry proposed for Mombasa should result in an important new export for Kenya.' Another industry still in an early stage of development which promises to be of great importance is the pulp and paper project centred on Broderick Falls.

In general, the best prospects for Kenya's development at present are in light industry. The former Minister for Commerce and Industry, Dr Kiano, gave a list of such possibilities at the time of independence: 'A most promising market for consumer goods is developing rapidly. Many of these are of the comparatively simple type and eminently suitable for local manufacture. Examples are enamelware, metal saucepans, cheap ready-made clothing, particularly shirts and cotton frocks, agricultural implements, oil lamps and electric torches. . . .' A number of such things are now being made in Kenya. There are big textile mills in Mombasa and Thika, and a sock factory also on the Coast. At the other end of the scale is an enterprising woman in Kisumu who started a combined dressmaking shop and dressmaking school which is an outstanding success on its small scale.

Many areas of Kenya will never have much industry and many others will not do so for a long time, because they lack an adequate infrastructure of communications, power and so on. The Italian Government experience with the Mezzogiorno schemes shows that it takes at least ten years to provide an adequate infrastructure for industry where none exists. In the case of Kenya, a good deal must be done to improve the infrastructure even of the relatively developed areas – at colossal expense.

If much infrastructure work is likely to be too expensive to be worth while, this does not mean that Kenya should be restricted to small-scale development. Sometimes several needs can be satisfied by one project. If these needs are pressing enough, it may be worth spending a good deal of money to satisfy them.

Kenya's most ambitious infrastructure project is the Lower Tana Hydro-electric Scheme. This is a long-term venture whose total cost will probably be about £38 million. Work has already started on the first stage, which will cost about £6 million. At present, Kenya imports power from the Owen Falls power station in Uganda. The Tana River scheme should make her self-sufficient not only for present needs but also for considerable industrial expansion. This alone might not make the project worth while – self sufficiency can be bought at too high a cost. But the Tana River (one of Kenya's three reliable rivers) also flows through a large area which at present is near-desert, but which only lacks water to become highly fertile, since the soil itself is good.

The total investment in the electricity generating industry, according to the revised development plan published last year, will be about £24 million including the major hydro-electric schemes. This is not as extravagant as it sounds, since the major schemes are aimed at making Kenya self-sufficient. Indeed many parts of Kenya do not have mains electricity at all. Until they do, these areas will not be in a very promising position for industrial development and most of their young people will tend to leave for less gloomy parts.

Apart from water, on which the revised plan foresees an expenditure of £4,673,000 in the five years which it covers, most of the expected infrastructure work will be in improving communications, which are increasingly inadequate. Of East African Railways and Harbours expenditure about £20 million

will be in Kenya. Capital expenditure on roads will be about
£21,500,000. Smaller sums will be spent on telecommunications
and air traffic.

As well as the problems she shares with all industrialising
countries, Kenya has a particular difficulty which (though it is
present to a lesser extent elsewhere) is intensified by the fact
that she has far larger immigrant minorities than any other
recently independent country. The blanket term for this
problem is Africanisation.

Africanisation is generally recognised as essential, and in
such fields as administration there is remarkably little to say
about it except that it is proceeding fast and without, on the
whole, too great a sacrifice of efficiency. But Africanisation in
industry, as in agriculture, presents more complex problems
than does a change in administration. It has already been said
that virtually all commerce and industry in Kenya is controlled
by immigrant groups. The first problem is how this is to be
overcome.

An NCCK survey of small industries divided the possibilities for
rapid African entry into business into three: common articles
of everyday use, with a small profit margin and high output;
tourist souvenirs with a local craft appeal, moderately priced;
and artistic crafts needing skilled work, with high profit-
margin and small output. Of these the first category is by far the
most promising. Apart from the fact that the second is aesthetically horrible, a mass-production industry in souvenirs is
relatively limited in scope. As for high-skill crafts, most are
confined to one-man shows which can hardly be called industrial. They will be most useful in giving employment to
women on a 'cottage' industry basis.

A field of endeavour which has hardly been explored is that
of blending objects in general demand with local craft techniques. Kenya would never be able to build up much of an
export trade in earthenware pots as such. But there is much
very pretty earthenware, decorated in black, produced on the
Coast. Since people in the developed countries seem willing
to pay almost unlimited prices for the grander sort of crock –

provided only that they can say knowingly that it is a *Mombasa crock* – a combination of traditional design and modern production might well succeed. There are a number of such possibilities in the luxury and semi-luxury field. A craft centre near Gilgil started tie-dyeing two years ago. Already the very attractive material produced is doing very well in the export market, although even in Nairobi it costs 84s. a yard. Still, this is a limited field; it can and should expand considerably, but it will never do more than supply a little extra economic jam.

The commonest difficulty facing Africans who want to start in business is finance. The Industrial Finance Corporation makes ceiling loans of £500 to businessmen who can show that they have adequate commercial experience and that there is a demand for the proposed business. Another way in which the Government is stimulating African participation in commerce is by means of the Kenya National Trading Corporation. This is a sort of super-wholesaler whose main aims as expressed by its general manager are 'to rectify racial imbalance in Kenya's trade; to rationalise distribution of commodities by elimination of unnecessary middlemen; and to help in the expansion of the country's export trade.'

A third way in which the small African businessman is to be encouraged is the setting up of 'Maduka ya Wananchi' (People's Shops), a sort of super semi-Government chain which is the KNTC's responsibility and is still at the planning stage. Another possibility which has been hinted at – and which will probably become a reality very soon – is that the Government or some Government agency should, if necessary compulsorily, buy commercial property in the centres of the big towns and let it cheaply, since African traders are at present limited to second-rate areas because of high rents. This has been successfully done in Kampala by the Uganda Development Corporation, and there seems no reason why it should not be equally successful in Kenya.

The revised development plan allows for the encouragement of African business partly by investment through the Development

Finance Company of Kenya. Another major scheme, to be run by the Industrial and Commercial Development Corporation, is the setting up of industrial estates at a cost of about £5 million at Nairobi, Eldoret, Kisumu, Mombasa and Nakuru. The total net investment in industry between 1965 and 1970 will, it is hoped, be about £45 million, of which all but £10 million will have to come from private sources.

The number of Africans who can as yet go into commerce on their own account is, however active Government encouragement may be, still relatively small. Africanisation in existing firms presents almost as much of a problem, though for different reasons. A certain amount has already been done. The *High Level Manpower* report stated that '51.6 per cent of the total high and middle level manpower employed in Kenya is African, which is an impressive achievement for a country so newly independent. Nevertheless, this percentage is far short of satisfactory distribution of these occupations among the races.'

Successful Africanisation of course depends on training. The number of small businessmen who have gone bankrupt through lack of skill in costing, accounts and so on has shown the need for commercial training. With the co-operation of the Japanese Government, the Kenya Industrial Training Institute is running courses for independent African businessmen and manufacturers at Nakuru. The number of suitable candidates is as yet small, even when there are viable projects and plenty of loan capital, but it can be expected to expand rapidly.

In major industries, as in big commercial enterprises, training depends largely on schemes run by individual firms. The intensity of such training varies. Although as the Development Plan says, 'Kenya is considerably ahead of many other African countries in its resources for stimulating and assisting industrial training programmes . . . and the development by employers of their own training organisations', technicians of all sorts are and will continue to be desperately short.

One reason for shortages in the skilled manual jobs is often said to be job-snobbery. At one time this was certainly true. In 1962 Mr Tom Mboya remarked: 'Over the years our schools have produced bookworms who thought that working with one's hands was not a civilised way of life.' In colonial conditions this was a natural enough conclusion to draw, since most Europeans worked with their heads and most Africans with their hands, but the attitude seems to be dying out. The Christian Industrial Training Centre in Pumwani, in Nairobi – which has been preparing young Africans for industrial jobs for some years – found that the first students were unenthusiastic about workshop training. Now, however, those who express views on how the courses could be improved ask for more practical work, more equipment, more specialisation in one trade. A survey which examined the lives of seventy young workers in Nairobi a few years back concluded: 'It is clear that the image of African preferences for white-collar jobs needs re-thinking. Young men in Nairobi are fully prepared to set their hearts on a practical career, provided that it is competently taught, made interesting, and seen to carry a respectable status in the modern world.'

One problem in persuading young Africans of the merits of skilled blue-collar jobs is the chaotic situation of the labour market. At present skilled artisans cannot be sure their training will get them a decent job. While few CITC trainees are out of work, one of the brightest could only get a job with an African-owned garage outside Nairobi where he was paid £3 a month. Another, a good deal less able, was employed as an office messenger by an oil company and was soon earning more than £30 a month. In conditions where lunacies like this occur, it is hardly surprising that the lathe does not attract.

Advanced training is given by individual large firms, by the Kenya Polytechnic, or in the case of very highly skilled jobs by courses abroad. Such training poses few problems except expense. What does pose a problem is the patchiness of big companies' response to the Government's call for training of Africans for important positions. On the whole the companies with the best record are the very big international firms, and public or semi-public bodies. Most firms have not done as much as they could or as is needed. In September 1966 the

Government announced moves to tighten up on work permits for non-citizens and to insist on more whole-hearted training schemes where there are no citizens qualified for a given job. If these regulations can be enforced, the situation should improve.

A genuine difficulty is the need for reasonable efficiency to be kept up even during the period of maximum Africanisation. The International Bank survey of Kenya's economic development remarked: 'The replacement of expatriate administrative and technical staff needed for management and operation of transport and communications by local people should be gradual, and replacement should be made only through the appointment of capable and well-trained officials.' Though this is most essential in public services, it applies throughout industry and commerce. Difficulty can arise when expatriates, who may tend to the assumption that Africans are too slap-happy for very responsible jobs, need to take a decision on Africanisation. This is not necessarily a matter of racialism. In England a man reaches a senior position after years of experience and learning through working. It is understandable if he is at times over-cautious about promoting somebody on the basis of two years' experience and a six-month crash course in Europe.

Yet Africanisation properly carried out can be of great benefit to the companies themselves, as some of the more forward-looking realise.

An industrial social worker put it this way: 'One day I was talking to a training officer of one of the big firms in Nairobi, and he said, "We are not training these Africans just because we want an African there. Economically it pays us to employ Africans." And he added, "When you have an African who can do the job, if you train him for three years, within one or two years you get back all the money you have spent on him. You can even afford to lose a third of the men you put into training." ' Expatriates come very expensive, with inducement pay, medical schemes, overseas leave and so on. Moreover, the mere fact that he is an expatriate does not guarantee that the man you have imported at great expense will not be a bungler. Putting it at its lowest, local staff are cheaper to sack.

Africanisation cannot be taken as an isolated problem. It is closely linked both with unemployment and with skilled manpower needs. At present Kenya is desperately short of skilled men for a huge range of jobs. She is in equally desperate need of jobs for a huge number of unskilled workers. The shortage of skilled manpower exists in most categories from university graduate to skilled artisan, but it is naturally greatest in the more esoteric trades. In the words of Sessional Paper Number Ten, 'The present situation can be indicated by noting that the Government now employs twenty-five highly trained surveyors, only two of whom are African, and has eleven vacancies; twenty-two hydraulics engineers, one of whom is an African, and has seven vacancies. . . .' It is obvious that if manpower needs are to be filled Africans should be informed of the vast variety of profitable careers open to them. Apart from anything else, ignorance about career possibilities leads to people going into unsuitable jobs, with a consequent wastage. As Whitaker writes in *Political Theory and East African Problems*, 'many people do not seem to know what they want to be, so that a person may train as a doctor, and end up by owning and running a chain of petrol stands. Somebody else may be a lorry driver one year and a baker the next.'

Behind demands for faster Africanisation lies the terrible unemployment situation. At the most recent estimate there were 200,000 registered unemployed, in a country which has only 536,000 people in paid employment in all sectors. To this very large number of adult unemployed must be added the 90,000 or more primary school leavers each year who have little prospect of work. Industrial expansion cannot provide a short-term answer. Even to double the number employed in industry would make very little difference, since it is so small at present. Anyway, the cost is fantastic. The Development Plan ended its survey of difficulties involved in creating industrial jobs by commenting: 'These data suggest that £8,757 of gross capital formation was necessary on the average to

create one new job.' The data referred to were for the period
1954–62, but things have certainly not changed for the better.

The major long-term answer to unemployment lies in expansion of the entire agricultural sector, including not only
farming proper, but forestry and fisheries. Examples of the
industries which can be based on agriculture have already been
mentioned. But the total effect on employment of a booming
agriculture does not rest only on the number of men working
on farms, nor on those employed in food-processing factories. In
the words of an NCCK seminar, a great deal more can be hoped
from 'the secondary employment generated by a high yielding
agriculture. . . . It is probably in these secondary effects that the
greatest number of paid jobs will be generated. Some of these
jobs will be in the villages, some will be in the industries supplying agricultural equipment and supplying consumption goods.
. . . The most effective way to industrialise is to create both
capital for investment and the purchasing power to buy industrial goods in the agricultural community; the effect of
rural development is to make industrialisation possible.'

All effective economic solutions are long-term, but at one
time the unemployment situation was so bad – and was
monthly getting so much worse – that urgent measures had to be
taken to provide a breathing-space. A daring experiment,
the Tripartite Agreement, showed how effective unorthodox
methods can be in desperate situations. One of the problems
in a country like Kenya is that if the appallingly low wages
earned by those in work are raised, the number without jobs
tends to increase. The Tripartite Agreement, to which the
employers, the unions and the Government were party, laid
down that for one year – later extended – there would be no
wage increases. Nor would there be any strikes. The employers
would take on ten per cent more staff and the Government
fifteen per cent. Nobody would be dismissed for redundancy.
It was hoped that this would provide early employment for
about 40,000 people.

Naturally such a scheme brought prophecies of doom, and
equally naturally, in many details the doom-merchants were

right. There were more than 200 strikes during the period; at a fairly late stage only 2,000 out of 10,000 employers had honoured the agreement; the Government – especially local authorities – never achieved its fifteen per cent target, partly because owing to tax defaulting it did not have enough money for the extra wages. Nevertheless, the Tripartite Agreement was an overall success. Its aim was to increase employment quickly, and this it did. In all, 38,300 people were found jobs. Equally important, only about ten per cent of the extra men taken on lost their jobs after the agreement lapsed, and even now seventy per cent of those taken on are still in work.

Africanisation, the localisation of commerce and industry, are entirely desirable aims. Nevertheless their success – unless the country booms to such an extent that commerce and industry more or less doubles in a short time, which is totally out of the question – is bound to be at the expense of the immigrant communities. The Europeans will not suffer a great deal of hardship, since they will be welcome elsewhere if they have to leave Kenya. Although general prospects for the Asian community are not too bad, the problem of the duka-wallas remains. Not only will large-scale Africanisation start in the small retail sector, but since very few dukawallas have taken out Kenya citizenship, they will get relatively little sympathy from anybody when their troubles start.

Mr Clement Lubembe is among the most outspoken Members of Parliament on Asian affairs – so much so that people tend to dismiss him as a racialist. His ideas on the subject are therefore of some significance. He is not insistent that 'the Asians must go', nor even that all the dukawallas must go. The almost total Asian domination of small trade must go, but he would be happy enough to see twenty per cent Asian participation in trade, provided that it is participation by Kenya citizens. For the others, 'I support wholeheartedly that the Indian Government must do as the British Government is doing (for farmers). The Indian Government must lend the Kenya Government money to buy out those Asians who want to go, so that we place in their position Africans in order to play a correct role in building our economy and in controlling our economy. . . . Now I don't mean all Asians: I mean those who have decided not to be citizens.' This is not a practicable scheme because the Indian Government has not the money to lend for 'rescue' operations of this sort but that it is suggested by somebody like Mr Lubembe indicates a certain concern that Asians should be treated fairly.

On nationalisation, which many Asian owners of major industrial enterprises used to fear, Mr Lubembe said: 'My feeling is that it would be wrong for us to nationalise these big enterprises, because if we nationalise we will deteriorate our relationship with the Indian Government, and we will be a gangster Government in the eyes of the world.' This laudable sentiment is given added point in that there are not sufficient Africans to run nationalised businesses competently as yet anyway.

The Asians themselves can influence other people's opinions by taking Africans into partnership, as they have been exhorted to do over the last couple of years. For small shopkeepers this is not easy since such businesses are family affairs, but it must come. At a higher level a good deal is being done by Asians to break their own monopoly. Although much Africanisation in both European and Asian firms is only token, genuine efforts *are* being made even if they are still too few. White Rose cleaners, an Asian concern, has for some time been issuing shares to its workers. On a much larger scale is Industrial Promotion Services, more than half the capital of which was found by the Ismaili community. It was founded in the spring of 1963. Already it has built and put into production a sock factory – the first in Kenya – on the Coast, and another factory manufacturing (not just assembling) electric light bulbs.

There are many more examples of real Asian attempts to hive off some of their exaggerated share in trade. Whether it can be done quickly enough remains to be seen. There are still among the dukawallas too many ignorant and frightened little men whose reaction to any threat is to sit tight and hope it will go away; but the success of those Asians who *are* making an

11a Siriba Teacher Training College, at Maseno near Kisumu, looks as though it had been transported from England. Its buildings are good, if stark, and its surroundings pleasant. Unfortunately neither Siriba nor the other colleges like it can train enough people to make good the terrible lack of teachers in Kenya.

11b There are times when game is exciting, and times when it is too exciting. This accident happened on the main Nairobi-Nakuru road near Naivasha.

12*a* Cow's blood mixed with milk still forms a major part of the diet of the pastoral Masai. The blood is drawn from a neck-vein by using a special, notched arrow which penetrates just far enough and no further.

12*b* Helped by Government loans, some African farmers are able to modernise their agriculture. But men like this one, seen learning about tractors at an agricultural show, often find modernisation presents its own problems when most of the profits in the early years go to paying back loans.

effort encourages others, and a snowball effect may yet develop.

An especially interesting feature of Kenya's industrialisation is labour relations. The tremendous problems presented by rapid social and economic change do not confine themselves to people's leisure hours. Industry has its share of these transitional strains. Though many of the problems in Kenya's factories are common to industry the world over, there are some which are not found in developed nations. Some of these are peculiar to a country most of whose managerial class is of a different ethnic origin from most of the workers. An industrial relations man described an example combining this with the special atmosphere caused by an overnight translation from peasant to proletarian.

'We were having a meeting and my colleagues referred to *kazi ya Mzungu* (Europeans' work), and I think this is the way most Africans have looked at wage employment. The foreigner is alien, he's a foreigner. He may be a good chap, he may not. You're working for him, but you don't get much out of it.'

The result of this attitude is often a 'going through the motions' which tends to produce inferior work.

The entry into industrial life can be disconcerting to a man who may go into a factory more or less straight from a two-acre smallholding. In the words of *The Church Meets Life in the Town*, 'coming into a plant as a new worker may be frightening indeed. The person may be greatly handicapped in hearing from his boss or teacher how he is to operate a machine. He tries to listen carefully but finds it extremely difficult. He may also find that he is unable to communicate with his fellow workers.'

Group attitudes are also affected by the newness of factory life, as is shown by the reflections of an English friend who was at one time manager of a large factory.

'The difference between the Them and the Us is very much different from the Them and the Us in a highly industrialised society like the UK. As far as the Africans are concerned Us is something completely different from the Us of the English working class because the African has got no background at all of the English social class system. He does not accept this, it

L

means nothing to him. Neither does a distinction like the distinction between management and employee . . . because after all the first advent of the European is only sixty years ago. . . .

'If you are going to establish yourself as a manager in industry in Kenya, the fact that you come from a particular social class in the UK, the fact that you have academic qualifications, the fact that you have had training as a manager in England and you are part of the executive social class, means absolutely nothing to an African. What you are judged by entirely is your natural ability as a leader, your ability to respond to Africans as a group, the ability to command their respect as a person and as a personality. Your ability, in effect, to be accepted by them as another African with the capacity for leadership, whether or not you have a white skin or a brown skin or a black skin.'

Most Europeans and Asians in Kenya are as yet lacking in this capacity. The results of management inadequacy in the field of labour relations can be considerable. The bulk of the managerial group is either 'old-hand' non-African or short-term expatriate. As far as the first group is concerned, its general inability to adjust is described in personal terms by the same speaker.

'Next door to me is one of my factory superintendents, a man who is responsible for about 150 people. Now he has been out here for a good ten years, and he is a very crude sort of person who was perfectly happy with the old set-up before Independence. But now that he finds himself in a position where he has to achieve leadership by consent, and not leadership by the authority of being a member of the white race, he is beginning to run into very serious personal difficulty, and at the moment he is in hospital with ulcers because he just cannot stand the strain, he is just incapable of making the adaptation.'

The newly arrived expatriate does not have the problem of adaptation to a changed situation. But even he must be ready to greet totally unfamiliar situations with aplomb, as this charming anecdote shows.

'I was absolutely shattered, with all the conventions of management training in the UK, to find some of the things that I was greeted with when I first arrived. I mean, with all the stuffiness of British industry, what would you have expected if you were greeted with something like this: when the second day after you arrived the union leaders called a meeting of the whole factory in the form of a party, and there was beer, and they read out to you a beautifully prepared speech in which they say that "this is a tremendous event, because you are going to be the first branch manager of this factory and we regard this as being very significant as it comes near the time of Uhuru, and we now in our own small way will have achieved Uhuru in our factory."

'And they go on to remind you about your responsibilities as a manager, because "in our African way of life we regard our-selves as a family and we regard the manager of this factory as the father of the family, the man who will protect our rights", and so on and so forth – pledge you their complete emotional support.

'Now you don't know until a situation like that hits you how you really are going to react. It does call for a degree of adaptation, even if you start off with the right principles. If you don't start off with the right principles you haven't got a chance at all.

'If you are a cynical type you could say: "Obviously all they are trying to do is to buy me, I'm not going to have any truck with this bloody nonsense," and you make a curt reply – and you lose your ability to handle them from that day onwards.'

That this man knew how to handle his labour force was shown when he resigned. The union branch got the mistaken idea that he was being victimised, and the entire factory came out on strike in his support, much to his embarrassment.

An inability to adapt can cause great difficulty in dealing with union branch officials. The common managerial attitude to union officials has been that they are power-mad or morons. Yet my manager acquaintance could say that 'my experience is that union leaders on the whole are a damn sight more responsible than many of the Europeans in senior management, in that they are very conscious of the powers they wield, of the role of trade unions in industrial relations, of the relationship of the trade union movement to the Government and to the ultimate aims of the Government. There is a very strong tendency for Europeans to regard union activities as being irresponsible because they are the direct target of those activities – this is one of the fundamental problems of industrial unrest in the branch in which I work.'

It is true that management's attitude has been coloured by the chaotic recent history of the union movement at national level – a history of power politics which has made two successive union federations useless.

At branch level, however, union leaders on the whole are responsible and more and more aware of the issues behind union affairs. As one industrial relations expert said, 'the unions are becoming more productionist-oriented, rather than consumptionist-oriented. The pressures are to get the union not to be fighting for more for its members but to be helping to create a bigger cake for society, and therefore certain limits on the conflict within industry and much more emphasis on the growth – and I think we are ahead of Britain on this one, frankly.'

The same man made it clear that the union men are well aware of the gaps in their knowledge. 'When we asked "What should the union be doing for you?" the thing which came above all was: more training in trade union matters, more training for shop stewards. . . . They were very much aware, and humble, that they didn't know all the answers as shop stewards.' This emphasis on training was repeated in every conversation I myself have had with union officials.

The sincerity of most junior union leaders is gradually being recognised by management. Since my managerial friend was speaking, a marked improvement has been made. When I quoted his remarks to a union leader in Nakuru, he replied, 'Previously, yes, it was happening; but at present most of the employers have changed. If they meet trade unions they give them their oportunity to state their case.'

As labour–management relations in a country where the executives are mostly immigrants are bound to be tricky, the progress which is being made in industrial relations, limited as it is, is hopeful. Given the right labour–management attitudes, many of the problems bedevilling Kenya's industrialisation programme can be solved with time. Time, of course, it will take, for industrial training as well as the building up of better attitudes rests on general education – and general education itself is faced with very severe difficulties.

9.

Game and the Second Industry

Elephants have right
of way
Unofficial road-safety slogan

. . . the less maritime kings
Mombasa and Quiloa and
Melind
Milton

The towns and farmlands of Kenya are islands in a sea of scrub.
Between them lies the bush.

'The bush' is one of those blanket terms covering a wide
range of landscape. Some of it is land which needs only water
to become fertile, some of it is rock, some of it is sand. To the
traveller the differences are less obvious than the similarities.
Whether between Mombasa and Nairobi, or on the road to
Uganda, or on the route south to Tanzania, the bush is the
characteristic backdrop to Kenya. It is so undifferentiated to
the inexpert eye, so unspectacular in anything but its size, that
after the first few journeys it becomes unnoticeable. Whether
broken on the horizon by hills or stretching apparently for
ever, whether dotted with acacia or broken only by lumps of
rock, or grazing game, its ultimate effect is of a uniform barren-
ness, a vast plain of scrubby grass, endless, useless; something
to be driven through – unless the big game which haunts it
strays near enough the road to be visible – as fast as possible.
It is beautiful, it is hypnotic, it is monotonous, and it is finally
irritating. There is a story about a man mapping a certain
region. He was helped by a sketch plan prepared by an earlier
traveller, which seemed pretty accurate until he came to a
vast plain. His precursor had written boldly on his sketch the
name Mamoba – but when the cartographer, who was a

conscientious man, tried to verify this, all the locals shook their heads. When the puzzled map-maker checked back, he found Mamoba to be more of a comment than a name: it stood for 'Miles and Miles of Bloody Africa'.

In fact, of course, the bush is infinitely varied – only its size lulls one into indifference. In the huge North-east Province it is mostly near-desert crisscrossed by Somali camel-trains. In the south and centre it is dotted with acacia and much of it, at least after rain, is covered with grass – often a singularly beautiful grass which from a distance seems like a mist knee-high above the ground – on which the Masai livestock graze. Almost everywhere it is a neutral zone where big game wander and the pastoral tribes herd cattle in an uneasy truce. It some-times gives one the feeling of a philosophical *Ding an sich*, self-justifying and monolithic.

There is an irritating tendency not only in the world outside, but among many Europeans in Kenya itself, to see the whole country in terms of the bush, and to attribute an exaggerated grandeur to what – though it is at times spectacular – is often merely large. To hear many people talk, one would think the country was one vast game reserve, cluttered in places with annoying humans. In fact, both the bush and its game are a nuisance as well as an asset.

In economic terms, big game is big business. Tourism is Kenya's second foreign currency earner, after agriculture. It is also, as the former Minister for Information, Broadcasting and Tourism, Mr Oneko, pointed out in an article in the *East African Standard*, the fastest expanding industry, and the one where the least investment can bring the most immediate and largest gains. In 1964 overseas visitors spent about £7,500,000 in Kenya.

At present an overwhelming proportion of tourists come to Kenya to look at game. They can be seen in Nairobi, climbing in and out of impressive four-wheel-drive vehicles, often dressed in faintly unnecessary Ernest Hemingway kits of khaki drill, accompanied by the enterprising descendants of the White Hunter. The curio shops of Nairobi are full of bric-a-brac made from the skins of wild animals. Clothes shops advertise safari clothes made to order, mostly sleeveless bush jackets and wide-brimmed hats with leopard-skin bands – the Kenyan equivalent of dude-ranch cowboy rig.

Of course, big game *is* spectacular in its natural setting, especially when the setting itself is impressive. On the road to Tanzania we once saw a giraffe standing contemplative on a huge outcrop of rock surrounded by a copse of dwarf acacias. Its impact was of an altogether different quality from that of giraffe grazing on the flat, which look odd but curiously mundane.

But wild animals pose a number of problems for Kenya. They can be a great nuisance to the people who live near them. The charm of the wild does not, for example, have a very powerful impact on a man whose entire crop has been devastated by baboons or elephant. The Masai whose cattle is being attacked by a lion does not see the lion as a dollar-earner for his country – he regards it as overgrown vermin. In some areas the problem is endemic and considerable. At one time the Member for West Pokot was demanding that his constituents be allowed to kill hippo on sight, since so much damage was being done to their crops. In 1963 the Pokomo threatened to kill off all wild animals unless a game reserve was created to contain them. A farmer on the outskirts of Nairobi one night in 1964 shot four lions, part of a pride from the Nairobi Game Park, which had got on to his land and killed some of his cattle.

The loss of a few cattle or the laying waste of a field or two may not be very serious to a reasonably prosperous farmer; to a poor man relying for six months' food on a small shamba, one night's incursion by game may spell disaster. And at times when natural food is short and such incursions become frequent, even a big farmer may be badly hit. The game protection laws recognise this. An animal may be shot if it is endangering life or threatening to damage crops. To stop anybody killing game for profit and then claiming it was being a menace, the trophy in a case like this belongs to the Government.

Though the right to shoot may help if you find a buck eating your maize, a small army would be needed to deal with a herd of baboon in a hungry mood. Unfortunately, the only really effective measure – fencing – is far too expensive to be practicable except in a few cases.

The difficulty is often two-way. Both farmers and game have their rights, and they can be mutually exclusive on a large as well as a small scale. This arises on the Tana River irrigation scheme, whose possibilities are still being investigated. On the one hand, enclosed farmland along the river would stop game getting at water. On the other hand, a whole new source of food – and increased water supplies – might attract enough game to devour the whole scheme.

Actual loss of life through attacks by wild animals is relatively rare. Even snake bite is not common considering how many poisonous snakes there are. Some time ago a woman was very badly gored by a rhinoceros at Dagoretti, a village actually within the Nairobi City boundary. At the beginning of 1966 a full-scale hunt was on for a leopard which had gone into a Masai manyatta near Kajiado and snatched a baby from its mother's breast. A wounded animal will occasionally turn on its hunters with fatal results. Game can be a traffic hazard. In the words of an unofficial addition to the Highway Code, 'elephants have right of way', and four lions once held up flights from Nairobi by sitting on the main road so that cars for the airport could not get by.

Only rarely are accidents caused by game, but a big animal darting across the road just in front of a motorist can bring disaster. A friend once had a narrow squeak. Having driven under what he thought in the twilight was an overhanging branch, he looked in the rear mirror and saw a giraffe crossing the road. The 'branch' was its neck. Giraffe seem to be particularly devoid of traffic sense. Another friend had one kick in his windscreen on a lonely road at night, and a few years ago a vet was killed in a collision with a giraffe.

Wildlife, being (like a drunken celebrity) an asset with built-in nuisance value, presents the authorities with a dilemma of some magnitude. The problem is increased by the fact that big game in Kenya shows alarming signs of dying out. The United Nations economic survey, in its section on tourism, said: 'There is a need for early measures of additional protection for wildlife if that important asset is to be of continuing value.'

Game reserves are by themselves no answer. As the Development Plan remarks, 'Kenya's wildlife population has been safeguarded less by sufficient wildlife sanctuary than by a reasonable degree of safety outside the reserves and parks. However this safeguard may be a fleeting one, and it will be necessary to increase the number and area of the sanctuaries.' This may merely clash with farming interests, however, unless the animals are given areas too poor for farmers – and thus the animals themselves – to flourish in. More important – though again not a complete answer – is the education of the public to regard game as a possession of which they should feel proud. This is to some extent being done through schools and on television; but the Pokomo, one feels, will take a lot of convincing.

Since tourism is such an important industry, the loss of much of Kenya's big game would obviously be a serious matter – and the economic aspect is reinforced by the ethical obligation for humans to preserve as much of the animal world as we have not so far destroyed.

Among the factors threatening game is poaching. Some of this is on a large scale for profit. Every now and then people appear in court charged with illegally possessing game skins or ivory. In a business as lucrative as this there is a considerable temptation to cut costs the easy and illegal way, a temptation the greater because poaching is almost impossible to stop. But a fair amount of poaching is done by people who are tired of having their shambas damaged by animals. An even greater amount is hunting for the pot. This is a particular problem: hunting is after all the oldest human method of gathering food, and is in itself entirely respectable. An uneducated man with an empty stomach cannot be expected to understand either the economic or the moral aspects of game protection. This kind of poacher is perhaps the hardest to stop, because his conscience is clear.

A related problem is that large animals need a very great deal of elbow-room – and while they can survive in fairly barren country, they flourish most among rich vegetation and ample water which also make for good farming. Kenya cannot afford to let any good farming land go unfarmed, but on the other hand the needs of the main exporting industry cannot be given total priority over those of the second industry.

Given the danger of game dying out, one apparent source of tourist revenue has to be forgone. In the words of the Development Plan, 'It is the Government's policy that the hunting safari should remain a high-priced, exclusive venture; to popularise hunting by lowering licence fees would only result in a serious depletion of Kenya's wild life to the detriment of the tourist industry.' A more civilised pastime, shooting game with cameras instead of guns, is of course being encouraged.

If big game is the main tourist draw, some of Kenya's less Westernised tribes are an important subsidiary attraction. Such pastoral tribes as the Masai and the Samburu fascinate the people of a Europe in which Jean-Jacques Rousseau's myth of the Noble Savage is not yet dead. This fascination is largely an unreal, not to say unworthy, one. For one thing – as is rationally but not emotionally accepted – the Noble Savage does not exist. The Masai and the Samburu have coherent and sensible ways of life which involve an effective political and social system; and allowing for differences in these systems, their concerns and worries are much the same as those of everybody else on earth. The average tourist is not taking an intelligent interest in a way of life different from his own. He leaves Kenya with a few photographs and perhaps a Masai shield or spear, but with no understanding of the Masai – how could he? He almost certainly has no opportunity of doing more than watch a group about such mundane activities as herding cattle, strolling along a country road, or trying to sell him a curio. Moreover, though the first sight of a group of Samburu in traditional costume is impressive, the novelty soon wears off and they become people like any other.

Still, the pastoral tribes *are* a tourist attraction, and this fact presents problems in an independent Kenya of which they are after all as much citizens as anybody else. These problems can be divided into the 'tourist' and the general.

Among the 'tourist' problems, the foremost is one of human dignity. In an independent Kenya, treating tribesmen as show-pieces is felt to be treating citizens with indignity. At the same time, the fact has to be faced that they *are* tourist attractions. The tourist literature has to reconcile these two factors. So far, nobody seems to have evolved much of an answer to this. The booklet *Tribes of Kenya* in its most recent edition has substituted the word 'people' for the word 'tribe', as in 'the Masai people', but this rather pointless exercise does not go to the heart of the matter. Perhaps the whole issue is too easily inflated. The English sense of dignity was not hurt by that rather absurd series of 'ye olde' BTHA advertisements which appeared in the *New Yorker* a few years back.

If the question has not been very well thought out, this is merely symptomatic of Kenya's unimaginative approach to its second industry. The whole rationale of tourism is built on one of man's most basic instincts – curiosity. If people were not deeply interested in what went on at the other side of the hill, there would have been no progress at all in any field. The experts tell us that the reason for Europe's early and sustained advance from the primitive was that – in days when boats were the easiest way of getting around – her peoples were given more chance to meet and exchange ideas and techniques because she has a longer coast line per square mile than any other continent. If, in other words, we were less nosey and all stayed at home, we should be the losers. And of course the more things there are in a country to be nosey about, the more of us go there. This being so, a country which depends to any significant extent on tourism must exploit this nosiness in every conceivable way. At present, such exploitation is almost totally lacking.

Basically, Kenya's tourist industry is caught in its own big-game trap. The *Overseas Survey 1965*, published by Barclays Bank DCO, says that 'The main tourist attractions are the country's game, its infinite variety of bird life and its wonderful coast with safe bathing, swimming, goggling, water-skiing and big-game fishing. Increasingly, however, tourists are becoming interested in the magnificent scenery, lakes and mountains as well as the peoples and their culture.' This is all true, but Kenya's tourist companies tend to complacency about it. Most of them give good service once they have laid hands on the tourist, but they fail in promotion. While Kenya's combination of attractions is unique, the fact is not rammed home in overseas advertising. Other countries have nearly everything which the Barclays Bank surveys mention. Especially as far as the sea-borne attractions are concerned, most of these countries are ahead of Kenya in the race for American and English tourists. Many – the West Indies, for example, or even Fiji – are also a good deal nearer to the most indefatigable travellers, the Americans.

It is not much use enticing people thousands of miles to see your big game, if big game is all you offer them, since most people get bored with big game after a few days. If you want people to spend a lot of money in your country, you must keep them there as long as possible. The countries which do this are the countries whose entire way of life is thought worth soaking up. Few people really go to France to look at Chartres Cathedral or the Chateaux de la Loire. Even those who think that is what they are going there for are really enticed by the whole aura of France. Kenya seems quite unaware of this factor. As we have seen, those 'peoples' who are used as an attraction – the pastoral tribes – are treated rather on a level with the big game. Even when the obvious African attractions like tribal dancing have been made interesting, much else remains. The whole of Kenya's situation, as a country between the past and the present, has endless fascination if this fascination is brought out. Take Nairobi – at present a place from which tourists set out to the game reserves. There is a whole culture developing down Racecourse Road; but how many tourists ever go and wander around there? The most exciting thing about Kenya – the fact that it is Africa and India and

England growing into a new and unique amalgam – is totally ignored.

If this is true of Nairobi, how much truer is it of the Coast? Here is an African Muslim civilisation unlike anything else in the world. It has a history going back many hundreds of years. Before Christ was born the Hindus, the Phoenicians and possibly the Assyrians and the Jews were trading with East Africa. Malindi was known to the fifth-century Chinese. When the Emperor was presented with a giraffe from Kenya the ambassadors who brought it were escorted back to Malindi by imperial envoys. Much later, '. . . the less maritime kings, Mombasa and Quiloa and Melind' were known to Milton and included in *Paradise Lost*. Mombasa, Kilwa, Malindi are still there, sleepier than they once were, but with the fascination of all ancient places. There is a description by a sixteenth-century European traveller of Mombasa which – except that Mombasans have lost their warlike nature – might have been written yesterday. And yet how many of the tourists on the Coast know this? If they go to the Portuguese Fort Jesus, a place with as much blood and romance in its history as any in the world, they may learn a little. The prehistoric site at Gedi, once a noble town, is largely given over to flies and snakes. There is a guardian there, but nothing has been done to make it the attraction it could be. And the Coast civilisation itself, which flourishes in Mombasa and Malindi and everywhere between, is totally unknown to most visitors. Its excellent and sophisticated food – a blend of African and Indian and Arab – is served in no hotel. Its music, in which fine poems are sung in Swahili to Afro-Arab melodies – even sometimes to Arabised Indian and European melodies – is a private affair of wedding parties and Muslim get-togethers. Even the parts of the Old Town which most tourists penetrate are not in fact old, but the nineteenth-century Indian shops on the fringes. Yet here are people of extraordinary dignity and friendliness. Even the rude little children which make the tourist's life a bane throughout the world are more harmless here than in most places – and more enchanting.

Of course, any tourist trade depends upon its facilities. Kenya has no hotels which could by international standards be called luxury hotels, but in Nairobi there are a number of excellent ones of the near-luxury variety, and Mombasa has one which is equally good. Compared with most African countries, Kenya is also very well off for simpler accommodation. In nearly every town on a main road there is a hotel – a little old, a little quiet, but comfortable in a plain way. Many of them offer good value for money. In terms of what the tourist has to pay in Europe, thirty shillings full board, with a menu running to five courses, is cheap. The food tends to be unimaginative-English, but it is usually better than the cooking was in most English hotels until very recently. These 'middling' hotels make up in willingness what they lack in polish. They are especially valuable since Kenya needs to attract more middle-class tourists – people who want to wander around on their own without being financially ruined or given food-poisoning.

Kenya aims to treble the number of her visitors by 1970. To this end a good deal of expansion of accommodation is going on. The Government has started a programme of providing tourist lodges and roads in the national parks, leaving the rest to private enterprise. The problem is not so much a shortage of beds; a recent survey showed that only in Nairobi were hotels more or less full most of the time. What is needed is to have beds in the places tourists want to go. Accommodation at Keekorok Lodge in the Mara Game reserve has been doubled. The two main hotels on the Mombasa Road, at Mtito Andei and Tsavo – both serving the Tsavo National Park – have carried out improvements and are of their sort excellent. Treetops, which became famous when the Queen visited it as Princess Elizabeth, has been enlarged to take thirty-six instead of twenty-two people.

All this is highly necessary, but the fact that so many of Kenya's hotels are half empty most of the time reflects less the dullness of the area in which they were built than the patchiness of tourist promotion. In some respects the tourist trade is modern enough. The package-tour idea was taken up – though by a German, not a Kenyan firm – to the extent that, as a colleague tetchily remarked, 'half the notices in Malindi hotels seem to be in German'. But although the money brought in by luxury visitors and package tours filters through to the economy as a whole, the class of tourist which spreads the money around fastest is lacking. This is the private visitor who hires a car and goes where he pleases. Kenya is an excellent place for doing this, but until a bit of intelligence is injected into tourist promotion, nobody abroad will be aware of the fact. If such visitors come, they will come not as a result of 'selling' big game, but of 'selling' that far more interesting whole of which big game is a fascinating part – Kenya herself.

10

Basis for Development

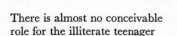

There is almost no conceivable
role for the illiterate teenager
in the towns
Church report

The next aim will be to
set our young people's
feet on a path of
instruction which will
correspond with the
requirements of the new
nation
Kanu Manifesto

For a very long time African education in Kenya – where it
existed – meant Church education. The missionaries were its
sole providers with the one exception – also religious – that on
the Coast and in the North-eastern Province, where there were
Muslims in large numbers, Koran schools provided education
of a sort. The few 'European' schools were also, if not Church-
run, pervaded with the sub-Christian ethos of British public
schools, and most of the Asian schools were also communal and
thus to a large extent religious. Until 1959, university education
did not exist.

This Church near-monopoly is symptomatic of what lies
behind Kenya's education problem – lack of Government
involvement in the past. Originally the colonial administration,
true to its policy of taking the line of least resistance, left
everything to mission schools in the 'unscheduled areas'. Even
when it began to take a part in education, the inevitable bias of
a settler colony led to the African's being, in the words of the
Kenya Education Commission's report (published in December
1964) 'the residual legatee of the nation's wealth. During the
ten years before Independence, more capital was invested in

M

European education, representing 3 per cent of the population, than in the education of the African 97 per cent.'

Before independence the voluntary bodies had relinquished or were relinquishing much of their responsibility to the Government, though a good deal of secondary schooling is still in their hands, totally or partly.

The Church role has for some time been unsatisfactory to both the Government and the Churches themselves, partly because denominational schools will almost inevitably contain a bias (usually unconscious), even if they are open to all. The old system in which a Roman Catholic School was open only to Roman Catholic children would be quite intolerable when schooling is in such short supply. A more basic objection than denominationalism is that, in a land more overtly non-Christian than European countries, education should be secular. With everybody's concurrence, the Government is taking over as fast as possible the responsibility for education, whether directly or through local authorities. 'As fast as possible' cannot, of course, mean very fast. Administrative problems aside, there is the question of money or the lack of it. A political complication is the fact that the Kanu Manifesto promised free primary education for all. No date was given for the achievement of this aim, but many people believed that it would be almost immediate. 'Free' education, like 'free' land, has remained a stick in the hand of critics of the Government, and was duly made one of the main planks of the Kenya People's Union platform. In fact, free education is a total impossibility at the moment. Kenya has not the resources to give adequate primary education to everybody who is prepared to pay the fees, let alone universally – and free education would naturally be pretty well universal.

For an Englishman, used to compulsory schooling, it is difficult to imagine a country nearly half of whose children at primary level never see the inside of a classroom. Although the proportion is highest in the country, even in some urban areas the attendance is less than half what it could be. There is therefore a very grave danger that the high illiteracy rate will be prolonged into the next generation, with serious effects on the country's attempts to develop.

Even so a great deal has happened since independence. In two years, primary education increased from 892,000 to 1,027,000. It is hoped that by 1970 the number of children in primary schools will have doubled. This growth is essential not only to individuals, but to the country as a whole. Nobody knows how many primary school entries are needed to produce one 'technological' man, but clearly with the base of the educational pyramid as small as it is at the moment, the skilled manpower shortage threatens to continue indefinitely.

For this reason and because an illiterate or semi-literate man is a man with little chance for a fulfilling life, universal primary schooling must be achieved as soon as is humanly possible. But the strain which this goal puts on a poor country is considerable, and Kenya's difficulty is increased by her high birth rate, which puts a terrible added burden on a country which will have enough of a job to raise to a tolerable level the standard of living of those already working.

This would be true even if it were only necessary to expand numbers. As it is, Kenya must not only provide schooling for those who at present have none, but spend a great deal of effort on improving what schooling there is. Some of her primary schools are as good as any in the world, with well-trained teachers applying modern methods in excellent buildings. These, however, are but a tiny minority. Many more are stark but adequate; the equipment, the buildings, the teachers may not be ideal, but they are good enough – if a little down-at-heel – to achieve the end result, a well-educated child. But conditions elsewhere, especially in the poorer country areas, make adequate teaching almost impossible, however devoted the teachers. A former primary school headmaster illustrated how what in more fortunate lands might be considered intolerable can in Kenya be a blessing. His school suffered all the difficulties of shortage of staff and the need for makeshift, but 'it was a good one, because it occupied buildings previously put up by security forces as a detention camp(!). But as I have been (Provincial Education) Supervisor, I can tell you that these buildings are really shocking. How can I describe them? Just some poles, mud, grass – they are huts. And teachers are sometimes forced, two or three of them, to share one tiny building.' The Education Commission, in its travels, found schools where 'classrooms were found without school furniture, in which the children squatted on the floor and wrote on logs or earth ridges.' Most of these very inadequate schools are those built through self-help, though even among self-help schools they are not the rule. The Commission reported that many school buildings put up by voluntary labour were wholly satisfactory.

Parental poverty adds to the difficulties put in a Kenyan child's way. In country areas a class which begins with, say, twenty pupils in February may have only five by June. Schooling is often paid for from the excess crop in a subsistence shamba. If there is a bad year there may be no excess crop – and no money for school fees. Anybody who employs a servant knows that one of the main reasons for which advances on wages are sought in Kenya is payment of school fees. Where there is no steady income a family may only be able to rely on the extended family to raise the pitiful sixty shillings or so which are so unattainable. Since everybody has to pay fees at the same time, even the extended family may not be able to help.

Poverty causes another serious problem: the lethargy of hunger. A headmaster told me that in one remote area where semi-famine is endemic, 'At lunch-time, when you are supposed to have a midday meal, you will find about eighty per cent of the pupils lying in the shade, just waiting for the afternoon. So as a result, in the afternoon you find nearly everybody in your class is without energy, feeble and uninterested, yawning and slumbering. In the evening they go home to have a meal – sometimes just porridge.'

A survey of twenty-seven schools all over the country showed that about forty-one per cent of children had nothing for breakfast, and that of these children fifty-six per cent had no lunch. Even those who did eat at lunch-time often had no more than a couple of bananas or a maize cob. These conditions show up not only in the health of the children but in the exam results – and in the wasted expense of an education from which they are too underfed to benefit fully.

The difficulties caused by poverty and backwardness are intensified when it comes to education for the pastoral tribes. The nomadic way of life makes regular schooling impossible, just as it makes adequate welfare services impossible. Yet these tribes need education more than the others if they are to progress, because at present they have less of it. In the President's words, 'In the old days the sign of ability was a spear and a shield. Today it is the exercise book and the pen.' Many pastoral tribesmen recognise this fact. In February 1965 the *East African Standard* reported that thirty-five Samburu moran 'shaved their long hair, put down their spears and marched off to Maralal school with fees in hands'. Alas, after a fortnight they were found to be too old and sent home, thus no doubt damping the local ardour for schooling for some time to come. This incident is a reflection of the need for flexibility in coping with nomads.

In the long run the only possible answer, as with agriculture, is to persuade them to settle down in one spot. In the words of the Education Commission, 'Until the people in these areas come to live in settled communities . . . educational progress on a large scale cannot be expected, for education itself is essentially a settled business, drawing upon human and material resources that only a permanent community can bring.'

A theoretical question of some importance which faces Kenyan primary schools is: what should they teach? Primary school, for the overwhelming majority of pupils, is not a period of preparation for secondary education. It is all the academic tuition they are going to get. In 1965 about 120,000 children left primary school. Only about 11,000 found places in secondary schools. Yet at present, since it is modelled on the English system, primary education in Kenya takes little account of this fact.

The problem was defined by Mr Zadok Otieno, in whose

work as Youth Secretary of the Council of Kenya it bulks large.

'We have got to face a primary education system which is at present geared towards every young person going to university. . . . We are not preparing these boys at the primary school level, though we jolly well know that ninety per cent are going to leave school anyway. This is my quarrel with our system. We should be conditioning the parents and children to know that they are going to leave school after seven years of education.'

Some people believe that since this is the case primary schools should frankly set out to give semi-vocational training for embryo peasants or workers. But already most schools provide an education which is barely adequate. To cut into 'three Rs' time would produce alumni so under-educated that one might as well save the money and not educate them at all. Moreover, the vocational training which *is* given is worse than useless. Most country schools have 'agricultural' classes; but as primary school teachers are not farming experts, lessons involve little more than weeding the school shamba – a proceeding which merely puts the pupil off country life for good.

What is needed, as Mr Otieno went on, is 'First a general primary school system, then a post-primary education for masses of our school leavers, geared to agriculture, to industries and all facets of development. At present every parent thinks his child is a potential graduate – and he's not.'

Such post-primary training is becoming increasingly needed as the school entry, and therefore leaving, age goes down. It has already dropped below the age at which it is legal to employ minors. This interim must be used to good purpose. Those who will go into industry are faced with the fact that as technology gets more advanced even semi-skilled labour demands more knowledge than a pass in the Kenya Preliminary Examination (the post-primary exam) guarantees to the employer. For the vast majority who will have no outlet but smallholder farming, training is equally necessary unless they are to become a lumpen-peasantry endangering the entire economic development of the country.

This is a problem which for lack of time has hardly yet been tackled, though the 4K Clubs cater for country primary leavers. Vocational training of a simple sort (including, for girls, subjects like domestic science) is planned, but for the moment it remains no more than a plan.

Most of the woes of primary education are suffered also by secondary schools, but at this level the shortage of places is by far the gravest difficulty. Partly for lack of money, partly perhaps because it was not envisaged until far too recently that Africans should need education much above literacy, the phrase 'secondary-school bottleneck' is one of the clichés of Kenya's educational world. So serious is the situation that the Government – for all the importance of producing skilled manpower – could only set as a target that by 1970 ten per cent of primary leavers should go on to secondary schools. The number of secondary schools (excluding 'Harambee' schools) was more than doubled between 1963 and 1965. This impressive figure, however, hides an increase from only 141 to 336 for a population of 9 million, more than half of which is under twenty one years old! The International Bank report on Kenya's economy recommended that the main effort be put into provision of secondary-level education – a recommendation which, in so far as it might mean cutting down on primary education expansion, is politically difficult. Parents being parents, they want the best for their children at all levels immediately, and are apt to get impatient with reasoned economic arguments.

The secondary-school bottleneck of course creates a terrific competition for places. This is not, according to the findings of the Education Commission, merely a matter of the largely mythical African insistence on the superiority of the white-collar job. 'The main impulse', it said, 'is a growing realisation that the KPE certificate alone is now almost worthless as a passport to the occupations of the modern world, in the excitement, the challenge and the benefits of which most young people long to share.'

That secondary school education is thought to be of prime

importance was proved by the Government in 1965. Instead of trying to rush into free primary education too soon, the first 'free' education it provided was in the senior secondary forms. This move stemmed partly from social conditions. Illiterate parents usually see the point of paying good money to have literate children. Even on the shamba, it helps to be able to read. But many, faced with twelve hours a day of back-break labour, on a small plot feel that their healthy young fifteen-year old son would be better employed giving them a hand than pursuing strange and half-understood studies which may only give him ideas above his station. When I lived seven miles outside Nairobi I used to give lifts to a number of secondary-school pupils. A score of times some young man whom I knew to be no scrounger would pluck up courage to ask if I could possibly lend him his school fees as his father had refused to go on 'wasting' sorely needed money. There are few sadder sights than a well-spoken, intelligent boy's face as he tells you that the decent job for which he is eminently fitted can never be attained because the school fees are not there, and that he is condemned to the heart-breaking round of unskilled job-hunting along with his 100,000 unemployed fellows. Conversely, one of the happiest sights I have seen was one such boy (who the day before had been begging me for a part-time job so that he could scrape up fee-money) as he told me that he was saved, that his schooling was free from now on.

Fortunately, illiteracy and conservatism are not necessarily bedfellows. The problem of the parent who 'doesn't see the point' affects too many children still, but they are a minority and a shrinking minority except in the pastoral tribes.

What does affect virtually all secondary-school pupils is the material results of poverty. If boarding schools have their advantages in England, consider the differences they can make in Kenya. In the words of the Education Commission, 'contrast the physical conditions of a boarding school, with electric light, evening study rooms . . . and a pervading atmosphere of study, with those of a day school, which the children must leave at 4.30 or 5 in order to get home in the light, often after a long, exhausting bicycle ride ... finding at home no light brighter than a single oil lamp and no place for study other than the crowded, family hut.'

As has been shown over and over again, a school can overcome almost any difficulty and still be a marvellous school, provided that it has teachers of high calibre. Unfortunately, Kenya is extremely short of teachers. With the coming of independence there was an exodus of the qualified to realms promising not only more money but better prospects – or apparent prospects – of advancement; politics of course, but also the higher reaches of the Civil Service. At the same time a number of expatriates retired early under the general compensation scheme. The shortage was made worse by the opening of new schools.

The lack of trained local teachers at both primary and secondary level is extremely serious. Fully thirty per cent of teachers in the primary schools are untrained. A school can cope adequately with one or two such people on its staff, but the shortages are such that the untrained must often be used in far too high a concentration.

An untrained teacher, in the Kenyan sense, is not a man or woman who lacks a degree and Dip. Ed. All too often he is a fifteen-year-old himself just out of school. Some are even younger. There is frequently far too little gap between what the teacher knows and what his pupils know. There may even be virtually no gap at all. At one school in Embu last year a Standard 7 pupil was teaching other Standard 7 pupils mathematics!

An untrained fifteen-year-old teacher is not merely too ill-educated to do his job really adequately: almost certainly he lacks emotional maturity in a job where above everything else it is essential. His age will also present him with discipline problems.

A crash programme is tackling the teacher shortage. The former British Army base at Kahawa, about eighteen miles from Nairobi, has been turned into a major teacher-training centre. At the same time, in-service training was undertaken to up-grade more than 200 primary school teachers. At the time of independence there were thirty-six teacher-training colleges in the country, but many of these were too small for efficiency. The Government planned to keep twenty five of these, expanding them to take at least 250 pupils each. The smaller colleges which could not be expended were to be turned into secondary schools, thus helping to solve another problem.

By 1965 a good deal of this reorganisation was complete. At the same time enrolment had increased by 1,236 in two years – and it is expected that there will be about 9,500 students at such colleges in 1970. The expansion of training facilities will go on as fast as possible for the foreseeable future, since the shortage of teachers above anything is prolonging the secondary-school bottleneck; it has been reckoned that in order to provide secondary schooling for half the children eligible for it, the number of teachers in training would have to be increased tenfold. The High Level Manpower report put forward various schemes for rationalising university level education, including one – which already exists in some fields – binding graduates to work for the Government for a certain number of years if they have received Government aid. The report calculated that if its recommendations were fully implemented, 'it should be possible to satisfy from 60 to 75 per cent of the total requirements for secondary teachers with qualified graduates in the next six years'. No plan in the world has ever been fully implemented, but even a more moderate percentage would transform the situation – provided that the 'binding' of graduates allowed them to work in the field of their own interest.

If the teacher shortage is ever to be solved entirely, another situation which must be remedied is the poor terms of service offered. The fact that teachers are employed by local authorities, and thus work in widely differing conditions, has led to the campaign by the Kenya National Union of Teachers for 'one employer' – the Government. In many cases teachers' salaries are totally inadequate. In all cases they are too low. The Secretary General of the CCEA, Mr Nelson Kivuti, found when he was a headmaster that, 'Through this poor salary teachers made full use of the spare time they had and did not bother about extra-curricular activities. They had to look after shambas and some even kept shops. As a result of this some of them didn't even mark the pupils' books, because they were occupied until nearly midnight.'

Complaints of teachers' neglect of their duties, and of even more serious misconduct, are not uncommon, and there is no doubt that the morale of the profession is low and must be improved if good minds are to be attracted to the schools. None the less, considering their difficulties – especially at primary level – Kenya's teachers show a remarkable devotion to duty. Ill-educated themselves, too young, underpaid, they work in inadequate schools with inadequate furniture or none at all, lacking textbooks and other equipment, so that one I heard of was reduced to making her own charcoal sticks for the art classes which, in spite of all, she managed to give. Yet they carry forward the essential task of providing the educational basis for Kenya's advance.

Bridging the gap in staffing is an army of expatriates. A number of 'traditional' expatriate teachers left the country at independence, making a bad situation worse, but many stayed. They have been augmented from several sources. The Government more than trebled the number taken under the Teachers for East Africa scheme, and arranged for others through the us Peace Corps and similar bodies. A recruiting drive in Kenya produced more. These expatriates work at all levels, but they are most numerous and most essential in the secondary schools. Without them, indeed, the country would have very few secondary schools at all. None the less, they do – especially the short-term expatriates – present a number of difficulties. With the exception of the volunteers, they are more expensive than local teachers. This is felt particularly at university level. Another problem is inherent in the contract system, especially when, as is the case with Unesco-sponsored teachers, Kenya has no say in how long they remain. A good teacher needs to be part of the community in which he works. What all too often happens in Kenya is that the expatriate, who is usually on a two-year contract, only reaches maximum efficiency halfway through it.

One problem posed by expatriates is frequently exaggerated: this is their supposed inability to see, and therefore teach, things from a 'Kenyan' point of view. The Education Commission dismissed this theory, pointing out that, 'The atmosphere of a school is created, not only by the staff, but also by the pupils. Secondly . . . a sensitive European headmaster and staff can go far towards building up, and preserving, within the school the ideals and spirit of Kenya. Fortunately, human beings do not live in such sealed compartments that they are incapable of absorbing a foreign culture, even while remaining faithful to their own.'

Another expatriate problem is left over from Kenya's former racialist structure. Until the very end of the colonial era, there were no less than four educational systems – African, European, Asian and Arab. Each of these was geared to the supposed needs of the community it served, in a society which saw the Europeans as being the top, the Asian the middle and the African the bottom of the pyramid. On the attainment of self-government, all schooling was integrated, in theory at least. But in fact the vast disparity between the standards of the different schools – and thus in the fees charged – meant that integration on any scale was impossible. This was accentuated by the fact that most African primary education was too poor in quality to allow many children to compete for places in 'European' secondary schools. To a lesser degree, this was also true of Asian schools. The result at secondary level in the 'European' schools is that although there are quite a few Asian pupils, there are very few Africans. After independence the 'European' schools very rightly resisted any idea that they should lower standards in order to integrate faster. The level of education is all too low, without interfering with the few schools which do have high standards. On the other hand, the fact that those few African children whose parents can afford the present high fees come of the new 'élite' is potentially harmful. For this reason the Education Commission recommended that the fees of high-cost schools should slowly be reduced to the national average. In order to do this without jeopardising standards, it suggested that economies could be made in the non-scholastic amenities. One of the chief recommendations was that these schools should look into the possibility of cutting down on food costs. This seems fair enough, since Kenya cannot afford 'élite' schools in the social sense.

Helped by a recent edict that half the new Form I intake of former mono-racial schools must be African, integration at secondary school level will be pretty well complete in about another five years' time, when the present crop of middle-class African children leave primary school. Then the problem will only be one of broadening the 'catchment class', so to speak. Integration of staff may, however, take longer. Shortage of local teachers makes it difficult. The former European and Asian schools themselves are willing to see an integrated staff, but there are too few African teachers with sufficient qualifications to make this possible on more than a very small scale.

If education at all levels has considerable bearing on Kenya's manpower needs, the problem is most acutely raised at university level. Kenya's university college was only started in 1959, and its ability to supply the country's need for graduates is still very limited. Of the 5,600 extra graduates which will be needed by 1970 about 4,600 will be foreign-educated. The clash between manpower needs and the traditional academic aims of universities presents a genuine dilemma. The University College cannot blithely ignore these needs as if it were a university in a developed country. At the same time, if it lowers its standards to produce a flood of graduates the degrees obtained will be worth very little, and the 'graduates' be graduates only in name. Another difficulty is that Kenya may soon find that while it is short of graduates in many fields it has too many in others. There was at one time a Government suggestion that students should be 'channelled' – provided with grants only if they agreed to study the subjects in which there are graduate shortages. Luckily nothing more has been heard of this plan. As the Vice Principal, Mr Samuel Waruhiu, commented, 'Universities are not there to channel the students into taking certain courses. We are there to provide facilities for them to discover themselves.' The University College can and should 'channel' its students by restricting its faculties to some extent. The only other solution to filling specific man-power needs is, as Mr Waruhiu observed, 'to make the profession attractive'. Graduate manpower is in fact not entirely a university problem, though it is usually treated as such. The University College's real difficulty is the universal one of finding sufficient money to do its central job properly.

At all levels, the desire for education is awe inspiring. It is seen as the key which opens all doors. Families scratching a living out of a pocketful of soil will scrape and pinch – and enlist the help of relatives and friends – to send at least the brightest son to school. The efforts made are often magnificent. One of my friends, who himself had to leave school when money ran out, spent nearly three years without a job. During that time he ran a shoe-cleaning stand from which he managed not only to keep himself and a younger brother, but also to put the brother through secondary school. Now he has, after a while working as a waiter, fought his way to a reasonable job.

But even if the money can be found, there are as we have seen far too few secondary school places to accommodate everybody. In this case parents will find, or try to find, the fees to send their children to private schools. A few of these private schools are very good. Too many are merely devices whereby the unscrupulous can take advantage of the thirst for learning to work a particularly unpleasant confidence trick. Such schools are from time to time discovered by the in-spectors and closed. The conditions revealed are sometimes appalling. One such place, ostensibly a commercial college, catered for 365 boarders and 100 day pupils. It was reported to be ridden with flies and mosquitoes, utterly inadequate in sanitation, cooking and medical facilities. Nairobi City Council was told that 'students were obliged to eat their meals in the cramped and overcrowded dormitories. No equipment other than typewriters was seen to be in use. The Manager explained that it was locked in the store. Two sick girls were seen, one lying under a blanket in the middle of the compound, the other slumped in a corner of the so-called dispensary.'

This school is an outstanding example of what can happen when an unscrupulous man discovers that there is money in people's longing for learning. There are, however, a good number of privately run secondary schools and commercial colleges the standard of whose teaching is too low and whose diplomas are therefore worthless. The owners of such places are not necessarily dishonest. Many believe that the tuition they are giving is of an adequate standard, and others say: 'I know that I cannot afford to give all I should, but without me what would these boys have? Nothing.'

Whatever the motives of the men who run them, these colleges – almost unregulated as they are at present – are undesirable. Government control is the only answer to them. If they needed to be licensed, and were inspected regularly, they would be forced to give value for money or close – though in a free country what one is to do with a boy who insists on paying for education for which he is not fitted, heaven alone knows. In present-day Kenyan conditions – in which the wage differential between a professional and a labouring man is about thirty times, whereas in England it is about four – the passion for education contains an element of desperation.

In African tradition if one wants something badly one does not shout for it as a gift, one provides it for oneself. We have seen how the tradition of communal work is being transformed in the self-help and community development schemes. One of the main goals of such schemes has been the provision of secondary schools. All over Kenya parents have got together to collect money, to provide materials and transport – one man responsible for iron sheeting, ten men for providing a little land, twenty women to build the mud walls and tamp them down – in order to build their own schools. The Education Commission reported: 'During our visits to different parts of the country, we have seen recent and impressive evidences of this spirit in the establishment and conduct of secondary schools. This spirit is not new. It is deeply rooted in the traditions and practices of tribal life. . . . It is, we believe, a source of gratification that this spirit is still alive today, for it is the mark of a virile and self-confident people.'

Although such schools were being built well before Uhuru, the independent Government's encouragement of self-help, as a method of providing essential services which the country could otherwise not afford, released a flood of energy. Too much, indeed. The authorities had not foreseen the results of the people's enthusiasm. They had indeed established community development officers to guide self-help schemes, but things got out of hand. Unregistered – and therefore illegal – schools began to spring up all over the place. Some schools were well planned in consultation with the local government, but too many were not. The result was that many of these 'harambee' schools, as they are popularly known, were a waste of money and time.

Though the buildings themselves were often inadequate, especially in that very few 'harambee' schools provided such essentials as laboratories, the principal problem was not this. First, the people who put up a school – and those who run it – are too often unaware that they are involving themselves in recurrent expense which they may well be quite unable to afford. They rush out in a fit of enthusiasm and build a nice school. But will they be so enthusiastic two years later, when they are still having to dig into their pockets to pay teachers, to mend the school roof, to buy new books? Enthusiastic or not, will they be able to do so? Again, too many harambee schools, lacking any equipment more sophisticated than secondhand textbooks, can hardly be called secondary at all. Like the commercial colleges, they lead to frustration, not fulfilment.

If these schools were only a small part of Kenya's educational set-up, they would be regrettable, but no more. As it is, however, they amount to about a third of all the secondary schools in Kenya; they therefore threaten to disrupt Government planning. This is especially the case as regards teachers. The

13a Part of an African-owned tea shamba. The expansion of Kenya's tea production will, if things go according to plan, be almost entirely in the smallholder section. In the distance on the left is one of those villages which make a characteristic if scruffy contribution to the Kenyan countryside. Such villages are rarely communities in any deep sense, but a collection of buildings without focus.

13b Coffee – one of Kenya's principal exports – is loaded into sacks by the shovelful at Etco House in Nairobi, the centre of the trade.

14*a* Kenya's pastoral tribes all live pretty near the starvation line. The Turkana, to whom these children belong, are more or less permanent candidates for famine-relief. The dried milk which is being doled out is almost the only good thing in a diet which would give a nutritionist nightmares.

14*b* An agreeable mixture of old and new. Two friends relax in a bar known as Lancaster House (after the conference), in one of the poorer quarters of Nairobi. What the law courts call 'African Intoxicating Liquor' is poured from one traditional container into another. *Pombe* is not only cheap, it can be quite good. Certainly it is more within most people's reach than the whisky advertised on the ash-tray.

Rev. F. R. Dain, who was until recently in charge of the CCEA, said: 'The Government's teacher-training programme doesn't provide for a single trained teacher in the Harambee schools. . . . They've got to live either by pulling out the primary school people, the best there, or making use of the refuse almost – the throw-outs – of the secondary system.'

The answer would seem simple, if ruthless: force the inadequate schools to close, forbid more to be built. If this were done, however, the entire concept of self-help would be menaced – and Kenya needs self-help. 'Look what happens', people would say. 'You urge self-help, and then when we provide it you tear down all our work. Next time don't bother to ask.' As a result nothing very drastic is being done about the harambee schools. It is hoped that the hopeless ones will disappear, and the better ones be quietly worked into the system. At the same time much greater emphasis is now being laid on central planning in self-help, so as to avoid similar situations in the future. This is reasonable, but it does not allow for the numerous harambee schools which will struggle on, still providing poor teaching, still poaching staff. It would be better if these schools were turned into primary schools releasing Government funds for secondary purposes. Given the need for vocational training, moreover, 'As and where full provision is maintained in certain areas for primary education, self-help impulses might be directed towards rural post-primary training centres, not aimed at academic examinations', as the Education Commission suggested.

The demand for education is not just a matter of parents seeking better things for their children. They want some learning themselves. Non-university higher education can be roughly divided into technical (principally for 'elderly' teenagers) and adult. Technical education is provided by the Polytechnic in Nairobi and by a number of technical and trade schools. The latter, which offer a two-year course, have not been doing very well, and the Education Commission has recommended that they be reorganised as four-year secondary schools, each specialising in subjects connected with a certain

N

industry. These 'secondary trade schools' would provide artisans with a good basic training in modern industrial techniques. This is very important for a developing country; for every potential investor who worries about politics, ten worry about the supply of skilled labour.

In a land like Kenya, adult education of a general nature is far more important than in England, for the very good reason that the average adult knows a great deal less. At the most basic level, adult literacy classes are needed to teach the seventy per cent of the adult population who cannot read, to do so. Such classes exist on all sorts of bases already. As in so many fields, the NCCK has contributed a good deal. In ten years more than 11,300 adults have learned to read at NCCK courses in the Central and Eastern Provinces alone, according to a report made last September. There are excellent university extra-mural classes. Agricultural training centres sometimes include them. The Government has plans whereby each Ministry will teach its illiterate staff – doormen and so on – to read. Students back in the village for the holidays teach brothers, or parents, or friends. The slogan 'each one teach one' is more attractive than practical, but something a little more modest is already in full swing.

None the less, adult education of all sorts, from literacy classes to technical part-time training, is in very short supply, especially in the country. In the long term, part-time education centres are needed at focal points outside the towns, each covering a large area. Obviously, however, this is for financial reasons only a dream at present. What can be done on a wider scale – it is already starting – is to use secondary school buildings. The main difficulty here will be staff: secondary school teachers are not as under-trained as primary, but they are just about as badly paid and overworked. Even though evening classes would give them a sorely needed extra income, the added hours of work would lower their efficiency. Still, the use of a single set of equipment (human or material) for more than one purpose is obviously a good way of getting round the shortage of both.

Radio is a field of immense potential for education in a country like Kenya. Thanks to the Japanese, who market one for as little as eighty shillings, almost anybody can by making sacrifices afford a transistor set. Radio classes solve many problems of equipment and staffing. A particularly valuable form of teaching – already begun – is the broadcast backed by a correspondence course. In the words of the Education Commission, 'Broadcasts can not only deal with new material in which a verbal explanation is likely to be particularly helpful, but also go over ground which is shown by the answers to questions set in the correspondence course to have been imperfectly understood'. Poor as most people are in Kenya, there is no area so poor that a village cannot get together to subscribe to a correspondence-radio course, and buy a communal transistor radio.

Broadcast education is not limited to the radio. Although the number of individuals who can afford a TV set is small, many social centres have their set. 'TV schools' have sprung up in many places. There is great scope for expansion. None the less, the radio will for many years reign supreme in this field, if only because with two main programmes (Swahili and English) and a third for vernacular broadcasts including Asian languages, it can reach those people who most need education – those who know nothing outside their own tribal life and language – and also avoid the problems inherent in teaching people in what is to them a foreign tongue.

In a country like Kenya, that rather nebulous exercise 'instilling a sense of national purpose' is an important part of education at all levels. In the words of the Education Commission, 'education is a function of the Kenya nation; it must foster a sense of nationhood and promote national unity . . . (it) must serve the people of Kenya and the needs of Kenya without discrimination.' Since the bias in the past was all away from 'Africanism' and towards Englishness, this process must sometimes lead to an insistence on the 'African' which can be misunderstood – though in a former colony a certain amount of flag-waving is understandable in the early years of indepen-

dence. On the whole, flag-waving is not a Kenyan vice. Most of
the Africanisation which is sought is purely practical. To give
an example, school syllabi are too firmly based on English needs.
Even textbooks are so foreign to what the child knows that they
can be a hindrance rather than a help. As Mr Dain remarked,
'The basic tools of learning are in themselves non-national. On
the other hand, these tools have got to be learned in a certain
context. . . . If you're reading English it's much more meaningful for a child if it's reading about children in a context they
understand, and you don't sing: "Here we go round the
mulberry bush on a cold and frosty morning!" '

Nice though it would be to use only East African textbooks,
this will clearly be quite out of the question for decades. Good
work is being done in publishing such books by the East
African Literature Bureau (a civil service department), the
Oxford University Press, and a local firm, East African
Publishing House; at school level, however, most textbooks
will remain foreign for a very long time.

A more fundamental problem is the appalling limitation in
scope of even the best 'African' education in Kenya. Even the
Alliance High School have for reasons of money and staff to
restrict their syllabus to the minimum. Mr Dain remarked,
'These chaps have gone through a desperately narrow programme.' There is none of the vast range of optional subjects
which an English school can offer – music, Russian, what have
you. He added: 'One of the contributions which the old
European schools made to the country . . . is an education where
you've got this freedom of choice and where you've got a
breadth of culture going on in the school.' We have seen the
strange void in the social life of Kenya's African élite: it is
partly due to the narrowness of African education in the past.
This narrowness survives everywhere except in the ex-European
schools. The emptiness which it creates is dangerous. Kenya
is moving forward with optimism, but in cultural terms, towards
what is she moving? And if the question cannot be posed in
cultural terms, in what terms can it be posed? If one of the
central ills of modern civilisation is indeed a loss of cultural

and spiritual values, Kenya can no more afford to ignore this question than can the rich nations. Though she may as yet have less time to worry about it, if she ignores it altogether she may find that 'tomorrow is too late'.

II

Art for What's Sake?

I do not believe in these
roles. . . . You are not trying
to convert the heathen
Rebecca Njau

It was art which taught the
Pan-African movement to go
back to the cultural background
European art expert

Two meanings of the word culture are frequently confused in African discussions, with unhelpful results. There is culture in the anthropologist's sense – a community's whole way of life – and there is culture in the layman's sense – the arts.

Kenya, like the rest of Africa, is as we have seen in a state of more or less complete cultural transmogrification, using the word culture in its broader meaning. Essentially this is the universal evolution from the peasant to the technological age, though very much speeded up and with many corners cut. What is not entirely compatible with the experience of other continents is the violence with which Africa was plunged into the process of change. The European arrival acted as a charge of blasting-powder – a very much larger charge than was necessary, and placed at random. It destroyed or half-destroyed a great deal which must now be re-examined to see if it is salvageable. The destruction has left people in a state of shock, even in countries where the traditional framework of life was left relatively undisturbed.

The effect of this cultural shock upon Africans is very hard to imagine for anybody used to the comforting assurance that Chaucer led to Shakespeare, who led to Dickens, and so on to the present day. The colonial era – whose effect was particularly intense in Kenya, a settler's country thought of as a 'white man's land' – was as cataclysmic in the arts as in other fields of life. Europe is full of certainties, of comfortable and on the whole justified assumptions about life: in Africa there are no certainties. It is in this context that the whole field of the arts in Kenya must be seen. It is in this context that African traditional art forms are searched for any contemporary relevance they may have.

When the British came to Kenya, they came assuming that they were colonising a barbarous land, without culture as without civilisation. There were always exceptions, men who believed that alien customs were to be studied rather than to be disapproved of; but most of those who came to East Africa genuinely believed that African music was gratuitous thumping, that African religion was blasphemous or childish. More disastrous because more positive, the missionaries, in combating the religious connotations in which all tribal cultural activities were rich, sapped the culture itself. This, with the best intentions, they did so successfully that in Kenya today nobody is a greater enemy of traditional music and dancing than the devout African member of the major denominations.

'For example you find dances connected with beer-drinking, and the mission considered drinking as a sin. If one belonged to the Christian society one had to abandon all these things. And you will find that some areas where the missionaries first started have lost completely quite a lot of their traditional songs and traditional way of thinking.'

The speaker was a young man whose father had once been a very good harp-player, but 'immediately he became a Christian he burnt all his musical instruments. And I remember before I went to England for my music studies I asked him to sing some of the songs which he used to sing. He was very shocked!'

In place of African tradition the Europeans, in so far as they put anything, put European tradition. In schools and colleges, Graeco-Roman art became the model, English literature the lodestar. Since few of the settlers were themselves cultured men the tradition they brought with them was weak. As a result

Kenya was on the way to becoming a land without culture, in which the arts are mere examination subjects – and useless ones at that.

Of course European models would have been followed in the arts even if Kenya's history had been different. Africa had no novel form, for example, and no substitute for it. European novels would necessarily have been the guide for young Kenyan writers. But in other parts of the world, even in other parts of Africa, foreign influences have been gentler. In Kenya one can hardly talk of influence at all, any more than one can talk about dynamite 'influencing' a cliff-face. Kenya suffered worse than cultural shock from the European experience: she suffered cultural amnesia.

In fact, though Kenya was culturally rich in the wider sense, she was artistically almost entirely barren. There were the usual crafts, of course. The Kamba were great chain-makers – an aesthetic activity since the chains were only used for orna- ment. The Giriama of the coastal plain did a certain amount of attractive beadwork. Artifacts like pots and water bottles were decorated, often quite agreeably. But of anything more – even on a purely decorative level – there was virtually nothing. Why Kenya should have been so arid when other parts of Africa – especially West Africa – are so rich not only in music and dance, but also in carving, metalwork and the decorative arts, is not clear. It may have been partly because most East African tribes believed in a God without a visual form – so the religious impetus behind almost all art was lacking – and partly because so many tribes were nomadic. Certainly even the crop-growing tribes are in most cases relative newcomers in their present areas. Certainly also, what art forms have developed – with the exception of Kamba drumming and dancing – are to be found in areas which have been settled for a long time: round Lake Victoria and on the Coast. On the other hand, the Luo, who are among Kenya's foremost music- makers, only arrived in parts of their present area within living memory. Wanderlust can therefore be only a partial explanation.

For whatever reason, the only art forms which flourished

before the arrival of the Europeans were music and the dance.
Kenya is not normally thought of when music is mentioned,
except perhaps for the Kamba drummers. But although the
height of achievement may be found in other parts, she has a
good, solid, varied musical background. The Luo and the
Baluhya are players of stringed instruments lyre-like in nature.
The Kamba are not the only drummers – the Giriama and the
Digo also use them effectively. And the coastal towns of East
Africa have a music of particular interest – Arab-based, with
strong elements not only of African music but of the music of
other settlers, both Indian and European – a Kenyan music in
an all-embracing sense.

But although all these traditional musics are still fairly
strong, they are losing popular appeal. The young men and
women of Kenya owe allegiance to Elvis Presley, Cliff Richard,
Jim Reeves, and to a modern electric-guitarred Swahili-
language popular music which stems from a curious mixture of
tribal and Anglo-American influence. This is a live and exciting pop music, but all the more dangerous to tribal music as
a result.

Tribal music and tribal dancing are becoming part of
Kenya's ceremonial life. Dancers perform whenever there is a
big diplomatic or political function, on anniversaries such as
Independence Day, or when the President tours the country.
But what will happen as transistor radios spread and the older
dancers and musicians die? Will traditional music disappear
completely, or linger on as a piece of dead ceremonial like a
cross between Morris dancing and the Beefeaters?

Nobody as yet has any answer to this question, but at least
it is being asked. Perhaps it is even being asked in time. One
of the few academically trained African musicians in Kenya,
Mr Gerishom Manani – who as a Muluhya comes of one of
Kenya's most musical tribes – has spent some time thinking
about the problem of traditional music. In any attempt at
conservation, the first step, as he says, is to make as wide a
collection as possible of what music exists at present. At the
moment far too little has been recorded to serve as a basis for

study, although the East African Institute has made some tapes and an enterprising local commercial company has put a few records on the market. The danger is that if this process of collection is delayed much longer, there will be no music left to collect. Manani feels it is essential that University College, Nairobi, should have a music department like that at Makerere. Moreover, as he remarked in a paper read to a seminar held a year ago, 'Every teacher-training college should have on its staff an enthusiastic musician capable of transferring his enthusiasm to his students. It should be part of his duty to collect, on tape, recordings of folk songs of the locality for subsequent transcription at university level.'

Such an operation, though it will allow future generations to hear what traditional music was like, will not in itself stop the music from disappearing. And unless it develops, disappear it will. Being not national but tribal, it is part of an overall traditional framework which is dying, and will inevitably die with it. There is virtually no Kenyan music for listening except the *taarabu* of the Coast.

Tribal music then needs to develop if it is not to die. What form this development will take is anybody's guess. Manani feels that any growth must be in the realm of harmonics, but beyond this he is not prepared to do more than ask pertinent questions. 'Will the theories of Western harmony suit the themes and feelings of African tunes, or must another theory of African harmonics be evolved, perhaps similar to Eastern music?'

There are other possibilities. Ghanaian musicians have experimented with forming an orchestra using traditional instruments but *en masse*, so that in Kenyan terms one might have a *lidungu* (lute) section or an *ngoma* (percussion) section. This sort of experiment is well worth trying even though instrumentation is only a minor part of the problem.

It is even possible that if African music survives it will not be through the efforts of the 'serious' musicians at all. Some Nigerian High Life bands – especially the Yoruba groups – use a great deal of traditional material, both rhythmic and melodic. The Congolese dance bands have come up with a rhythm known as the *dingidingi* which does something similar. Many Kenyan Swahili pop songs are 'semi-folk' in nature, and the more frankly pop styles draw from them. *Taarabu* bands, traditional as their music is, are amplified to the eyebrows. Perhaps the development of African traditional music is under way, ignored.

Popular music is not just a matter of nightclubs. The little Christian and sub-Christian sects which broke away from the missionary groups did so partly on genuine though half-understood cultural grounds. In Manani's words 'Their hymns really fit the African rhythms. You will find they keep the same (Western hymn) tune, the same words – but the rhythm changes quickly, with the drums to make it more alive. . . .

'I think to some extent this was a cultural revolt.' This cultural revolt may have a bearing on the future of African music. African hymns – whether sung to the drums by the Roho Israel sect or to the guitar by the African Inland Mission – are not European in approach, nor are they traditional. They may be the first steps in the growth of a modern African non-dance form. Certainly on a popular level – sacred and secular – a very lusty Kenyan culture is growing, almost totally ignored by the intelligentsia, who too readily equate culture with education.

If Kenya is a musical country, it cannot be claimed to have any literary tradition worth consideration. True, there are fine legends and folk-tales – but so there are anywhere in the world. Apart from these tales, which are not much of a base for literature in any serious sense of the word, there is only the traditional Swahili poetry of the Coast. This poetry, which goes back some centuries, is not to be sniffed at: but it appears at present to be stultified by its own past, so that modern Swahili verse reads like exercises in an earlier style. Moreover, it is a good deal more Arab than African in influence, and most of it comes from Tanzania anyway.

The whole question of Swahili is one which has aroused a certain amount of nationalist feeling. East Africa has a right to feel proud of what is perhaps the continent's only non-tribal language, a language moreover which is at present a more widespread vehicle of communication in Kenya than is English. Some people have insisted that it should become the national language, and hoped that in the end it would become the country's sole tongue. At present, however, this attitude seems to be dying. While suggestions that Swahili is incapable of becoming a technological language are not well-founded (if English could create words needed from Greek and Latin, so can Swahili), Kenya already has a technological language in English. To abandon the most important international language in favour of one spoken only in East Africa (and even there, except in Tanzania, not very well) and the eastern Congo, would be a foolish nationalist parochialism. This seems to be subconsciously realised, since everybody who can talk English, does so. Without belittling Swahili, which is a beautiful language, one cannot regret the present development away from it. It seems likely that Kenya will develop a linguistic pattern a little like Switzerland, in which the tribal languages continue as 'hearth and home' tongues, and English is the national medium. Swahili is extremely useful at present, and it will presumably survive as long as it continues to be so. When it dies . . . well, nobody seriously suggests that Latin and Greek could have been preserved artificially. Attempts to preserve Swahili are rather irrelevant fumblings for a cultural identity.

Although traditional culture is far more lacking in Kenya than in most other parts of Africa, aspects of the past way of life which can be translated into modern terms cannot be allowed to go by default. For years, the British seemed to be saying to Kenya: 'You must try – though you won't succeed – to make yourself as English as possible.' Many people were tempted to accept this proposition. Any group dominated by another tends to feel that the ruler's customs must be in some way superior to its own. Now that Kenya is independent, an African State able to be as African as it knows how, the need for Africanness is felt. The question remains: What, in terms of the twentieth century, is African? As yet, nobody can give a convincing answer in any detail. It is impossible to go back to pre-colonial modes, even if anybody wanted to. At the same time, to proceed as if Kenya were a black England, which is more likely to happen in the arts than in any other field just because there is so little that is traditional, is psychologically out of the question. Apart from the fact that such an assumption is clearly not true, it would be regarded as wounding to the dignity of the country and of every individual in it. National pride is essential to any country. Kenya still has to find out what she has to be proud of, but her Englishness is an improbable candidate.

In the search for an identity, a certain amount of rejection of European models is likely to take place. As the painter Elimo Njau, speaking to an artists' workshop at the short-lived Chemchemi Creative Centre, once said: 'The African wants to show that God can also express himself powerfully and afresh through African hands on African soil. He wants to be left alone in all cultural matters so that he can discover his soul for himself. When a person is looking at herself in a mirror, she had better be left alone. Africa is now examining herself culturally in front of a mirror. A European friend may have bought her the mirror, but the African now resents to be disturbed while she looks at herself.'

Basically, the search for a cultural identity is not artistic but psychological. Yet the idea of an African Personality, an African Image, is by now hopelessly interwoven with artistic theory – especially in the somewhat stultifying formulation known as Negritude. Indeed the search is carried out simultaneously in the psychological, the artistic and the political fields. For until one knows what, in the deepest sense, is a modern African, how can any political theory be tailored to suit his needs?

'The country must ensure that the culture which must and will be developed is rooted in the soil and way of life of the people.' This remark, made by the then Minister of Education, Mr Otiende, when he opened an art exhibition at the time of Kenya's independence, is characteristic of many statements about the arts by Ministers and other representatives of the official Kenya. When a speech is made by an official at an artistic function, the emphasis is usually on the need for Kenyan art to reflect the Kenyan (African) way of life.

Mr Otiende went on: 'While Kenya will turn to other nations for technical advice and help in the development of skills, she must be jealous of her artistic integrity.' That this fear of cultural domination from abroad is a real one is shown by a remark made a long time ago by Mr Murumbi: 'Africans should not try only to imitate European art forms, but should strive to produce an art that is a true expression of African feelings.'

It is difficult at first sight to understand why this official fear of alien influence should be so great, since art, we are usually lead to believe, is universal. It seems to me that the basis of this concern lies in an unexpressed feeling that Kenya's artists must help show what *is* the African way of life in a modern context. If this is the case, overmuch influence from abroad represents a very real danger. Otherwise, it is hard to see what the fuss is about.

Admirable as this official concern with the arts may be, it is not very relevant to the real problems of the artist in Kenya. Politicians anywhere have a way of talking which tends to generalisation, so that one is apt to forget that artists are individuals with their own problems, and that art is too personal for generalisation about their role to be of much value. It is furthermore difficult to listen with any patience to official pronouncements about art since whenever the Government has had an opportunity to do something practical for Kenya's artists it has totally failed to do so. The murals in the Parliament Building were, it is true, by local artists. Even these artists were, though good, both European and artistically 'safe'. When a statue of the President was wanted no chance was given to local sculptors to compete for a commission. The commission went to London. The result was expensive, foreign, and artistically abysmal.

In Kenya, which is after all a small country as well as a new one, there are few who write, and these few are at the beginning of their careers. The first novel by a Kenya African – *Weep Not Child*, by James Ngugi – was published only a couple of years ago. Rebecca Njau and to a lesser extent Grace Ogot are 'names' – and yet they have published only a handful of short stories, and in the case of Rebecca Njau had a few short plays performed. The same is true of poets like Joseph Kariuki or John Mutiga. This small output is neither surprising nor regrettable. Prolixity is not much of an artistic virtue.

In spite of their limited production, these writers already show certain qualities in common. The most important is a lack of emotional side-taking. *Weep Not Child*, which deals with the time of the Mau Mau rebellion, is not concerned with showing one side or the other as evil. Even the white settler who is in a sense the villain is not seen as intrinsically villainous. For a first novel, the characterisation is fairly subtle. The same can be said of Ngugi's other novel, *The River Between*, and of the short stories and plays of the two women writers. Most of these concern the strains inherent in a changing society, either explicitly or implicitly, and treat them in an unrhetorical, deeply felt and at times ironical way. At the same time language is used with an emotional confidence which is afraid neither of extreme simplicity nor of rhetorical flights.

Of the painters – who suffer less than the writers from Kenya's lack of artistic outlets – only Elimo Njau, who is a Tanzanian anyway, is well known outside East Africa. Names such as Louis Mwaniki or Asaph Ng'ethe are known abroad only to those who frequent the exhibitions put on by bodies like the Commonwealth Institute in London. And yet East Africa – to talk of Kenya alone in painting is pointless: Njau is Tanzanian, Eli Kyeyune Ugandan, but they work in and influence Kenya – is as highly developed in painting as Nigeria in novel-writing.

These painters are extremely different one from another. Njau seems to be tending to a semi-mystical expressionism. Kyeyune makes bold and incisive statements about the appearance of things, using a palette which inclines to pure and singing colours, and drawing emotion from the immense solidity and unexpectedness of life. Ng'ethe paints in dark, almost drab browns a harsh and grinding world, relieved by a Christian faith as dogged and tenacious as the Kikuyu peasants who are so often his subjects. And all three are unmistakably though indefinably *African*. It is impossible to point to any quality in their work and claim that it links them, but it is equally impossible to suggest that their Africanness is not the basis of their work.

Perhaps the only way in which one can appreciate this Africanness fully is by going to a gallery like the New Stanley Art Gallery in Nairobi, where works by African, Asian and European artists hang side by side.

The New Stanley is one of those smooth, modern, character-less hotels catering mainly for airline passengers, whose entrance hall – full of little heaps of luggage and faintly lost-looking travellers – is lined with cubby-holes of shops: a bookstall with the usual international magazines, a safari organiser's, a miniature airline office. Among the discreet notices – GRILLROOM, BAR, and so on – is one incongruously reading ART GALLERY.

The New Stanley Art Gallery is intended as a shop window for East African painters. In its exhibitions are examples of the work of Kenya's best painters, African, Asian and European. But the gallery has to pay the rent – and what pays the rent is a style of painting best called Elephant Landseer. The Elephant Landseer is usually a painstaking work with big-game in characteristic poses in the foreground, assorted scrub in the middle reaches and often Mount Kilimanjaro in the background. Such paintings are larger than photos and little inferior, though much more expensive. They are all painted by Europeans.

Elephant Landseer does not at first sight seem much of a threat to serious painters. But Nairobi is not a town in which art is, so to speak, in the air. Elephant Landseer is extremely popular with the 'I know what I like' brigade. Its effects on African artists (who are themselves no abstractionists) are I believe twofold. First, it siphons off a certain amount of money which might otherwise come the way of serious painters. Second, it

15*a* The Latin-American-based dance music of the Congo is the rage throughout Kenya, but uninhibited gaiety such as this is the prerogative of people who do not have to keep up appearances. Grander dances are a good deal duller.

15*b* Asaph Ng'ethe is one of the better painters in a painter's country. His work is as dour and strong as the Kikuyu peasant life which inspires so much of it.

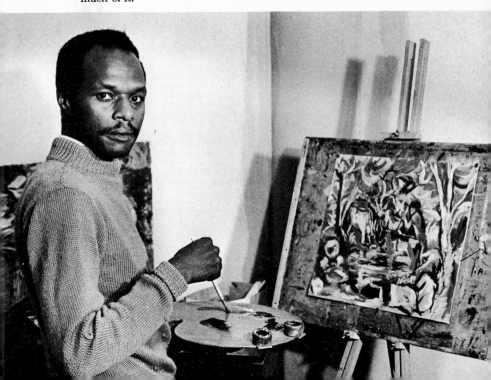

16a To a large extent, the change-over from European to African ownership of Kenya's big farms was amicable enough. This outgoing owner may not have got the price for his land that he would have liked, but the two families sealed the bargain unofficially in a very English fashion.

16b Women of *Roho Israel* – the Spirit of Israel, a sect which came into being partly as an unconscious cultural revolt against a Christianity whose outward manifestations were too European.

provides a false scale of comparison. Most of the young African painters in Nairobi are talented and hardworking. They are not, in the pejorative sense of the word, painstaking. Since many Europeans still labour under the delusion that Kenyan Africans are still at the elementary stage of learning to do things, the result may be that African painters suffer not only financially, but also in their reputations, by comparison with a bunch of palette-knife photographers. This is a pity, especially since they are in fact the leaders of Kenya's art world in quality and meaningfulness. None the less the problem of Elephant Landseer is just the local version of a universal problem. In Kenya the week-end painters paint animals; in France, men fishing on the *quais*.

None the less, Kenya's African painters are in a relatively fortunate position. For the writers, the situation is still much more unsatisfactory.

Talking about her own work, Rebecca Njau says, 'I don't like to write for the European market. I think the temptation with us, if you want to make money, is to look for the subject-matter that will make your book popular. I know Europeans think the African is very simple . . . so "let me make him naïve, let me make him answer things in a naïve way, like a simpleton, like a child" . . . and you know, that is wrong, because really the African is not simple.'

The same idea is expressed more fully by Jonathan Kariara when he says: 'There is a danger among African writers – in wanting to use English they will possibly want to present the picture that is acceptable to that vague but important society they hope to write for. You get a kind of simplification of the African, which I think is partly because you are writing to a foreign people and you dare not bog yourself down in the psychology and complexity of seemingly simple people, because this will rather tend to detract from the bigger issues you are writing about. And this can be a great weakness.'

This is the basic dilemma of Kenya's young African writers. Since most of the proportionately few Kenyans who *can* read and write are quite uninterested in literature, the local market

o

for novels would be very small even if there were much in the way of local publishing, which as yet there is not. Apart from the socio-literary magazine *Transition*, published in Uganda, there is no regular periodical outlet for serious writing. A writer who wants a reasonably large audience – and this means all writers – *must* publish abroad, with the grave danger to his integrity which Rebecca Njau expresses.

As far as local publishing is concerned, the Oxford University Press's Nairobi branch is mainly concerned with textbooks; the East African Publishing House is planning a series of works by local writers; and the Literature Bureau of the East African Common Services Organisation – which mainly publishes educational books in vernacular languages – will in theory at least publish fiction. And although the problem of limited readership will remain for some time, the literacy rate will increase.

With all the practical difficulties in the way of African artists, the problems posed by the African Image and the need to develop an African art might seem unimportant; and in fact, such questions seem to be raised mostly by non-artists.

One young journalist and writer, asked whether he thought talk of the African Image had real meaning, said: 'Of course it has. . . . If African writers keep on imitating the foreigners we will forget our culture, our old customs and many things which happened or which are happening in the African world, and will find within a very short time that we are absorbed by the Western or Eastern way of living.'

But this man is in a minority. Kyeyune takes the line that the whole thing is inevitable: 'If an artist is African, his picture will automatically look different from that of an artist who is in Europe, because of what surrounds him.' Beyond this, 'he should not simply try to be an African artist. He tries to express himself, and knowing which group of painters or artists he belongs to will be automatic. . . . I do not think our problems are local problems.'

The whole question of the role of the African writer was dismissed out of hand by Rebecca Njau: 'There is no role. You know, I do not believe in these roles. Roles for what? You are not trying to convert the heathen. I would like to write something that would make people read and feel; but I don't believe in these roles.'

The question of European influences in African art is not one about which it is easy to be dogmatic. On the one hand, to quote the former Director of the New Stanley Gallery, 'It is very difficult in a country like this, which has no tradition of art, for an artist to start from scratch and evolve his own artistic philosophy – it is impossible, because the artist must be a gregarious person: each artist learns from another, the idea of art revolves from a group. If you haven't got an immediate tradition, then you have got to get your information from whatever source offers.'

A quite contrary view is plausibly expressed by a Czech artist working in Kenya, who has spent thirty years studying African art, Professor Frank Foit.

Professor Foit is something of a voice crying in the wilderness at present, but there can be no doubt that what he says is relevant to the concern with an African Image in art. Basically, he maintains that art education at school level in Kenya is drastically wrong, based as it is on European art. Admitting that all art is made up of cross-influences, he says: 'If you speak about influences on European art, you must consider that we have background – a very strong background of Graeco-Roman art; so modern European art has a scientific and creative basis. But Africa has no original modern art, because the artists have no background except a foreign one. If they could start from traditional African art, they could develop a really African modern art . . . they could use the old African traditions such as the African anatomical canon, philosophy of form, philosophy of life – these are very important things which should be there in painting.'

A modern Chinese or Indian painter is both modern, *and* recognisably Chinese or Indian: the same should be – and he feels is not – true of African artists.

But most theories about what African artists should be

doing are the products of people who are in one way or another outsiders. What matters in the long run is what the artists themselves think they should be doing. Kenyan painters on the whole believe their job is to paint, in spite of Njau's cultural mirror. But Kenyan writers seem fairly unanimous that – in a sense far removed from the social realism of writers such as Zola – their role is social. One explains it as 'first of all, educating my people; making my readers, mostly Africans, not to forget their old customs and culture'.

James Ngugi once described the function of the author as 'to probe his society and capture the conflicts and tensions within it'. This classic vision of the artist's position – in so far as he has a recognisable position – *vis-à-vis* his society is shared by most of Kenya's young writers. In one sense, they are in agreement with the African Image theorists, in that they see themselves as dealing with the strains of Kenyan society, and at present these strains, as Ngugi says, have much to do with the clash of old and new – which frequently means, with the clash of traditional African and modern industrial (and thus to a large extent foreign) ways.

On the whole the search for an African identity as such is regarded as incidental to the writer's more traditional pre-occupation with the human condition as a whole. Ironically, what efforts have been made elsewhere to take the bull of Africanism by the horns have been heavily flavoured with European modes of thought. Nothing could be more French in its intellectual framing than the theory of Negritude. The effect of such theories on writing is often sheer disaster. Much of the work even of a man like Leopold Senghor sounds like an archaeologist making a bad guess at the liturgy of a long-dead faith. Kenya is fortunate to be free of what on purely pragmatic grounds appears almost entirely harmful to the arts.

So far the artists and writers mentioned have all been African. Kenya being now – for the first time in any meaningful sense – an African nation, what is done by Africans is relevant in a way which the activities of the minority groups – however admirable – are not. But it is not adequate to say 'Kenya is an

African country' and blandly ignore the work done by these very large minorities, as some people try to do. Kenya *is* an African country. She is not, however, African in quite the same way as Nigeria, say, is African: and both she and the world would lose something if she were to become so. Her potential as a *purely* 'African' country is no greater than that of many other lands. Her potential as a multi-racial society is considerable.

Kenya has only just begun to create a united whole from African, Asian and European strands. The unique balance of races in East Africa may one day result in an art which will be individual while remaining in the main stream of world art – as English and Italian Gothic, though national styles, were recognisably part of a greater European Gothic. Such a vision is still many decades from fulfilment. Aesthetically it can be dangerous to treat an individual artist too much in terms of his group background. What is important is his work. But an artist's work is within the context of the whole of his life, and of his community. When Kenya is integrated, there will in a true sense be Kenyan artists. At present there are African artists, European artists and Asian artists, and the two last groups on the whole still work entirely within the aesthetic framework of their ancestors.

There are nevertheless individual artists of significance. Robin Anderson, for example, has developed a batik technique which she uses with great power for representational subjects which are often however, abstract in feel. She is a person who must be taken into account in any serious conversation about Kenyan art; not only on grounds of merit, but because she is a *Kenyan* artist – her eye, her aesthetic sense, call it what you will, has been made by Kenya.

Another painter of some interest is a Kenya-born Asian woman, Nirmala Gautama, whose style is clearly Indian in many respects and yet owes much to Africa. Nirmala Gautama is perhaps a pointer to how things may go in the future with minority-group artists, because her quite unmistakable Indian-ness is, as she says, 'more environment than inheritance – by seeing these Indian movies and so on, and by leading a life which is semi-Indian as well, I think some influence of the East is bound to come into my work'. If minority artists in Kenya are to have any relevant role in Kenyan art, it must be by bringing the different flavours of the minority communities into a distinctively Kenyan context.

European Kenyan writers are few and far between. Elspeth Huxley stems from the Kenya of the past, and her work is in a way part of history. On a lesser aesthetic level, a novel on a Kenyan subject appears from time to time, but there has as yet been nothing of any consequence. Perhaps the best known novel about Kenya is still Robert Ruark's *Uhuru* – a masterpiece of wrongheadedness.

The only Asian writer of any note in Kenya is the Mombasan Kuldip Sondhi, whose plays have the dubious distinction of being performed more often by the BBC African Service than they are in Kenya. Sondhi, a writer of deep sensibility though over-literary style, may one day become a major name in Kenya's drama – if Kenya ever develops a drama. His play *The Undesignated*, which deals with personal and public pressures on a young African whose talents are needed in more than one field, has its technical faults; but not only is it superior to anything else in a theatre where talent is thin on the ground, it is entirely Kenyan in its terms of reference. Another work, *With Strings*, examines mixed marriage in a Kenya–Asian context.

Sondhi's lack of adequate recognition is at least partly a result of prejudice – of a rather nebulous feeling, easy to recognise but impossible to prove, that in an 'African' Kenya outstanding talent among the minorities is an embarrassment to be played down. Such an attitude is in the long run more harmful to Kenya than to the individual talents concerned. Kenya, to put it crudely, needs all the good men she can get.

If European and Asian artists are often misunderstood by the African majority, this is by no means entirely the majority's fault. Undoubtedly, most of those who think of themselves in any deep sense as Kenyan are aware of the need to cut loose from their own little cultural worlds; but many are in the position of the bather faced with a cold sea. They know that the plunge will be invigorating, that it will do them nothing but good. But they are still standing on the edge, dipping a tentative toe. Sooner or later – probably sooner – there will be a splash as the irrevocable effort is made: but except (possibly) in the case of Sondhi, it has not been made yet.

Commitment always takes courage, but as far as Kenyan minority-group artists are concerned, the choice is between total commitment to a 'Kenyanism' whose form nobody can yet foresee, or genteel stagnation in a rapidly silting communal backwater.

A minority problem which is much more that of the Europeans than of the Asians is the all too frequent feeling – which is probably stronger on an unconscious than a conscious level – that he must continue to guide the faltering footsteps of the African: Now that you're free old chap, do what I advise and you'll be all right.

To people who are used to the feel of the tiller, it is genuinely difficult to feel complete confidence in the untried new helmsman when they hand it over. The temptation to go and sit in a lifeboat is very real. None the less, the crew's job is largely to do what the helmsman says, and there is really no other choice – except some form of disaster.

In the arts, however, the doctrine of Africanisation is pointless if pushed too far. The only realm in which it has any real meaning is in the corporate arts like the theatre. Here, as we have seen, nothing is being done. In most of the arts, African leadership is hardly more relevant than talk of the African personality. Inevitably, in a healthy cultural atmosphere, the lead will be given by the best painters and writers. These may just as well be of one race as of another. Fortunately, the arts are essentially non-racial, and so are most artists. The greatest difficulty of African artists in getting acceptance in Kenya lies not in the attitudes of the minorities, but in the apathy of the educated African public. Mr Mboya, speaking at an old boys' dinner a couple of years ago, was caustic about the failure to support cultural activities: 'I am very much of the opinion that it is the lethargy and laziness of educated Africans in failing to come forward which is primarily responsible for the continuing dominance in so many institutions by non-Africans.'

There is no doubt whatsoever that this is still true, though it is not altogether to be wondered at. Cultural activities at the best of times only consciously concern a minority in any country. And since the arts in Kenya are still in process of finding their true place in society, it is even less to be expected that the general public should take an interest. It is up to the artists – with African artists firmly in the lead – to create a strong culture. Then the public will (perhaps) follow.

Obviously the principal way in which artists create a strong culture is by doing a lot of good work, and making sure it is seen. Ancillary activities never do any harm, however, particularly in a country like Kenya. The African public, being ignorant of any art forms other than music, at least does not get the wrong end of the stick as easily as the public in a country like England, which has a few half-understood aesthetic theories to trip over. The teaching element is not without its importance in Kenya – though exactly how this teaching should be done remains an open question. Chemchemi Creative Centre, which was opened in 1963 with the South African writer and critic, Ezekiel Mphahlele, as director was intended to encourage cultural activities by whatever means possible. Chemchemi is now closed. Public indifference undoubtedly contributed to its failure, but so also did concentration on educating children at secondary schools level – a job which could be best done by the schools themselves.

A more promising venture has been started by Elimo Njau, a man of whom an enemy once said: 'He is a prophet, that man, not a painter' (Kenya can use prophets). Njau, after opening an art gallery in his home village on the slopes of Mount Kilimanjaro, has started the Paa-ya-Paa gallery in Nairobi. Paa-ya-Paa hangs paintings because they are thought to be good, and for no other reason. Njau, who spent some months in Paris and came back in prophetic mood about the influence of the artists' café, has hopes that if he can get permission to sell coffee and so on Paa-ya-Paa may become a place not only where there are paintings to be seen, but where poems are read and shouted about, where theories are erected and dismantled, where in fact a dialogue is maintained. If anybody can pull off this idea, it is Njau; not only because he has the enthusiasm, but because he is a painter with a writer wife and a ready-made circle of acquaintance in both worlds.

Such places as Paa-ya-Paa are needed. Kenya has much that could, with time, grow into a strong culture. The presence of three communities each making its distinctive contribution may enable her to develop something rich and unique. On the other hand, the dead hand of the TV suburb lies heavy on Kenya as a whole, and especially on Nairobi – which must inevitably be the dynamo. If the dead hand is thrown off, most of the credit will go to the individual artists who are fighting it with very little support.

It Gets Everywhere

We all must struggle
together to build a
united nation.
Kanu Manifesto

Kanu is the party
for the satisfied.
KPU speaker

'Politics gets into everything in Kenya', so the cliché runs. In so far as this is true – and there is a lot in it – it is a compliment. To say the least, a country in which every party and every bar is loud with theorising and dispute – informed and ill-informed – is not a country with a 'When I jump you jump' régime. Anyway, in a sense everything *is* politics. Agriculture, industrialisation, social welfare, all are matters for policies and thus politics.

Those who talk as if the love of intrigue was the mainspring of Kenya politics, or as if either the Government or those opposed to it were in business for the benefit of Cold War strategists, are making a fundamental mistake. With all its personalities, plotting and scandal, Kenyan politics is concerned with genuine policy disagreement. The recent breakdown of single-party government was caused by dissension on basic attitudes to a number of issues, but especially the two issues which are nearest to the hearts of the electorate – land and education. The Kenya People's Union has – like all parties in Opposition – thought it necessary to produce its own policy on every aspect of Kenya's development. From the statement of policy made by Mr Odinga last May, it is quite clear that in many of these fields the KPU does not really have an independent policy. On subjects like university education it confines itself to bromides like: 'KPU will step up higher education and will emphasise training in science and technology, which the colonialist denied the youth of Kenya.'

On the major issues of land and primary education, however, the KPU is merely giving voice to views which have been held by the radical wing of Kenyan political opinion since Uhuru and before. Briefly, the land policy involves the issue of free land to squatters, where necessary by 'acquiring' land from European settlers; a ceiling on the number of acres which may be owned by one person; and a ban on land ownership by non-citizens. The KPU education policy involves the introduction of free primary education 'immediately after KPU forms the Government'. Apart from this there is little which differs from Kanu's official policy.

It is true that since, in the words of the Manifesto, 'Kanu intends that every child in Kenya shall have a minimum of seven years' free education', free primary education is in a sense not a real policy issue – a point naturally enough seized on by Kanu itself. Differences of priority, however, can in politics be quite as important as differences of ultimate aim. Free primary education is not regarded by the Government as being possible until about 1980. The KPU is joined by a large number of people in wanting it now.

As far as land is concerned, the KPU claims that settlement of 35,000 families on 1,000,000 acres is inadequate since at the time these schemes began, European settlers owned 8,000,000 acres. As we have seen, success in the high-density settlement schemes depends heavily on the co-operatives. This is another field in which the KPU attacks the Government, claiming that owing to 'capitalist' policies, the co-ops received only 6.7 per cent of Land Bank loans, and only 5.3 per cent of Agricultural Finance Corporation loans.

Whether or not KPU policies are good ones or bad, they rouse much sympathy and not just among the landless, nor just among the more Marxist-inclined intelligentsia. Many people feel that Kenya is too like what it was before independence. Some of these are unaware of the difficulties involved in changing from a foreign-dominated to an indigenous economy: but others believe that no serious start has been seen to be made on Africanising industry, for example. These people claim that lecturing small businessmen on their duty to train Africans is not a realistic approach to the problem – and it is hard to disagree with them. KPU's loss of support indicates dissatisfaction with the party leaders, both because some of them are regarded as too involved with Communist countries and because the party generally has proved incompetent and disunited. It does not mean that the Government's very cautious pragmatism is universally admired.

The principal argument against KPU policies is not that they are wrong, but that the KPU has taken no account of whether the country can afford them – or more important, whether she could raise aid to carry them out. It is certainly true that so far no attempt has been made by KPU spokesmen to dispute the findings of the Education Commission, whose opinion is that for shortage of teachers and facilities as well as of finance, free primary education cannot be introduced more quickly than is at present envisaged. Inevitably the KPU would expect to rely on foreign aid for much of this money, just as the Government does at present. Since America and Western countries in general could hardly give more aid than they do at present – and perhaps more important, since they would almost certainly be disinclined to give more aid to a Government headed by Mr Odinga – the extra aid would need to come from the Iron Curtain countries. While there is nothing wrong with this in theory, Kenya's experience of Iron Curtain aid so far has not been happy.

In fact, however, the two main voices of the political dialogue are not ideological as such. As far as policy is concerned, free land only excepted, KPU members argue that Kanu has betrayed its own policies, and thus that KPU is calling for what Kanu was elected to carry out, rather than pushing something new. The other voice is more personal. Many of the KPU leaders have become so associated with views more radical than the majority of the present Government is prepared to accept that the Cabinet was functioning more like a rather strained coalition than a united body. Similarly, opinion within Kanu was becoming so varied that it was a single party only in name. Unity having in practice vanished, it is a great deal healthier that political opinion should have polarised than that the whole battle should have been fought out by cabals and hidden alliances under the Kanu umbrella. The breakaway, even if it had done nothing else, would still have had the merit of giving the voter a chance to say what he thinks about the whole matter. It seems a pity that KPU proved so inept that a few months after its formation it was already showing signs of collapse.

In a sense, the one-party interlude was a necessary step in the progress from an Opposition which did not really correspond to any serious political needs, to one which (however inadequately) does. For the Kenya African Democratic Union was a product not of policy disagreement (most of such disagreement as there was, was very much 'same difference') but of tribal fears. As tribalism slowly receded from the forefront of the political scene, Kadu became an anachronism. The death of Kadu was therefore not the sign of an attack on freedom in Kenya. Even as a one-party State Kenya had a political freedom rare among African countries. When she became a one-party State on the eve of becoming a republic, she did so not by legal action but because Kadu voluntarily dissolved itself.

Though it appears not to suit Kenya (for reasons partly irrelevant to the system itself) a one-party State can in theory be as democratic as a two-party State – and a good deal more democratic than many multi-party States, where three men backed by a few hundred voters can overthrow the Government on the most frivolous of grounds. A one-party State, so the African theory runs, is a logical development of the traditional African method of coming to a collective decision and is one of the realms in which Africa will do better to adapt her own traditions than to adopt those of others. When a village, or a tribe, or any African social unit, had to make a decision, everybody discussed the matter until a solution was found which satisfied all schools of thought – or as many as could possibly be satisfied. This decision was then accepted unanimously.

The one-party State works along the same lines. The party grows from the grass-roots, from the individual Members of Parliament, as well as from the branch and sub-branch officials. Debate and criticism come from within the party, and if the backbenchers disapprove of something which the Government proposes, they vote against it.

This system being both traditionally African (or at any rate seen as such) and reasonably democratic in nature, there is no reason to expect the 'Westminster pattern' to be adopted. Anyway, the former colonies have no first-hand experience of democracy à l'Anglaise. Englishmen tend to forget that though they themselves are ruled democratically, their rule over other people was entirely autocratic. Far from teaching their dependencies about democracy, they taught them about dictatorship. Kenya's entire colonial history could hardly have been more effective in instilling contempt for the Westminster pattern. A colonial government is inherently undemocratic, and the settlers' approach to the subject was put by one European politician of the late fifties with fine, if unconscious, irony. The European answer to African nationalism, he said, was 'reasonable democracy – not a total democracy, but one controlled by us'. It is hardly surprising in these conditions if the Westminster pattern did not 'take'.

However democratic the one-party State may be in theory, in practice it is wide open to a drift to tyranny. On the other hand, *any* system can be manipulated, as Hitler was not the only man to prove. The fact that a system can be used by the unscrupulous to defeat itself means nothing. Democracy depends not on electoral regulations but on the citizens' and government's enthusiasm for letting people have their say. In some African countries this enthusiasm has been lacking – though it is dangerous to jump to conclusions about tyranny too quickly even where the single-party system is backed by law, as the Tanzanian elections showed. In Kenya, the cynic might say, the enthusiasm for saying one's say has been almost too great. As Mr Mboya put it in an article in the *East African Standard* on Republic Day, 'Let any foreign journalist sit in our Parliament and note the freedom of expression which Government backbenchers enjoy when debating Government Bills. Let them compare this with the conduct of the party yes-men in the British House of Commons.' The Kenya backbenchers were always aware of the danger that they might, if they did not exercise their rights, end up as 'rubber stamps' automatically approving the Cabinet's wishes. They have been known to outvote the Government largely in order to show that they were not prepared to be ignored. In any debate in the House of Representatives all the relevant issues – and a fair number of irrelevancies into the bargain – are thoroughly aired. Members have never shown much sign of being afraid of being un-popular with the Cabinet (though some are too open to carrots and horse-trading). Many indeed seem to welcome it as an indication that they are looking after their constituents' interests.

The role of the party in a one-party State has never been defined with any closeness. Kanu's structure is plain enough, from the sub-branches up to National Headquarters. But this structure is independent of, or at least unrelated to, the Parliamentary structure. The branch officials are elected by ordinary party members. Members of Parliament, though they are party members, are elected directly and are not necessarily party officials. This being the case, does the MP for an area have any duty to the local party branch? If so, this weakens his position as direct representative of the whole electorate (not necessarily all party members). If not, does party discipline have any hold on him?

This question obtains right through the dual hierarchy of party and Parliament. Some time ago the then Kanu national vice-chairman, Mr John Keen, said that the Cabinet should be subservient to the party. Such a subservience would of course create an intolerable situation: but the question to which

Mr Keen was trying to give an answer is a real one. For if the Cabinet is answerable only to the President and to Parliament, what in the long run is the reason for the party's existence, beyond picking official candidates for elections? Unless democracy is to vanish and only one, official, party candidate be allowed for each seat, the party has little role in elections except to lend its prestige (if any) to the official nominee.

In Kenya the party has until recently played very little part in the affairs of the country. Sessional Paper Number Ten, the Government's basic policy statement, was produced by the Cabinet, not by Kanu. The party leaders might act as mouthpieces of the ordinary man, but this is also the role of the backbenchers, who moreover have the power to make themselves felt by voting against the Government. When there was no Opposition all that the party officials could do was to exercise personal influence or issue Press statements – an activity the less effective since it is something of a Kenyan national sport. There were two scaffolds of power, the Parliamentary and the party, and the party scaffold seemed for practical purposes of no use whatsoever.

In fact, whether in a single- or multi-party system, the most valuable task Kanu can perform is to act as the medium through which Government and people are kept in touch with each other. This is something which MPs cannot carry out effectively, because each is responsible for so large an area. In a country like Kenya there is a fairly wide gulf between what the voter wants and what can be done. If the Government is not to get the reputation of ignoring the needs of the common man, there is need for a continual process of explanation of why this must be done and why that is out of the question. The party is ideally suited for the sort of dialogue between the man-in-the-street and the authorities which is necessary if misunderstanding is not to develop. Questions like the role of tax should be debated at sub-branch level, so that ordinary party workers and the people who select them gain insight into the process of economic growth. Kenya's leaders frequently point out that sacrifice is needed if Kenya is to prosper, but they do not explain why, in terms understood and recognised as valid by the ordinary people. This is a task for the party.

Again, the party can interpret the Development Plan in terms of the local situation, relating national targets to local communities, and local needs to overall targets. Another possible job is the changing of local attitudes, especially the sort of traditional attitudes to diet or farming which delay progress. It is no good, as happens at present, senior officials from Nairobi lecturing people on what they should be doing. All that happens is that the crowd, in a spirit of politeness, passes any resolutions that may be desired. Then everybody goes home and carries on as before. Party branch and sub-branch officials being known and in most cases respected in their areas, can hammer away until an effect is felt.

Kanu means little to the average man, except momentarily during a big rally. It is significant only to the actual party workers. The apathy of the public was shown at the by-elections in the part of Central Nyanza which is the heart of 'Odinga-land', and where some exciting politics might have been expected. In the event, only about ten per cent of the electorate bothered to vote.

A good deal of this apathy was caused by the Government's attitude to Kanu. It was clearly felt that to give the branches too much say would risk pressure from the 'wild men' for the execution of all sorts of politically or economically impossible ventures. The party was, therefore, tacitly ignored. This may yet prove one of the gravest political blunders which the Government has yet committed. Most of the party branch officials are dedicated men. Though some of their notions may be impracticable, the best way of handling them is not to leave them out in the cold, but to bring them in, use their talents, and put their ideas right where necessary.

By the time the Government realised this fact and began belatedly to prepare for the reorganisation of Kanu, the damage was done. While the issues go deeper than this, there can be little doubt that much of the support for the KPU stemmed from people's awareness that Kanu was being ignored and that they

P

therefore had little say in affairs. There is a danger – inherent in Africa, where a small élite is supported by a largely illiterate mass – that the educated may underestimate the political awareness of the man in the shamba. In other countries, where the ordinary man has altogether been denied a voice, the result has been instability and *coups*. The Kenya Government believes sincerely enough in the right of every man to say his say, but it is too quick to assume that the result will not be worth listening to. In this respect it is very like an over-bossy board of directors, which has the interest of the shareholders at heart, but is inclined to try and stage-manage the annual meeting.

This resemblance to a board of directors is heightened by the role played by the President himself. Kenyatta has much of the charisma of most great men. Kenya would in all probability not have dealt so successfully with the rifts and dissensions left by the Emergency if Kenyatta had not been there. This was, if not the man who suffered most from the Emergency, the leader of those who suffered. He enjoyed a tremendous prestige among people of all tribes and he used it entirely in the interests of conciliation.

Perhaps more impressive than the fact that Kenyatta turned people's minds from the past to the future is that he did not do so by means of visions of glory or easy promises. He said in his speech to the nation at independence: 'Many people may think that, now there is Uhuru, now I can see the sun of Freedom shining, richness will pour down like manna from Heaven.

'I tell you there will be nothing from Heaven. We must all work hard, with our hands, to save ourselves from poverty, ignorance and disease.'

The African liking for honorifics, and the more fundamental attitude behind it – the seeking, in personal life, of the traditional figure of the chief or elder – are not in themselves a bad thing, but recent history has shown what trouble they can lead. In theory, Kenyatta ought – so at least visitors to Kenya feel – to be a dictatorial old man. In fact, Kenya is about as far from dictatorship as it is possible to be: a good deal further from personal rule than was Britain under Churchill. Asked whether since he held so much power there was not a danger of his becoming tryannical, Jahwarlal Nehru of India remarked coldly: 'I am not of the stuff from which dictators are made.' This is eminently true of Kenyatta. He has never stressed his position, and has always emphasised that he, the government and the people are all members of a team. In his Uhuru speech, he continued: 'Now the Government is ours. Maybe you will now be blaming Kenyatta, saying: "Kenyatta, we elected you, but where is this or that?"'

'But you must know that Kenyatta alone cannot give you everything. All things we must do together. You and I must work together to develop our country . . .'

Kenyatta's belief in conciliation has often been misunderstood. Time and again people have started to say: 'The old man's losing his grip.' Faced with a Cabinet containing elements as immiscible as Odinga, Gichuru, Mboya and Achieng Oneko, he always sought to hold things together, to avoid showdowns. Part of this may be an old man's dislike of argument, but mostly it is a genuine belief that much must be tolerated in order that disunity should not hamper the country.

This chairmanlike attitude has its drawbacks. Many people allege that in the interest of holding the ring and not upsetting people, necessary reforms have been delayed and that this is principally the President's fault. There may be something in this. None the less, his role in Kenya continues to be remarkable. From being the one man who could hold the country together he has been very slowly withdrawing into the background, letting his Cabinet do the work, acting the Head of State in the role's formal aspects. When people in Kenya start worrying these days, they usually say: 'But what about when the Old Man goes?' It may be that when he does go, we will see that his greatest service was bringing Kenya to a position where he is no longer needed. Perhaps even the fact that these days he commands perhaps more affection than respect is deliberate.

None the less Kenya's relative lack of slogans is not the work of one man. It was the result partly of the one-party period, during which there was a faintly artificial ideological lull, and partly of hard political realities. Before independence, for instance, Kenya in common with other African States used African nationalism as a political lever. But in fact, there is no such thing as an African nation, except in so far as a tribe can be said to be a nation. In other words, nationalism exists before the nation. Clearly, to spend much time shouting nationalist slogans when it was obvious that most people still thought to a large extent in terms of a tribe would be a little ludicrous. Slogans do not materially alter opinions. The Government therefore concentrated on the practical things which bring a sense of nationhood nearer, and tended to play politics down in favour of economics.

Much the same is true of the East African Federation. The optimism of 1963 is long gone. It is realised that even without the political differences between Uganda, Tanzania and Kenya, federation would be a slow process. This does not mean that Federation will never come about, but that nobody is now prepared to say when it will be or what form it will take. In the meanwhile the talks between eleven nations of East Africa with a view to setting up an Eastern African economic community are proceeding with a caution which is promising. In May 1966, the articles of association were signed. Nobody is prepared to say what form this community will take (a lesson learned from federation). Its aim is merely to promote a co-ordinated development of the countries' economies with free trade as the ultimate aim. This plan is important because at present all the countries involved compete with each other for overseas aid and manpower, as well as for trade.

If many of the elements of African ideology were played down because their immediate relevance was slight – and have recurred now mainly as ammunition for party-political in-fighting – the theory of nonalignment has considerable practical importance. As far as foreign policy is concerned, nonalignment or positive neutralism in its positive aspect means refusing to side automatically with either power bloc. Strict nonalignment in the sense of backing neither side would of course be practically impossible as well as morally reprehensible. When evil is done, ignoring it cannot possibly be defended. Moreover, most countries are likely to be aligned on one side or the other. This is not necessarily cynical. Which side seems right more often than the other depends on one's own point of view. In this sense Kenya is on the whole 'nonaligned to the West'. This will not, however, prevent her voting with the East on any individual issue in which she thinks the West is wrong, such as Vietnam. When one contemplates the British Government's contortions over Vietnam, this attitude seems the only one compatible with dignity.

In one respect Kenya is especially Western-leaning, and that is in respect of the aid she receives. In hard economic terms the East is not much use as an aid giver, since both China and Russia lack convertible currency. Russia tries to give a fair amount of aid, dodging the currency problem by complex barter arrangements which Kenya refused to agree to, since they would land her with a great deal of unsaleable merchandise to get rid of. The example of Ghana, much of whose financial trouble is said to have been caused by such 'barter aid', shows how reasonable Kenya's suspicion is.

Western aid, on the other hand, is liberal and in hard cash. It ranges from the £60 million 'independence dowry' given by Britain to thousands of individual gifts like the Volkswagen ambulances ones sees running around with 'A gift from the People of West Germany' painted on their sides. There is no end to the ways in which aid is given. It is not necessarily Government to Government. The us Agency for International Development, for example, has offered the town of Thika half the cost of an £11,000 community centre being built there if the local people will find the other half. Aid in money, aid in machines, aid in manpower – especially in skilled technical advisers – pours in. It does not go unrecognised. Mr Murumbi commented last April: 'I know that on our side we do not lose an opportunity of asking for more, but I sometimes wonder how long the process can continue.

'Whatever our differing view on the relations between our two countries (Britain and Kenya) may have been in the past, let me quite frankly say now that the concept of disinterested assistance by the rich nations of the world to the poor ones – without the sinister strings which have sometimes been found attaching to it – is one which is of vital necessity' – and one, he added, in which Britain led the way with flexibility and adaptability.

'Aid with strings' has been a rallying cry for the more foolish of the world's population. None the less, strings *are* frequently attached to aid offers. Nor does the only meddling in the affairs of a country like Kenya come from the Iron Curtain countries. Attempts to win the allegiance of the Afro-Asian countries by fair means or foul are bound to increase with their growth in voting importance at the United Nations. Unnamed (but clearly Eastern) countries were said by the Minister for Home Affairs, Mr Moi, to have spent £400,000 for subversive purposes in Kenya within eighteen months. Much of this was however aid to the KPU which, however reprehensible a meddling with Kenya's affairs, was not necessarily subversive. The strings which attach to aid are usually more complex than outright subversion, though not necessarily less serious in the long run.

One little-recognised way in which foreign countries try to influence Kenya's future is by earmarking aid for certain specific purposes. It is entirely reasonable that an aid-giving country should make sure its money does not go to line the pockets of a lot of crooked operators. It is not reasonable – if one pretends one's aid is disinterested – to use it to guide the direction of economic development. Both the US and Western Germany are said to have been guilty of this sort of practice. KPU complaints have some validity in that Kenya's co-operative movement is suffering in comparison with the small businessman because these countries – especially Germany – give so much aid on the understanding that it shall only be used to build up the individual entrepreneur. While the Kenya Government is at fault for not refusing these conditions, it is too much in need of

money to be able to do so lightly. The aid-giving countries
are the main culprits, in that while claiming they want Kenya
to develop as she thinks best, they are laying weight behind the
private sector at the expense of the co-operatives.

If both East and West in one way or another try to meddle
directly in Kenya's affairs, a greater long-term threat lies in
unconscious influences. A country like Kenya is in a curious
position. As we have seen, she depends heavily on foreign
teachers for her secondary schools. The American Peace Corps
and the US and British Teachers for East Africa organisations
are doing excellent work. Most of their volunteers are dedicated
and reasonable people. Still, the fact remains that too many
Americans or British in the secondary schools risk unconsciously
giving a pro-American or pro-British bias. When this difficulty
is spread over all the fields in which foreign technical advisers
are at work, it becomes a sizable one. What can be done about
it, except to try to acquire one's experts from as many different
countries as possible, it is hard to see. To some extent the
problem can be avoided by recruitment at international level,
through Unesco, the FAO and so on. This is not a complete
solution, however, since international resources have to be
spread very thin.

The need to avoid foreign influence is primarily practical,
but it is reinforced by ideological considerations. The desire
at long last to be truly 'African' is a strong one in the political
field as elsewhere. It lies behind much pan-African thinking,
of course; but more especially it lies behind the phenomenon
known as African Socialism.

African Socialism is one of those expressions which cause a
lot of misunderstanding. It is regarded by many people as
meaningless – by Communist sympathisers because it is not
'scientific socialism' (an expression with just as little or as much
meaning), and by those who regard all African Governments as
idiotic, just because African Governments use it. Others regard
it as almost Holy Writ, holding that it is the Third Way
between Communism and Capitalism, and thus sometimes
falling prey to the mistake of buying anything, provided it has

the right label. In a sense, the expression *is* meaningless as is the word socialism itself, or the word democracy. In all three cases, 'it all depends what you mean'. But in general terms African Socialism does represent a distinct concept – or at least a distinct ethos. Democratic socialism takes on the colours of the separate countries which adopt it, being in Sweden a very different thing from in England. There is a socialism in England which shares recognisable tenets and basic assumptions with the Swedish variety, and yet which is distinctly English in character. There can – and indeed should – be a socialism which shares the same basic tenets but which is distinctly African. In turn, there will within the general phenomenon of African Socialism be differences of form or emphasis in different countries. Kenya and Tanzania share common assumptions as to what society should be like in the future. These assumptions are African, as we shall see, and they are socialist within the wide limits of definition which socialism allows. But they allow for a very wide range of policy-making.

The basic assumptions of African Socialism are summed up in the Sessional Paper Number Ten. It must draw on the best of African traditions, be adaptable to new and rapidly changing circumstances, and must not rest for its success on a satellite relationship with any other country or group of countries.

'There are two African traditions which form an essential basis for African Socialism – political democracy, and mutual social responsibility.' The latter is perhaps the most important, since tradition in African societies had a far more radical concept of it than traditional European societies. On the other hand, mutual responsibility is a traditional *socialist* concept throughout the world. African traditions may dispose Africa to adopt this aspect of socialism without question, whereas it is an assumption which is often questioned in Europe.

Differences of emphasis are no reason for asserting that African Socialism does not exist. Socialism as a whole is like the elephant in the legend – not argued out of existence just because the man feeling the trunk cannot agree on definitions with the man feeling the leg. The same is true of African socialism.

Within Kenya itself one school of thought has always challenged the general (if rather superficial) acceptance of African Socialism. This is 'scientific' or Marxist – socialism. 'Scientific' socialism rather seemed to have died away in the last year, but with the return of an Opposition it was resurrected until its advocates got frightened of seeming too openly Eastern-aligned. Its classic Kenyan statement was in a pamphlet called *Our Way to Socialism*, published in early 1964 and more or less entirely ignored. Basically this is an attack on African Socialism and a dogmatic statement of the position that the only true Socialism is Marxism. It does contain a few sections of special interest, however.

The kernel of *Our Way to Socialism* occurs in a passage about a third of the way through: 'The advocates of African socialism use the slogan of socialism in order to perpetuate the colonial capitalist system and thereby frustrate for ever the achievement of a socialist society. African socialism is indeed a reactionary ideology used by some of the national bourgeoisie to hold back progress.' It is interesting, though hardly surprising, to find this view partly endorsed by the KPU policy statement.

Our Way to Socialism is an oddity because hard-line Communism is rare in Kenya. The country's danger is less a Communist takeover than that – as has too often happened elsewhere – a genuinely nonaligned (if 'Eastern nonaligned') KPU or other radical Government be taken as Communist-inspired by the West. If this happened and Western aid decreased, such a régime might indeed be forced to depend more and more heavily on the East until it was in the position of a satellite. It is conceivable that such a fate might befall Kenya if the Kenya People's Union were to gain power. This would be a pity for everybody concerned. The KPU should not be seen merely in terms of the Cold War. It forms a genuine – even though an over-emotional and inept – radical alternative to the present Government. Moreover, some of its supporters attract a good deal of sympathy even from people who do not believe in its politics. Bildad Kaggia was sacked from a parliamentary secretaryship because he persistently attacked the Government's agricultural policy. This happened at a time when to fall out with the Government apparently meant political oblivion. As a result, he is thought by a number of Kenyans – by no means all particularly radical – to be a man prepared to sacrifice the sweets of office for a principle. Though he is not trusted by the 'man in the shamba', as his opponent's 20,000 majority in the election showed, he may yet emerge again as a figure of importance. Kaggia was once described to me as a 'solar plexus thinker', but although his insistence on 'free' land will not hold water, it would be wrong to dismiss him. Kaggia, and a number of other dissidents of the younger generation, are not at all in the same category as Odinga, whose politics have a faintly old-fashioned air.

It is not probable that, unless it takes to illicit means, the KPU will drive Kanu from office in the immediate future. None the less it has from the start performed a very useful function. In spite of the official line on unity, people never seem to have been very happy with even so democratic a one-party State as was Kenya's. In its early days there was a great deal of sympathy for the KPU among people of all sorts, not because they supported its policies, but because it was an Opposition reminding the Government that it was not perfect. It is interesting that a year before the KPU was formed an opinion poll had shown fifty-nine per cent of the sample as thinking an Opposition necessary – this only a few months after Kadu had collapsed. One of the principal results hoped for by many people was achieved by the formation of the KPU. It gingered up the Government, one of whose faults was to assume that since it knew things were getting along nicely, there was no need to let people know what was going forward in the development line.

As soon as the KPU was formed, a whole stream of information about development projects began to flow from the Ministries. All these projects were already in hand, but nobody had been giving progress reports. As a result the KPU line that the Government had done little to implement its election promises, although nonsense, gained credibility. If the Kenya Cabinet has tended to act rather like a bossy board of directors, the value of the KPU as spokesmen for the dissatisfied shareholders has been considerable, even if it has been mainly nuisance value.

Whatever happens to Kenya's politics in the future – and the most likely happening is a Leftward move to take in the more moderate and intelligent radicals, with the concomitant dropping of some of the ultra-Conservative especially if the country finally reverts to one-party status, so that the radical opposition goes back to work from within Kanu – Kenya has so far survived successfully the great temptation besetting one-party Governments in a similar position. This is the temptation to use preventive detention not to deal with subversives (in whose case there is a possible, though shaky, argument in its favour) but to frighten if not actually to muzzle genuine critics. With the exception of the American wife of one of the KPU leaders, the activities of the first detainees are pretty well known in Kenya, though the law of libel prevents the knowledge from reaching public print. I have heard nobody non-political raise an objection to their confinement. Nevertheless, it is a very great pity that the Government found it necessary to introduce such an act. Although the present rulers appear genuine in their intention to use it to cope with subversion, once such a law is in existence the definition of the word subversion can too easily be stretched beyond all justification; and even if the present Government avoids this temptation, who can guarantee that the next will do so? A bad precedent has been created, and the authorities have failed to provide any convincing reason why the usual sedition laws and court procedure would not have been sufficient to handle Kenya's security situation.

None the less, for all the shadow cast by this Act, Kenya is still an open society, where freedom of speech is abundant and therefore underlying stability considerable. Of course, as one cynic put it, 'The trouble is that in Africa you've always got to allow for the General who wakes up one morning and decides it would be nice to be President.' Even if this should happen, all is not lost. There has been a recent tendency to talk as though Africa had 'failed', as if such a thing were possible. Mexico's history was as bloodstained as any, before she emerged into 'success'. Tomorrow she may be plunged back into 'failure'. Nations do not succeed or fail, they have ups and downs. Just as it would be wrong to talk of Kenya as a 'success' after three years of independence, so it would be wrong to talk of 'failure' if things went wrong for a while.

In the past, Kenya's pragmatism has led to a certain vagueness about objectives. As one young man – not a political activist – remarked:

'You hear all this optimism about Kenya. I have never quite found out what people are being optimistic about, what is going to happen to Kenya. Whether it is going to carry on the traditions which were left behind by the British or whether we are being optimistic about finding a new way of life with the material we have got here. And even on the personal level I think this still is a problem.'

If (as is quite possible) Kenya still has upheavals to come, this lack of a sense of identity and purpose will undoubtedly lie beneath them, however much the situation is complicated by Cold War or other factors. This is the reverse side of the managerial approach to government. The obverse can be best expressed, ironically enough, by the words of one of the leading European Right-wing politicians of the past, the late Group Captain Briggs. Speaking in 1959, he said: 'Make no mistake about it, we shall stay in this country and be governed by a Government of experienced and responsible people.' In quite another sense from what he intended, he was entirely right.

Index